Westward Watch

Pergamon Titles of Related Interest

Related Journal*

(Free sample copies available upon request)

DEFENSE ANALYSIS

Westward Watch

The United States and the Changing Western Pacific

NORMAN D. PALMER

PERGAMON-BRASSEY'S
INTERNATIONAL DEFENSE PUBLISHERS
(a member of the Pergamon Group)
WASHINGTON · NEW YORK · LONDON · OXFORD
BEIJING · FRANKFURT · SÃO PAULO · SYDNEY · TOKYO · TORONTO

U.S.A. (Editorial)	Pergamon-Brassey's International Defense Publishers, 8000 Westpark Drive, Fourth Floor, McLean, Virginia 22102, U.S.A.
(Orders)	Pergamon Press, Maxwell House, Fairview Park, Elmsford, New York 10523, U.S.A.
U.K. (Editorial)	Brassey's Defence Publishers, 24 Gray's Inn Road, London WC1X 8HR
(Orders)	Brassey's Defence Publishers, Headington Hill Hall, Oxford OX3 0BW, England
PEOPLE'S REPUBLIC OF CHINA	Pergamon Press, Room 4037, Qianmen Hotel, Beijing, People's Republic of China
FEDERAL REPUBLIC OF GERMANY	Pergamon Press, Hammerweg 6, D-6242 Kronberg, Federal Republic of Germany
BRAZIL	Pergamon Editora, Rua Eça de Queiros, 346, CEP 04011, Paraiso, São Paulo, Brazil
AUSTRALIA	Pergamon-Brassey's Defence Publishers, P.O. Box 544, Potts Point, N.S.W.2011, Australia
JAPAN	Pergamon Press, 8th Floor, Matsuoka Central Building, 1-7-1 Nishishinjuku, Shinjuku-ku, Tokyo 160, Japan
CANADA	Pergamon Press Canada, Suite No. 271 253 College Street, Toronto, Ontario, Canada M5T 1R5

Copyright © 1987 Pergamon-Brassey's International Defense
Publishers, Inc.

First edition 1987

Library of Congress Cataloging in Publication Data

Palmer, Norman Dunbar.
Westward watch.
Includes index.
1. United States—National security. 2. Pacific
Area—Strategic aspects. 3. East Asia—Strategic
aspects. I. Title. 86–306–78
UA23.P265 1987 355'.00335'73

British Library Cataloguing in Publication Data

Palmer, Norman D.
Westward watch: The United States & the
Changing Western Pacific.
1. Pacific Area—Strategic aspects
2. United States—Military policy
I. Title
355'.0335'73 DU30

ISBN 0–08–034957–9 (Hard cover)
ISBN 0–08–034956–0 (Flexicover)

*Printed in Great Britain by
Hazell Watson & Viney Limited,
Member of the BPCC Group,
Aylesbury, Bucks*

[I]f you want to understand the future,
you must . . . understand the Pacific region.

—*Secretary of State* GEORGE SHULTZ

Contents

Preface

THE growing importance of the Western Pacific as a major world region and of the countries of the region as international actors is now widely recognized, and there can be no doubt that this important dimension of international relations will continue to receive increasing attention in future years. It is essential for the United States to give greater attention to and gain a deeper understanding of the realities of the new era in the Western Pacific and to reassess and reorient its approaches and policies toward the region, including security policies, in the light of these new realities. In their rhetoric U.S. policymakers have shown an awareness of these new directions and new imperatives, but they have not yet adequately reoriented their policies or their thinking. They must certainly take a broader approach to security than they have thus far demonstrated, and they must relate U.S. security policies in the region more closely to those in other parts of the world and also to other aspects of overall policy. These are challenges that have not yet received adequate responses.

For the United States the Western Pacific is probably the second most important region in the world. It is perhaps the most highly militarized part of the world. It contains some of the world's most dangerous conflict zones. It is the region in which the superpowers and two other major powers, Japan and the People's Republic of China, interact most directly in various ways. It was the second major theater of conflict during World War II. It has been the scene of the two major wars in which the United States has been involved since 1945. It is not surprising, therefore, that with respect to this region security considerations have been uppermost in the minds of many American policymakers. But it is becoming increasingly apparent that these considerations must be more closely related to political, economic, and other policies and interests.

The security environment in the Western Pacific is changing significantly. Moreover, threat perceptions continue to vary greatly among countries of the region and between the United States and most of these countries, even including U.S. allies. Approaches to security are taking on new and more comprehensive dimensions.

Fully realizing the special problems and risks involved, I have tried to write a book that will have some value and appeal for the specialist, the policymaker, and the general reader. The subject of this volume should be of interest and concern to all of these audiences, in the United States, in the Western Pacific, and elsewhere. For the specialist there may be some value in having a work that provides an overview of U.S. security policies and relationships in the entire Western Pacific region, as viewed from the countries of the region as well as from Washington and elsewhere in the United States. From this perspective there are no specialists on the entire subject, although there are many on various aspects of it. For the policy-maker, who in all probability is not an expert on the region nor on security matters in any real sense of the term, a comprehensive overview may be of both immediate utility and long-range value. For the general reader it may provide important background information, analyses, and perspectives that may help in understanding the nature and dimensions of a subject that is rapidly coming within the purview of almost every informed person in the United States and elsewhere.

In the preparation of this volume I drew extensively on my own vol-uminous files and on official statements, reports, and other documents and materials from the United States and the major countries of the Western Pacific region. I intensively analyzed a vast number of published works by American, Asian, and other authors. For information and insights regarding a rapidly changing scene I relied on an extensive reading of current literature, from such obvious newspapers and journals as the *New York Times* and the *Far Eastern Economic Review* to published sources less well known and more specialized. My frequent visits to the Western Pacific region began during World War II, when as a naval air combat intelligence officer I served for many months in the Pacific combat theater. I have benefited greatly from my own continuing contacts with scholars, officials, and other knowledge-able persons in the United States and the Western Pacific countries. This "endless dialogue" and these continuing direct encounters have been espe-cially stimulating and informative.

I am indebted to many good personal friends, to many officials in the U.S. government and in the governments of Western Pacific countries, and to many research centers in the United States, the Western Pacific, and elsewhere, for helping and stimulating me in more ways than they can imagine. I am particularly grateful to Joseph G. Whelan, senior specialist in international affairs, Congressional Research Service (CRS), for making available to me at an early stage the six lengthy reports prepared by him and Michael J. Dixon, research analyst in Soviet and East European affairs in the CRS, with the assistance of a number of colleagues in the CRS and on the staff of the Committee on Foreign Affairs of the U.S. House of Representatives. These reports were first published in 1985 by the Government Printing Office for the use of the House Committee on Foreign Affairs under the title "The Soviet Union in the Third World: Threat to World Peace?," and in 1986 were made available in book form, under the same title, by Pergamon-Brassey's International Defense Publishers.

I am also especially indebted to my long-time friend and former colleague, Robert L. Pfaltzgraff, Jr., president of the Institute for Foreign Policy Analysis (IFPA) and a professor at the Fletcher School of Law and Diplomacy, for making available to me a number of relevant reports and studies issued under the auspices of the IFPA, sometimes in collaboration with other research institutes in this country and in the Western Pacific.

Donald C. Hellman of the University of Washington (associated with the Political Science Department and the Jackson School of International Studies) was most helpful in providing two important unpublished reports of study teams representing the Pacific Forum in Honolulu. These study teams spent several weeks in East and Southeast Asia. Professor Hellmann was the major author of one of these reports. He also contributed to my consciousness raising by giving me his personal impressions of the changing situation in the Western Pacific and its implications for U.S. security and other policies.

Over the years I have gained new insights into the major themes addressed in this volume through my association with colleagues at the University of Pennsylvania and at a number of major research centers in the United States, including the Council on Foreign Relations and the Foreign Policy Research Institute. More recently I have benefited from my participation in the discussions organized by the Pacific Northwest Colloquium on International Security.

During my visits to various countries of the Western Pacific I have been able to confer with many scholars, officials, and others on matters relevant to the present volume. My recent contacts with such knowledgeable people in South Korea were particularly fruitful. I should like to acknowledge my special indebtedness to Ambassador Park Kun (a former student) and others in the Institute of International Relations in the Ministry of External Affairs, to a remarkable internationalist, Chancellor Young Seek Choue, and the fine group of scholars at the Graduate Institute of Peace Studies and the Institute of International Peace Studies at Kyung Hee University in Seoul, and to several key officials in the Korean Association of International Relations.

For two opportunities in recent years to confer with scholars and officials in the Soviet Union about security problems and U.S.–Soviet relations, including security relations in the Western Pacific, I wish to express my appreciation for the invitations of the Institute of Far Eastern Studies of the U.S.S.R. Academy of Sciences, which made it possible for me to obtain at first-hand insights into Soviet thinking, policies, and basic policy motivations and objectives. Thanks to the arrangements made by the Institute of Far Eastern Studies I was able to exchange views with leading Soviet specialists on Western Pacific and security affairs in that Institute, the Institute of Oriental Studies, the Institute of World Economy and International Relations, and the

Institute of the U.S.A. and Canada, all affiliated with the Academy of Sciences, and also with several key officials in the Soviet Ministry of Foreign Affairs (especially Mikhail Kapitsa, now a deputy foreign minister) and in the Communist Party of the Soviet Union.

I have used some of the material in this volume to prepare the article "The United States and the Western Pacific: Understanding the Future," published in *Current History* (vol. 85, no. 510, April 1986).

For their personal interest as well as their professional guidance and assistance I am indebted to Franklin D. Margiotta, President and Director of Publishing, and Don McKeon, Jr., Editor, Pergamon-Brassey's International Defense Publishers, and Angela Piliouras, Production Editor, Pergamon Press. Mr. McKeon guided me through all the final stages of the preparation of the manuscript and was always available for consultation and advice. Ms. Piliouras supervised the copyediting of the manuscript and the production of the book.

May I venture a personal word in conclusion? After spending most of my life looking at Asia and the Western Pacific from several places on the Atlantic seaboard, with frequent visits to various countries of the Asia-Pacific area, I am now living in retirement (?) in the Western Seaboard state that enjoys the closest geographic—and perhaps also psychic—access to the countries on the other side of the Pacific Basin. About one-fifth of its labor force is dependent on international trade, especially with Western Pacific nations, and it has a large population of Asian origin. The San Juan Islands in the far northwestern part of this country provide an excellent vantage point for a "westward watch". Looking out over the Strait of Juan de Fuca, I can see in my mind's eye the vast expanse of the Western Pacific. It is as helpful and consciousness raising to view the region from this perspective as it is to look at the United States from the other side of the Pacific rim.

All Americans, not merely those with special interest and first-hand experience in the Western Pacific, including those in high policymaking positions, must be concerned with and better informed regarding the unfolding drama in the new era in the Western Pacific region, a drama that is changing the character of the region and is making it a major international stage. This drama has security dimensions that the United States cannot disregard, especially if the concept of security is given the broader and more comprehensive interpretation required for the promotion of true national interests, international cooperation, and greater prospects for human and national survival in an increasingly interdependent and shrinking world.

Norman D. Palmer
Friday Harbor,
San Juan Islands
Washington, U.S.A.
April, 1987

Acknowledgments

FOR permission to quote from the following publications, I am indebted to: Oelgeschlager, Gunn & Hain: *Asian Security in the 1980s*, edited by Richard H. Solomon, 1980; Council on Foreign Relations and Yale University Press: *Soviet Policy in East Asia*, edited by Donald S. Zagoria, 1982; Westview Press: *U.S. Foreign Policy and Asian-Pacific Security*, edited by William T. Tow and William R. Feeney, 1982; Jeffrey Record and Pergamon-Brassey's International Defense Publishers: *Revising U.S. Military Strategy: Tailoring Means to Ends*, by Jeffrey Record, 1984; *Current History*: "The United States and Southeast Asia," by Gareth Porter, December 1984; Pacific Forum, Honolulu: "Northeast Asia Trip Report," 1984, and "Australia-New Zealand Trip Report," 1984; *The Economist*: "Did You Say Pacific . . . ?," map in issue of February 16, 1985; *The Seattle Times*: "Rival Naval Bases in the Pacific," map in issue of September 28, 1986.

List of Maps

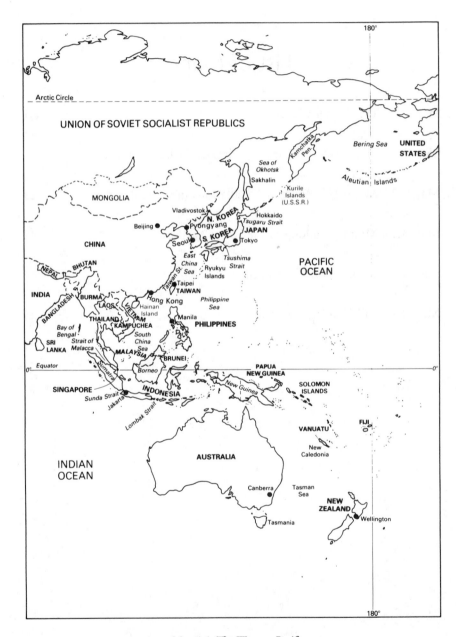

Map 1.1. The Western Pacific

CHAPTER 1

The New Era in the Western Pacific: Security Implications for the United States

A NEW era is dawning in the Western Pacific, and the United States would do well to make a greater effort to understand its nature and implications. In economic terms, and to a lesser but growing extent in political and security aspects as well, this vast region, especially its East Asian subregion, has become a major theater of U.S. contacts and interactions.

As the Pacific Basin becomes increasingly an area of international attention and activities it is only natural that relations among the countries of its eastern and western rims should become closer and more extensive. This is particularly true of the major nation of the eastern rim—the United States—and of the major nations of the western rim—Japan and China. It is also true of the United States and the Soviet Union, because these two superpowers have a formidable presence and influence in the countries of the Western Pacific and in its adjoining waters in the Pacific and Indian Oceans. The relationships and interactions of the superpowers in this region are, of course, only a part, and not the most important part, of their overall relations. These relations are still more centered on Europe than on the Asia-Pacific area, and, more important, on global more than on regional considerations.

In this larger perspective the Western Pacific will assume an increasingly important place. It is the homeland of some of the world's oldest and most complex civilizations, and of more than one-third of the human race. It is also the locale where some of the major political and economic developments have taken place in relatively recent years (especially since World War II) and where problems of political, economic, and social development, of demographic and ecological challenge, and of the reconciliation of tradition and modernity—in other words, the problems that constitute the present world *problematique*—have assumed gigantic proportions. It is the region that has the dubious distinction of being the site of the first use of the atomic bomb in warfare and thus, in a sense, of ushering in the nuclear age. It is a region where some of the most innovative and future-oriented contemporary ideas and inventions—such as those associated with the communications and computer

1

revolutions, in which the United States and Japan have pioneered, and other major scientific and technological advances—have germinated and been applied.[1]

NEW ERAS IN THE WESTERN PACIFIC SINCE WORLD WAR II

During the less than one-half century since World War II—a brief period indeed in the time span of the region's long and crowded history—the Western Pacific has already experienced several new eras. They seem to come almost every decade. They are the result of a large number of significant internal, regional, and international developments that have changed the political, economic, and security environment in the region almost beyond recognition. These eras have also been marked by the increased impact of external powers and events upon the region—an impact with both helpful and deleterious effects—and by the gradual but growing roles and influence of the countries of the region and of the region as a whole on the changing international system.

World War II and its immediate aftermath was an obvious watershed. The war brought the entire region into the vortex of the first truly global conflict, and it changed the political map of the region in innumerable ways. It also brought the United States and the Soviet Union, the two countries that emerged from the global struggle as the only superpowers, into the region, as major actors and major intervening powers in increasing conflict and confrontation with each other in this region as in other parts of the world. Both countries, to be sure, had long been involved in the Western Pacific, and especially in East Asia, but their wartime and postwar involvement has been of wider dimensions and of greater significance and impact than ever before.

Immediately after World War II, Japan, which had emerged as the first Asian world power, ceased to exist as a sovereign nation and became an occupied country. China survived as a nation, but eight years of war with Japan and continuing conflict between Nationalists and Communists left it in a weakened condition. Korea passed from a long period of Japanese rule to division by the United States and the Soviet Union along the Thirty-eighth Parallel, with what were in effect puppet regimes established in both parts of the divided country. Taiwan, also under Japanese rule for many decades, became the place of refuge for—and of domination by—the Nationalist Chinese. In Southeast Asia the former colonial rulers returned to Vietnam and the Dutch East Indies, but their days were numbered and no Western support for their continued control could offset the tide of nationalism and growing demand for independence.

In the late 1940s and early 1950s, a new era began. The People's Republic of China was proclaimed on October 1, 1949. The Korean War (1950–53) brought the United States and the new Chinese Communist regime, as well as the rival Korean regimes, into direct conflict. The allied occupation of Japan ended, and a peace treaty was signed with Japan (to which the Soviet Union and India did not adhere); Japan re-emerged as a sovereign nation, and the U.S.–Japan security treaty was signed in 1951 and effected in 1952. The new era also began with the failure of France's effort to continue its hold on Vietnam, was followed by conflict between the Viet Minh and the Bao Dai regimes and some involvement of the United States, and saw, finally, the emergence of several new nations in Southeast Asia and elsewhere in Asia and Oceania.

These were all major developments. They changed the political, economic, and security picture in the Western Pacific, and they brought the entire region more centrally and more conspicuously into the orbit of world attention and global interactions.

In this era the confrontation and tension between the United States and the Soviet Union in the Western Pacific and elsewhere and the division between the Communist and noncommunist regimes in the region became more marked. The new Communist regime in China entered into a treaty of alliance and cooperation with the Soviet Union in 1950 and proclaimed itself to belong to "the anti-imperialist camp headed by the Soviet Union". Several of the most important noncommunist states of the region entered into security arrangements with the United States on a bilateral or multilateral basis. Major examples of bilateral security arrangements were the U.S. security treaties with Japan (1952) and South Korea (1954). Major examples of multilateral security arrangements were the ANZUS pact (1951), concluded by the United States, Australia, and New Zealand, and the Manila pact (1954), under which the United States, Britain, France, Australia, New Zealand, Pakistan, Thailand, and the Philippines became associated in the Southeast Asia Treaty Organization (SEATO).

A third era began to be apparent in the late 1950s and early 1960s, with the Sino–Soviet split and the beginning of large-scale American involvement in Vietnam. The Sino–Soviet split was one of the most surprising and most important developments in post-World War II international relations. It has had a wide impact on the world power struggle, as well as on the situation in the entire Western Pacific. Although it was not clearly realized at the time, large-scale American involvement in Vietnam during the Johnson administration (whose beginnings can be traced to the Kennedy and perhaps previous administrations) had fateful effects on the situation in Indochina and elsewhere in Southeast Asia and on the U.S. role and influence in the Western Pacific region and beyond.

A decade later another new era was marked by the Cultural Revolution in the People's Republic of China; the beginnings of the dramatic reversal in Sino–American and Sino–Japanese relations; the American withdrawal from Vietnam (a significant blow to U.S. influence, prestige, and credibility in the entire Western Pacific, leading to a marked decline in the American presence and interest in the region); the emergence of Japan as an economic, but still not a political or military major power, and the impressive economic progress of some of the smaller states of the region, notably the "four little tigers of Asia"—South Korea, Taiwan, Hong Kong, and Singapore, whose economic growth was more impressive than their political development.

The next era, in the late 1970s and early 1980s, was characterized by the continuance of the "economic miracle" in all of these countries, with some evidence that other states of the region such as Malaysia and even Indonesia had also made a quantum jump in economic if not in political terms, and that even Communist China, after the Cultural Revolution and the death of Mao Tse-tung (Mao Zedong), was embarking on a new, more pragmatic, and more promising economic road featuring a strange mixture of socialist and free market policies while still within the ideological framework of the Chinese version of Marxism-Leninism.

In retrospect, the first conspicuous signs of the present era dawning in the Western Pacific began to appear during the two previous eras. The signs of the present era are many and significant.[2] In almost every country of the region, large and small, even in some of the Communist countries, these signs include perhaps first and foremost a growing preoccupation with internal problems and needs and a more pragmatic and realistic approach to these internal problems, illustrated by China's "four modernizations" program and the "national resilience" program of Indonesia. Next in importance—and perhaps of primary importance from a global and security perspective—is the growing tide of self-confidence, of linking basic traditions, values, and cultures to contemporary realities, of self-assertiveness, of independence, of a more selective reaction to external influences and practices. A new kind of nationalism is emerging, a nationalism that seeks to preserve one's own identity and to capitalize on growing internal strength while at the same time recognizing the limits as well as the opportunities of external relations and activities in an interdependent world. In the Western Pacific, as in every other part of the world, we are confronted with one of the supreme paradoxes of the contemporary era—the paradox of growing nationalism and inward-turning, on the one hand, and of increasing regional and international linkages and interdependence, on the other.

The United States has not yet made the requisite policy adjustments to these outstanding features of the present era in the Western Pacific.[3] This is not surprising, because the United States leadership has not yet demonstrated that it understands the nature, significance, and dimensions of these changes in a region of growing international importance and certainly of growing importance to the United States. In fairness to U.S. policymakers, it should be noted that the outlines and course of this new era are still not clear, even to the leaders of the Western Pacific countries or to indigenous or external specialists on the region. Hence even if American policymakers were less preoccupied with other matters and more familiar with the Western Pacific scene, their failure to make important adjustments in existing policies toward the region and toward the countries in it would be understandable. But they must pay more attention to the region, to the great changes that are under way there, and to the implications for U.S. policy. This task must be given a far higher priority on their agenda of concerns than it has received to date. Thus far their policies have not matched their rhetoric.

THE CHANGING SECURITY ENVIRONMENT IN THE WESTERN PACIFIC .

In the current era the problem of security in the Western Pacific must be viewed from a broader and more balanced perspective.[4] Security is a major consideration for the countries of the region as well as for the United States. In the existing regional environment the wider dimensions of security and its relation to other dimensions of national, regional, and global interests and policies must be more generally recognized. The military aspects of security will still be of central importance, but other aspects—political, economic, cultural, psychological—must also be integrated into security planning and policies. Here a possible difference in perspective and orientation between the United States and the Soviet Union, on the one hand, and most of the countries of the Western Pacific, on the other, will require more careful attention. In general, a prevailing view in the region is that the superpowers take a dangerously narrow and technical approach to security, emphasizing military aspects. Conversely, there is widespread belief among policymakers in both superpowers that most of the Western Pacific countries, even those allied with one or the other, do not attach sufficient importance to the military dimensions of security and tend to emphasize nonmilitary aspects, not so much because these weaker countries have a more realistic and accurate approach to security but because these countries are searching for ways to compensate for their relative weakness and avoid the hard decisions and commitments that a more adequate military posture would entail.

Any adequate security planning and implementation measures in the new era must be based on a recognition and an understanding of the changing security environment in the Western Pacific, and of the significance of this changing environment from national, regional, and, at least in the case of the superpowers and China and Japan, global perspectives.[5] The nature of this changing security environment has already been the subject of extensive and continuing consideration and analysis in decision-making circles in all of the countries involved in the region and by scholars and research institutions in the region and elsewhere. That changing environment is being shaped by a large number of major developments and trends in recent years. Among these are:

- The changed relations between the Soviet Union and China, between the United States and China, and between Japan and China;
- The American withdrawal from Vietnam after the failure of a decade of

intensive military operations in that area, and the impact of this development on U.S. policy in the entire region and on the attitudes of the countries of the region toward the United States;

- The rise of Japan to the position of the world's second-largest market-oriented economic power and the slowly emerging signs that Japan is beginning to be less ambivalent and hesitant regarding its proper political and military posture and role in the region and globally;
- The many changes in alliance relationships and the emergence of other patterns of alignment, well short of formal alliance;
- The developments in Vietnam since the U.S. withdrawal and the end of the Vietnam War, including the Communist consolidation of control over the entire country, the tragic happenings in Cambodia/Kampuchea, including internal brutalities and Vietnamese military occupation, the strong support of Vietnam by the Soviet Union, and the continuing hostility toward Vietnam of China and the United States;
- The emergence of ASEAN as an increasingly significant and active regional arrangement and regional actor, and its increasing use, thus far more indirectly than directly, as a forum for the consideration of security as well as economic, political, cultural, and other forms of cooperation;
- The new and unexpected strains in relations between New Zealand and the United States and the consequent crisis in ANZUS;
- The major military buildup of the Soviet Union in East Asia, the adjacent seas, and the western reaches of the Pacific Ocean;
- The increasing militarization of the region;
- The impressive economic growth of Japan and several of the smaller countries of the region; and
- The continuing political and social instabilities in and uncertain political future of most of the nations of East and Southeast Asia.

To this lengthy, but still highly selective, list should be added the two factors that have been mentioned as perhaps the most important general portents of the new era, namely (1) the growing emphasis in most of the countries of the region on internal problems and concerns, including political, economic, and social development, internal tensions, and the reconciliation of national values and identity with increasing interdependence and modernization goals; and (2) the growing self-assertiveness, self-confidence, and independence of almost all of the countries of the region.

Major developments and trends outside the region have also had an obvious impact. Among these are the continuing tensions and the escalating arms race between the superpowers, the oil price rise following the 1973 Yom Kippur (Arab–Israeli) War and more recent slump in oil prices and production and other evidences of a growing energy crisis, various crises in the international economy of most major Western economic powers and to some extent of those of the Western Pacific region, a rising tide of protectionism and other "beggar-thy-neighbor" policies, the Soviet invasion of

Afghanistan, the increasing naval presence and confrontation of the United States and the Soviet Union in the Pacific and Indian Oceans, and a growing world malaise reflected in widespread doubts about the future.

Obviously the United States must continually reassess the changing security environment in the Western Pacific and in other parts of the world and shape its security and other policies toward the countries of the region in the light of the changing realities. To do this it must consider the security and other interests in the Western Pacific from a broader and less ethnocentric—and Eurocentric—perspective than it has demonstrated to date. This also requires greater attention to and a deeper understanding of the concerns and interests of the countries of the region, as those concerns and interests are perceived by these countries themselves. A standard criticism in almost all countries—including those of the Atlantic community—is that Americans do not really try to understand the perceptions and viewpoints of other countries and peoples, and in fact do not even listen to what others are saying. This criticism is quite pervasive in the Western Pacific region, where the genuine concern of the United States for the welfare and security of the countries and peoples of the region and the desire of Americans to understand the basic realities of the region are seriously questioned, as well as are the reliability and credibility of U.S. commitments.

DIFFERING THREAT PERCEPTIONS AND SECURITY PERSPECTIVES

It is particularly important for the United States to recognize that the security environment in the Western Pacific is a complex as well as a changing one, and that there are, in the region, many different threat perceptions and security perspectives that differ rather substantially from American views and assessments.[6] These basic considerations have been especially stressed and substantiated by American as well as by indigenous specialists in Western Pacific affairs, but they have not yet been adequately incorporated into official U.S. thinking and planning. Official attitudes still are so dominated by global concerns and suffer so much from a lack of understanding of or deep concern for the views of the countries of the Western Pacific that they are not properly geared to the needs and new realities of the Asia-Pacific region in this new era.

In U.S. official circles the United States seems to have a very clear idea of the basic security threat in the Western Pacific. In this region, as elsewhere, that threat is the Soviet Union. Soviet policies in the region, especially the growing military buildup in East Asia and the Pacific, extending into Southeast Asia and the Indian Ocean, have only confirmed the American view of the number one threat to the region. But that view is shared only to a limited degree by some of the Western Pacific countries and regarded as a dangerous and unwarranted American preoccupation—or obsession—by others. Even in countries with which the United States is allied, including Japan, South

Korea, and Australia, and in other countries whose leaders have been particularly critical of the Soviet Union, such as Taiwan and Singapore, concern about the Soviet threat is less deeply felt and is given a less exclusive priority than it is in the United States. Even the leaders of the People's Republic of China, who after the break with the Soviet Union and particularly after Mao's death warned the United States and the world against the dangers of Soviet hegemonism, now take a less obsessive view of the dangers from the Soviet Union than does the United States. In other words, no country in the entire Western Pacific region completely shares the views of the United States regarding the priority that should be given to the threat from the Soviet Union.[7] Some are more concerned with potential threats from the other major powers in or involved in the region, particularly from China, but even, in the longer run at least, from Japan and the United States. This perspective exists in most countries of the region and is particularly discernible in most of the noncommunist states of Southeast Asia, perhaps more notably in Malaysia and Indonesia. The United States cannot promote its cooperative security relationships in the Western Pacific without giving more consideration to these multiple-security perspectives and threat perceptions and to the very different and complex views regarding the Soviet threat.

In many of the Western Pacific countries immediate and localized external threats are of greater concern than those from major powers, including the Soviet Union. For example, South Korea is primarily concerned with the threat from North Korea, although recognizing that this threat is aggravated by external support of the North from China and the Soviet Union and is mitigated by the support that it receives from the United States and, to a lesser extent, from Japan. The ASEAN countries, and particularly Thailand, are primarily concerned about the threat from Vietnam, aggravated, to be sure, by Soviet backing of Vietnam. The island mini-states of Oceania are more concerned about the pervasive presence and influence in their area of the United States, France, and Britain, and especially about the nuclear policies and activities of the United States and France in their oceanic areas, than they are about the relatively limited Soviet presence, influence, and pressures.

Perhaps the most important differences in threat perceptions and security perspectives between the United States and the countries of the Western Pacific are those between the global approach to security of the United States and the regionalized and localized approaches of most of the countries of the region (with the possible exceptions of Japan and the People's Republic of China, which are emerging as important international as well as regional actors). The United States is necessarily concerned with global interests and threats. As a high-ranking American official stated in 1984, "We have no choice but to view our strategic interests from a global perspective."[8] U.S. concern about the Soviet threat is a global one, with the Western Pacific as an area of lesser concern, except during periods when conflicts in that region involved the possibility of Soviet–American conflict. Heretofore, in American security thinking and planning, the Western Pacific, except for limited crisis periods, has been given a lower security priority than Western Europe and the Middle East, and sometimes Latin America as well. Quite understandably, some difficulties in security approaches and cooperation have arisen because the Western Pacific is only one of the major world regions with which the United States is concerned, whereas naturally for the indigenous nations it is the region of primary concern.

As has been noted, Western Pacific nations also place much greater emphasis than does the United States on internal security threats.[9] Indeed, many of these nations attach the highest priority of concern to internal threats, and many seem to view external threats mainly in the context of the extent to which these exacerbate their problems of internal stability and security. These internal threats are many and varied; they usually include threats posed by internal dissident and insurgent groups, political instabilities, economic underdevelopment, population pressures, and social and ethnic tensions. In many of the countries, governments in power—often shaky authoritarian regimes with little legitimacy or base in popular support—regard opposition groups generally as internal threats. This raises the much-discussed question of threats to governments in power as contrasted with threats to the countries themselves. The two are not necessarily synonymous. Leaders of governments in power believe, or pretend to believe, that threats to them are also threats to the nation, whereas opposition leaders and groups often contend that the most serious threats to the nation, internal or external, are the very governments and leaders that are in power.

For the United States such concern with internal security threats and differences of views regarding them pose serious security dilemmas—indeed, place the United States in a kind of Catch-22 situation with respect to nations with which it has special security interests and relationships. If it tries to intervene or exert influence too directly, it will be accused of unjustified interference in internal affairs. If it does not include internal conditions in its agenda of security concerns, it will be accused of ignoring basic dimensions of security and of national policy. It must work with the government in power in every country with which it has relations, whatever its views of that government may be. If it fails or refuses to do this, it will be unable to get the access and cooperation that it will need to further mutually agreed-upon goals. But if it works too closely with a government, it will be accused of giving undue support and approval and will alienate critics of that government at home and abroad. In any event, in addition to recognizing that the countries of the Western Pacific do not give as high a priority to the Soviet threat as it does, the United States must recognize that most of these countries are primarily concerned with internal problems, even from a security perspective. Recognition of both conditioning factors must be a central part of U.S. security planning, policies, and activities with reference to the Western Pacific region.

These introductory comments have concentrated on main background

themes and considerations. A general conclusion for U.S. policy that under-
lies this entire overview is the importance of continuing reassessment of
security and other policies in the light of these background considerations
and new realities. This general theme should be borne in mind as we now turn
to an overview of U.S. security policies and relationships in the Western
Pacific and undertake a more detailed analysis of these policies and relationships, first with respect to the other major actors and then with respect to
other countries in this complex and increasingly important world region.

Notes

[1] An American specialist on Pacific affairs has called attention to several major social and
scientific innovations that mainly originated and reached their fullest development in the
Pacific region: "Perhaps the most exciting aspect of the emergence of the Pacific Basin as an
influential area is its creative contributions to innovations and new trends with dramatic
implications for future culture and civilization. The microprocessing revolution, robotics,
Theory Z and industrial democracy, ecotopia, cultural democracy and *dependencia* are
significant new concepts and theories all having their origins in the Pacific Basin." Gerald W.
Frey, "The Pacific Challenge: A Transnational Future," *Asia Pacific Community* 21 (Summer
1983): 37.

[2] Perceptive analyses of the new era in the Western Pacific, especially as viewed by leading
officials and scholars in the countries of the region, with concise commentaries on the
implications for United States policy, are contained in three reports of study teams of the
Pacific Forum in Honolulu: (1) "Pacific Forum Northeast Asia Summary Report," report of "a
study and investigative tour of the Republic of China, the Republic of Korea, and Japan . . .
from September 3–15, 1984" (Rear Admiral Lloyd R. Vasey (Ret.), president and executive
director of the Pacific Forum, and Professor Donald C. Hellmann of the University of
Washington, joined by Admiral Thomas B. Hayward (Ret.), vice-chairman of the Pacific
Forum, during the visit to Japan); (2) an untitled report of a two-person team (Admiral Vasey
and Professor Donald E. Weatherbee of the University of South Carolina) that visited all of the
ASEAN countries except Brunei between July 14 and August 4, 1984; and (3) "Australia–New
Zealand Trip Report," report of a two-person team (Admiral Vasey and Professor Henry S.
Albinski of the Pennsylvania State University) that visited Australia and New Zealand between
October 23 and November 11, 1984. For official U.S. perspectives on the changing scene in the
Western Pacific, see "The U.S. and East Asia: A Partnership for the Future," an address by
Secretary of State George Shultz before the World Affairs Council of San Francisco, March 5,
1983; Bureau of Public Affairs, U.S. Department of State, *Current Policy*, no. 459; "The Asia-
Pacific Region: A Forward Look," address by Michael H. Armacost, under secretary of state
for political affairs, before the Far East–America Council/Asia Society, New York, Jan. 29,
1985, in *Current Policy*, no. 653; and "The Pacific: Region of Promise and Challenge,"
address by Paul D. Wolfowitz, assistant secretary of state for East Asian and Pacific affairs,
before the National Defense University Pacific Symposium, Honolulu, February 22, 1983, in
Current Policy, no. 660.

[3] For overviews of U.S. relations with and policies toward the countries of the Western Pacific
and the region as a whole, especially in the 1970s and 1980s, see: Lloyd R. Vasey, ed., *Pacific
Asia and U.S. Policies: A Political-Economic-Strategic Assessment* (Honolulu: Pacific
Forum, 1978); Raymond H. Myers, ed., *A U.S. Foreign Policy for Asia: The 1980s and
Beyond* (Stanford, Calif.: Hoover Institution Press, 1982); William T. Tow and William R.
Feeney, eds., *U.S. Foreign Policy and Asian-Pacific Security: A Transregional Approach*
(Boulder, Colorado: Westview Press,, 1982); James S. Hsiung, ed., *U.S.–Asian Relations: The
National Security Paradox* (New York: Praeger Publishers, 1983); Robert L. Downen and
Bruce J. Dickson, eds., *The Emerging Pacific Community: A Regional Perspective* (Boulder,
Colorado: Westview Press, 1984); Robert A. Scalapino, "The US and East Asia: Views and
Policies in a Changing Era," *Survival* 24 (July–August 1982), reprinted in Robert O'Neill, ed.,
Security in East Asia (Aldershot, Hants.: Gower Publishing Company, for the International

Institute of Strategic Studies, 1984); and Norman D. Palmer, "The United States and the Western Pacific: Understanding the Future," *Current History* 85 (April 1986).

4 See *The Growing Dimensions of Security: A Report by the Atlantic Council's Working Group on Security* (Washington, D.C.: The Atlantic Council of the United States, 1977); *Common Security: Report of the Independent Commission on Disarmament and Security Issues* (the Palme Commission) (London: Pan Books, 1982); and *Report on Comprehensive National Security*, by the Comprehensive Security Group (Tokyo, 1980). See also the introductory essay by Robert A. Scalapino in Robert A. Scalapino, Seizaburo Sato, and Jusuf Wanandi, eds., *Internal and External Security Issues in Asia* (Berkeley, Calif.: Institute of East Asian Studies, University of California, 1986).

5 For good general analyses of the changing strategic environment in the Western Pacific, see Richard H. Solomon, "American Defense Planning and Asian Security: Policy Choices for a Time of Transition," chapter 1 in Richard H. Solomon, ed., *Asian Security in the 1980s: Problems and Policies for a Time of Transition* (Cambridge, Mass.: Oelgeschlager, Gunn & Hain, 1980): Donald S. Zagoria, "The Strategic Environment in Asia," chapter 1 in Donald S. Zagoria, ed., *Soviet Policy in East Asia* (New Haven: Yale University Press, 1982); and Peter Polomka, "The Security of the Western Pacific: The Price of Burden Sharing," *Survival* 26 (January–February 1984).

6 For good overviews of differing threat perceptions and security perspectives in the countries of the Western Pacific, and between these countries and the United States, see Charles E. Morrison, ed., *Threats to Security in East Asia–Pacific: National and Regional Perspectives* (Lexington, Mass.: Lexington Books, 1983); and Mizanur Rahman Khan, "Security Threats and Responses in the Asia-Pacific Region," *BIISS Journal* 5 (July 1984). (*BIISS Journal* is the organ of the Bangladesh Institute for International and Strategic Studies, Dhaka, Bangladesh).

7 This important fact was brought out clearly in the reports of the three study teams of the Pacific Forum in 1984 that are cited in note 2.

8 "NATO and the Challenges Ahead," address by Michael H. Armacost, under secretary of state for political affairs, before the thirtieth meeting of the Atlantic Treaty Association, Toronto, October 10, 1984; Bureau of Public Affairs, U.S. Department of State, *Current Policy*, no. 620, 4. In this address Mr. Armacost was "asked, in particular, to comment on the security situation in the Asia/Pacific region." *Ibid.*, 1. Reflecting the usual orientation of official American spokespersons, he placed particular emphasis on the Soviet threat, in the region and globally.

9 This view was brought out clearly, and forcefully, by the Southeast Asian contributors—Jusuf Wanandi and M. Hadosoesastro (Indonesia), Zamil Abidin B. Abdul Wahid (Malaysia), Carlos F. Nivera (Philippines), Lau Teik Soon (Singapore), and Thanant Khoman, Sarasin Virophol, and Somsakdi Xuto (Thailand)—to Morrison, ed., *Threats to Security in East Asia–Pacific.*

CHAPTER 2

The United States and Western Pacific Security: An Overview

In terms of security policies and planning, the concerns of the United States have been global in scope and nature, centering mainly on the problem of achieving security in the nuclear age against the perceived threats from the other superpower, the Soviet Union. In general, therefore, it has been more concerned with global than with regional security; but because the global challenge has often centered on particular regions, notably Western Europe, East Asia, and the Middle East, its global security concerns have had a strong regional focus.

The relative importance attached to the world's regions in American security thinking has varied greatly as a result of changing perceptions and circumstances. Priority among the world's regions has usually been given to Western Europe, because this is the region with which the United States has long had special interests and relationships, and it has been the potentially most dangerous theater of superpower confrontation. The Western Pacific, especially East Asia, has sometimes been an area of high priority, but despite lip-service recognition of this fact on the part of American political leaders, many observers would agree with Stephen B. Gibert that those leaders "have consistently undervalued the importance of Northeast Asia in world politics."[1]

THE UNITED STATES AND THE WESTERN PACIFIC SINCE WORLD WAR II

The situation in the Western Pacific has been particularly complex and changing, and particularly bewildering, to Americans, who are far less familiar with its people, its politics, and its cultures than they are with Western Europe and European civilization. Yet the Western Pacific was the second major theater of World War II, and also the theater of the two main wars in which the United States has been centrally involved since the end of World War II. The impact of the Korean War and the Vietnam War upon the United States, and indeed upon the whole order of power and influence in the world, has been profound and continuing, in innumerable ways.

After the truce in Korea in 1953 the United States recognized its inescapable and continuing involvement in the Western Pacific. After the end of the prolonged war in Vietnam, however, it sought to achieve a partial disengagement from the region, at least from its commitments to the security of the countries on the Asian mainland. This attitude was seemingly confirmed and elevated to the level of doctrine in the "Nixon Doctrine" of 1969. But even before American troops left Vietnam in 1975, the United States had begun to show a growing recognition and acceptance of the fact that it was too deeply involved in Western Pacific affairs, in military, political, economic, and other respects, to permit any significant disengagement from the region. More recent developments have brought the security of the Western Pacific even more closely within the orbit of American policy concern. These include the new relationship with China, the changing relations with Japan, and the Soviet military buildup in East Asia and the adjacent Pacific waters. The heightened apprehensions regarding Soviet policies and intentions in that region were in part a result of the spillover effects of the increasing globalism of the Soviet Union, its active intervention in areas of unrest and disturbance in Africa, the Middle East, and elsewhere, and above all its military intervention in Afghanistan.

Many informed observers in Western Pacific countries and in the United States and elsewhere as well think that, as Stephen B. Gibert contended in the early 1980s, the United States still underrates the importance of the Western Pacific region to its own security and to the preservation of security in the world.[2] They believe also that the United States has not laid a sound basis, either in a military or in a psychological sense, for a more satisfactory and continuing relationship with a very important world region, despite frequent professions by American policymakers that they attach great importance to the region and regard its security as vital to the United States. Frequently these professions are couched in terms of a recognition of the growing importance of the entire Pacific Basin region, not only to the United States but to the entire world. Recent American presidents have talked about the advent of the "Pacific Era." In October 1984 President Reagan said that "that is where the future lies."[3] There is a growing recognition of the fact that U.S. relations with the countries of the Western Pacific are quite extensive and are rapidly changing, but unfortunately there is less evidence that U.S. policies and perceptions are truly adjusting to the new circumstances and importance of this part of the world. A few cardinal facts, however, have penetrated the American consciousness. Among these are the facts that U.S. trade in the Asia-Pacific region is now even greater than that with any other part of the world, including Western Europe. A second is that the new U.S.–China relationship is developing erratically, with many difficulties and disappointments, but also with many encouraging prospects. A third is that the Soviet military buildup in the East Asia–Western Pacific region has reached alarming levels. Not so well known is the fact that, if the Soviet military strength in this area is included, East Asia is now the most highly militarized region in the world.

Official U.S. spokespersons frequently refer to the new era in the Asia-Pacific region and assert that the American position and presence in that region are growing in importance and in acceptance. The official view was well expressed by Secretary of State George Shultz in an address before the Los Angeles World Affairs Council in October 1984:

> There is one striking success of the past couple of years that gets little publicity and, therefore, may be virtually unknown to the American people. We have begun to build a network of new ties with our friends in Asia—relationships that could well prove to be one of the most important building blocks of global prosperity and progress in the next century. Only a decade after Vietnam, the United States has more than restored its position in Asia. Our alliances in East Asia are strong, and our friendships there are remarkably promising. . . .
>
> Today, a sense of Pacific community is emerging with a potential for greater collaboration among many nations with an extraordinary diversity of cultures, races, and political systems. Certainly this is not as institutionalized as our ties with Europe, but there is an expanding practice of consultation, a developing sense of common interest, and an exciting vision of the future. We may well be at the threshold of a new era in the Pacific Basin.[4]

Sympathetic commentators on both sides of the Pacific have sometimes pointed out that this kind of approach is much too rosy and overlooks many of the difficulties and limitations in U.S. relations with the countries of the Asia-Pacific region. More critical analysts, including some Americans, believe that a very different assessment, especially of the policies and orientation of the Reagan administration, would be closer to the truth. A rather extreme sample from a reputable American scholar claims that "The United States is today playing the role of the 'sick man' of the Pacific under policies of the administration of President Ronald Reagan. . . . [P]olicies in Washington seem destined to erode the influence of the U.S. in Asia and the Pacific in the late 20th century. . . . [T]he Reaganauts have taken a narcissistic view of Asia and the Pacific that is sharply at variance with what is taking place. . . . [T]he countries of Asia and the Pacific are becoming increasingly disenchanted with American saber rattling to maintain hegemony." The same commentator also believes that '[T]he Reagan administration has paid less attention to Asia and the Pacific than to any other regions of the world," which seems rather inconsistent with the charge that the United States is carrying out a deliberate policy of "saber rattling to maintain hegemony" in the region.[5]

Whatever the verdict regarding recent U.S. policy in the Asia-Pacific area should be—and clearly it should be somewhere between the official and the ultracritical views—the main tasks before the United States with regard to this important region, as delineated by Sheldon Simon, are: ". . . the problem of sorting out Asian priorities; the degree to which the region's integrity is important to U.S. security; the probable threats to that integrity; appropriate American policies toward friendly and hostile states; and finally the force deployments needed to sustain the region's freedom."[6] The main threat to the Asia-Pacific region, as elsewhere, was perceived to be that emanating from the Soviet Union, and U.S. policies and strategies in the area were designed primarily in the light of global rather than regional considerations, commitments, and capabilities.

The United States has been heavily involved in the security of the Western Pacific region since the Japanese attack on Pearl Harbor in December 1941. Its military and strategic objective in the region during World War II was quite clear: the defeat of Japan. Since then its broad goal has been to maintain an order of power in the region that will be conducive to peace, order, and stability in the region and in the world, and that will not present formidable security threats to the United States. Two other general goals and objectives in the Western Pacific are: (1) to encourage and support the emergence of the region as a major actor in the international system, and the trends towards greater peace, stability, and development, and increasing cooperation on national, subregional, regional, and global levels; and (2) to develop and enhance the already extensive pattern of political, economic, security, cultural, and other forms of contacts and relations with the countries of the region. More specifically, the goals and objectives may be summarized as follows:

- In cooperation with its allies and other friendly countries (notably the People's Republic of China), to maintain a sufficient military presence and strength in the region to deter and, if necessary, counter any major military action by the Soviet Union against any nations in the region, or against the United States, in the region or beyond;
- To maintain and strengthen its bilateral or trilateral alliances with Japan, South Korea, the Philippines, Thailand, Australia, and New Zealand; to attempt to deal with the problems and complications that have developed in all of these alliances, and to expand and deepen its security cooperation with other nations of the region;
- To strengthen the alliance and other ties with Japan, and to work more cooperatively with Japan in dealing with the many problems that have arisen in this key relationship;
- To develop its new relationship with the People's Republic of China, on a cautious, limited, but expanding basis, with an emphasis on parallel interests and on recognition of the limits as well as the possibilities of this unique relationship;
- To develop its growing ties with the ASEAN states, and with ASEAN as the most promising regional arrangement in the Western Pacific, and to support the economic and political development as well as the security of the Southeast Asia subregion;
- To continue its security and other connections with South Korea, its unofficial but still substantial ties with Taiwan, and its special relationships with the Philippines and Thailand, constantly stressing its mutual interests with these countries and their people but not necessarily its support of existing authoritarian regimes; and
- To attempt to resolve the impasse with New Zealand and to restore the ANZUS alliance, now at least temporarily in abeyance, and, whether these objectives prove to be realizable or not, to cultivate its bilateral

relationships with Australia and to develop its relations with the smaller island nations of the Southwest Pacific and Oceania.

There is widespread consensus in the United States regarding the desirability of these major goals and objectives, but the United States has never been able to evolve coherent and generally supported policies designed to achieve these agreed-upon objectives. It has, instead, made a number of efforts to reshape its Western Pacific policies in the light of changing circumstances and changing capabilities and interpretations of its national interests.

Its first post-World War II effort was based on the Rooseveltian assumptions that China would be the keystone of security and stability in the region in the postwar era and that Japan, in the aftermath of its defeat, would be restricted to a secondary role. These assumptions became untenable after the People's Republic of China was proclaimed in October 1949 and associated with the Soviet Union to form what was regarded by the United States as a dangerous communist monolith of power and expansionism.

Another appraisal was forced upon the United States by the outbreak of the Korean War in mid-1950, by the heavy American military involvement in that war, and by Chinese intervention and the added possibility of direct Soviet participation. This changed the whole American approach to East Asia and to that region's security needs and dilemmas. It was a major factor in the rapid buildup of American military strength after the post-World War II retrenchment and in the evolution of the concept of massive retaliation in the mid-1950s, associated with Eisenhower's secretary of state, John Foster Dulles. By this time the American occupation of Japan had ended, and the United States was linked to Japan in the security treaty of 1952. No adequate strategy of overall policy was developed to meet these changing conditions.

In the 1960s and early 1970s American preoccupations in the Western Pacific were increasingly focused on Vietnam, which became a quagmire for American forces and a nightmare for America's political and military leaders, demonstrating increasing disparity between goals and actions and causing gradual loss of support on the home front as the agonies of Vietnam belied the claims of official American spokesmen.

[T]he deepening American involvement in Vietnam gradually distorted almost all aspects of U.S.–Asian relationships and created deep divisions not only between the United States and many Asian countries, but also within American society. . . . In the 1970s, the Nixon and Ford administrations made further efforts to reshape policies toward Asia. The emphasis was placed, as President Nixon stated in his fourth report to the Congress on U.S. foreign policy for the 1970s (submitted in May 1973), on ending conflicts (mainly in Vietnam), strengthening partnerships (especially with Japan), and building new relationships (referring to the opening to China). These efforts had some success, but they did not add up to a coherent or consistent policy. Moreover, they had inherent difficulties and inconsistencies, which were complicated by some of the diplomatic mistakes of the U.S. administrations and by the adverse reaction of Japan, America's major ally in Asia, to such moves as the "Nixon shocks" of 1971. The United States did not give Asian relations and problems the kind of priority in its overall foreign policies that many Asian leaders felt was essential, and the "withdrawal mood" in the United States increased Asian doubts about U.S. credibility, capabilities, and will. Watergate and its aftermath led to virtual paralysis in the final months of the Nixon administration, and Nixon's successor, President Ford, was never able to give adequate attention to Asia or to do much more than begin to assuage Asian doubts and hurt feelings.[7]

The withdrawal mood was manifest even before the withdrawal of U.S. forces from Vietnam in the mid-1970s. It was reflected in official policy as well as in the public mood. The "Nixon Doctrine," or Guam Doctrine, first enunciated by President Nixon in an interview with journalists on Guam while he was en route to Asia, in July 1969, and elaborated in his first foreign policy report to the U.S. Congress in February 1970, seemed to reflect this mood, although Nixon always insisted that it in no way represented a renunciation of U.S. treaty and other commitments. As Jeffrey Record has observed, the mood was evidenced throughout the decade of the 1970s: "The U.S. impulse to retrench in Asia continued for eight years, culminating in President Carter's proposal, successfully resisted by the Congress, to withdraw the Army's one remaining division in Korea."[8]

Carter's announced decision to withdraw most of the American ground troops in South Korea was the most highly publicized aspect of his Asian policies, and the one that created the most concern and criticism on the part of most of the non-communist states of the Western Pacific. Although it was reversed two years after it was announced because of strong protests both in Asia and in the United States, it profoundly affected Asian images of America and did lasting damage to American prestige in that part of the world. It was, however, only one aspect of Carter's approach to the East Asia–Western Pacific region. He professed the desire "to improve the American image and the credibility of the United States in Asia and to reassure Asians that the United States had no intention of withdrawing from Asia (except in a limited military sense) and also that it recognized the new realities, changing circumstances, and growing importance of Asia."[9]

The withdrawal mood abruptly ended even before the end of the Carter administration. This was a consequence of many factors and many new developments, both in the Western Pacific (such as the growing concern over the Soviet military buildup in the area) and in other parts of the world (notably the Soviet invasion of Afghanistan and its aftermath). It was also a consequence of the basic approach of President Reagan and his administration, which gave a high priority to the Soviet threat, regionally and globally, and to the need to rebuild American military strength and capabilities after long years of relative neglect. This world view led to a more activist – some would say more hard-line and interventionist—approach to the world generally, and to the Soviet Union in particular.

The Reagan administration has repeatedly affirmed that the United States is a Pacific power and intends to remain one. It has placed special emphasis on U.S. military and other relations with its allies of the Western Pacific, especially with Japan, South Korea, and Australia. It has sought to develop its relationships with the People's Republic of China and has even offered to provide some military or military-related assistance. It has shown a new interest in establishing closer relationships with the ASEAN countries, while maintaining a hard line toward Vietnam. But it has also experienced many difficulties in its relations with its major allies in the Western Pacific, and its relationships with the People's Republic of China and the ASEAN countries are still quite tentative and uncertain. On the whole, however, it feels that it is in a much stronger position than previous administrations have been in military and other respects and that developments in East and Southeast Asia have been more favorable to it and its noncommunist allies than to the Soviet Union.

Some American spokespersons have even argued that the Soviet military buildup in the Western Pacific is more an indication of basic internal weaknesses and of frustration at Soviet inability to exert effective influence abroad by other than military means than it is of growing Soviet strength and influence. But there can be no doubt that the Reagan administration is alarmed by growing Soviet military power and military interventionism wherever it has occurred, as in Africa and Afghanistan, or where it may occur, as in the Western Pacific where formidable military forces and weapons, conventional and unconventional, are based.

No "Reagan Doctrine" has been expounded, although a "Second American Revolution" has been proclaimed. The basic approach of Reagan and his associates is a pragmatic one, even though the language is often highly ideological. This may be a welcome change from the preachments of the past, and from the dilemmas created for American foreign policy by Carter's insistence that the promotion of human rights was a cardinal principle of American foreign policy, even in dealing with the Soviet Union, South Africa, and indeed almost all of the Communist and Third World states, where human rights violations are built-in features and practices. But such a pragmatic approach, anchored in a basically anti-Soviet "operational code" and in an internal policy-making environment in which basic consensus seems to be lacking, is not conducive to the evolution of long-range planning or policy.

The American experience in Asia, especially during and since World War II, is an essential background for an understanding of the current U.S. approach to problems of security in the Western Pacific. These problems are more difficult to deal with because of a lack of basic policy and because of continuing U.S. ambivalence and misperceptions and misunderstanding regarding the Asian scene.

From a regional perspective American policy generally, including security policy, has been and still is strongly Eurocentric. This creates special difficulties in U.S. relations with other parts of the world, especially the Western Pacific, now a major theater of U.S. involvement and concern. As Peter Polomka has perceptively pointed out: "The dangers of seeing Asia through European eyes, of sinking into the quicksands of oversimplification which Western political systems seem to require to function, and of being overinfluenced by the political dynamics of one's own environment rather than the forces at work in Asia itself, may well explain a good deal that went wrong with US policy in Asia in the post-1945 period."[10]

As the United States reexamines its security and other policies and approaches in the Western Pacific in the light of the changing scene in this increasingly important world region, it must seek to avoid "the quicksands of oversimplification," and reverse its tendency to look at this region almost exclusively from the perspectives of its own internal environment and its relations with Western Europe and the Soviet Union. The existing fluidity in the Western Pacific region opens up possibilities for a fruitful reorientation of U.S. policy, as well as new problems and dangers. The objective should be a more informed, realistic, and balanced policy—or policies—better attuned to the new realities and the ongoing changes in a dynamic region.

To what extent have responsible policymakers been able to articulate the main outlines of U.S. policy, including security policy, in the Western Pacific? Do their public statements support their claim that the United States does indeed have a Western Pacific policy, or policies, within the framework of global policy, or do they confirm the assertions of critics that the United States does not have a foreign or a security policy for the Western Pacific? What are the aspects of U.S. foreign and security policy that these official spokesmen emphasize when they speak of the United States and the Western Pacific? For answers to these questions we shall turn to major public addresses in the mid-1980s by the secretary of state and the under secretary for political affairs.

SECURITY POLICIES AND CONCERNS

Two broad objectives and main concerns of U.S. policy regarding the Asia-Pacific region have been stated repeatedly by high officials in every American administration since the end of World War II. As Professor Russell Fifield wrote in September 1984, "The basic objective since 1940 has been to oppose the domination of East Asia by any major power or combination of powers hostile or potentially hostile to American interests."[11]

Until the Sino–Soviet conflict broke out into the open in the late 1950s and early 1960s, the United States was primarily concerned with working with noncommunist states of the Western Pacific in dealing with the continuing threat of the two Communist giants, either individually or in collusion. When the U.S. reversed its policy of hostility and virtual noncommunication and began to work out an entirely new relationship with the People's Republic of China, China ceased to be regarded as primarily a threat and instead was viewed as a country with which at least tentative and limited relations and some cooperation in economic and military as well as political spheres were possible. The Soviet Union then came to be regarded as the supreme threat, in the Western Pacific as elsewhere. This view was shared by a few of America's allies and other noncommunist states in the region, but seldom if ever with the same degree of conviction and commitment.

Throughout the post-World War II period security considerations have usually been uppermost in the American approach to and appraisal of the Western Pacific region. At times, however, as during the Carter administration, other factors such as human rights have been given equal or even higher priority. And in relations with Japan, which the United States came to regard as the keystone power in East Asia, economic and political—and psychological—issues have often been more compelling than the military dimensions of security.

After Reagan assumed office the Pacific region was recognized—in words if not always in fact—as a region of growing importance in the world and of high priority in U.S. policy. The American approach to the region again reflected a heavy emphasis on military and security considerations, but it also reflected an awareness of the growing dimensions of the U.S.–Western Pacific relationship. This is clearly brought out by a content analysis of a few of the many statements by leading spokespersons of the Reagan administration.

In March 1982 Reagan's secretary of defense, Caspar Weinberger, described U.S. policy in the Asia-Pacific region as a "six-pillar edifice."[12] Pillar I was the U.S. commitment to remain a Pacific power. Pillars II, III, and IV symbolized the United States' special relationships with and interests in the major noncommunist states of East Asia, Japan, and South Korea, and the largest communist state in the region, the People's Republic of China. Pillar V focused on ASEAN, a newly discovered pillar of the U.S. edifice in the Western Pacific. Pillar VI—the Rapid Deployment Force—was outside the Western Pacific region, but presumably Weinberger thought that it was important for this region as well as for the Persian Gulf and the northwestern reaches of the Indian Ocean. He may have been thinking primarily of the security of the sea-lanes from the Gulf to East Asia, as well as to Western Europe and the United States.

A similar approach to the Asia-Pacific region was enunciated by Secretary of State Shultz a year later, in a highly publicized address before the World Affairs Council of San Francisco.[13] Shultz had just returned from a trip to East Asia and the Western Pacific. After expressing his conviction that "if you want to understand the future, you must . . . understand the Pacific region," he called attention to "the dramatic change that has marked the region in recent years," including a new dynamism and "a new self-confidence . . . born of economic success and of an emerging political maturity." He also affirmed "the direct interest of the United States in this region." The countries and peoples of the region, he declared, "have an important future, and we should be part of it." The major portion of his address was devoted to discussion of four lessons for the present and the future. Two were directed primarily at the nations of the region—"the need for a global, not merely a regional, point of view," and "the importance of economic and political freedom for the region's progress and security." One was advanced as a lesson primarily for the United States, namely that "our policy must reflect the growing community of interests among nations there in preserving peace and promoting economic progress." And the final lesson was a reminder to both Americans and the peoples of the Western Pacific that "the United States has both vital interests and a unique and critical role to play in the area." In conclusion the secretary foresaw a larger role for the Western Pacific in the future: "Our Asian Pacific partners are developing relationships not only with us but with each other. They are also joining with us in cooperative efforts that extend beyond the Pacific region and increasingly bring their positive influence into the world at large. These steps are the basis for a global role that will fit the region's growing strength and responsibilities."

Obviously the secretary's approach to his topic—"The United States and East Asia: A Partnership for the Future"—was quite positive and upbeat, with a deliberate intention to emphasize the encouraging developments and aspects, and with only passing references to the more discouraging aspects of the situation in the Western Pacific. Obviously, too, he spoke largely in terms of generalizations and impressions.

More specific analysis was presented by Michael Armacost, the under secretary for political affairs in the State Department, in two important addresses in 1984 and 1985.

On October 10, 1984, in an address before the Atlantic Treaty Association in Toronto, on "NATO and the Challenges Ahead,"[14] Armacost linked the problems of security in the Asia-Pacific region, which he said he had been asked to include in his discussion, with those of the NATO region and with East-West and U.S.–Soviet relations. After stating that "our security continues to require an equilibrium in Asia, and no such equilibrium is foreseeable without American participation," he pointed out that the West in general had "an interest in preserving the independence of our partners in Asia," in assisting in the region's "continued economic development," in "the strengthening of Asian political institutions," and "in the protection of those sea lanes over which vast trade flows now move between East Asia and the Persian Gulf and Europe and the United States." After calling attention to a few encouraging trends, notably with reference to Japan and China, and a few discouraging ones, notably the "steady Soviet military buildup in Asia and the Pacific," he returned to the theme of "the increasing significance of East Asia from the global strategic perspective," and suggested that "the approach of the Atlantic allies to developments in the Asia/Pacific region" should show a recognition of this important fact. "The resilience of our friends in Asia," Armacost continued, "clearly contributes to a favorable global balance of power. North America, Western Europe, and our friends in Asia have sufficient common interests to warrant a wider framework of cooperation in many spheres." Hence his special message was that "the West should encourage Asia's awareness of the broader community of interests that link it with both North America and Western Europe."

A more comprehensive and more detailed explanation of the changing situation in the Western Pacific and U.S. policy in the area was given by Armacost on January 29, 1985, in an address before the Far East–America Council/Asia Society in New York, entitled "The Asia-Pacific Region: A Forward Look."[15] After referring to "the growing interest of the United States in East Asia" and the "growing national consensus regarding the importance of our ties to the Pacific," he singled out eight regional developments as of "major consequence." Four of these he thought encouraging, and four had "a less sanguine appearance." The encouraging developments were: (1) "the extraordinary economic dynamism of the region"; (2) the continuing assumption by Japan of "a political role more commensurate with its economic power"; (3) 'China's acceleration of its "modernization efforts" and its inauguration of "a stunning program of economic reform"; and (4) some "hints of change in the relations between North and South Korea." The "less sanguine" developments were: (1) the continuing Soviet military buildup in East Asia and the Pacific—a development that is almost always mentioned by official U.S. spokespersons in their statements on the situation in this region and that obviously is a major factor conditioning U.S. policies and activities in the region; (2) the fact that "the Vietnamese show no signs of reducing their military pressure on Cambodia" or of a willingness "to negotiate a political solution to the problem"; (3) "the prospect of political transitions in several important countries," with the unhappy possibility that "succession politics" will become "a source of uncertainty and potential instability in those countries where political institutions are weak"; and (4) the growth of "antinuclear sentiment in the South Pacific," which has created major complications for U.S. policy toward New Zealand, the ANZUS alliance, and the South-Southwest Pacific region as a whole.

Against this background of favorable and unfavorable developments Armacost briefly itemized some opportunities and risks for the United States. The opportunities that he mentioned were stated in terms of policy objectives: to "expand commercial and investment opportunities," to "associate Japan even more closely with the West," to "propel China toward patterns of closer cooperation with us," to "work constructively with regional groupings in the area, particularly ASEAN," and to "foster a dialogue on the Korean Peninsula." The risks that he selected for special mention were that "burgeoning trade deficits will stimulate increased protectionist sentiment and protectionist trade measures in the Congress," that "succession crises could lead to political instability adversely affecting our financial flows, economic development, and strategic interests," that "antinuclear sentiment could check our naval access to New Zealand and vitiate a key alliance," that "failure to redress the imbalance within the Cambodian resistance could undermine future possibilities for a political solution," and that "the Soviet

Union will continue to build its military strength in Asia while playing for any diplomatic and political breaks that may come along." Armacost did not elaborate on these risks and opportunities. Nor did he point out that very slow, if any, progress is being made in developing the opportunities, whereas all of the risks that he itemized are becoming more rather than less likely and serious.

The bulk of this address consisted of comments on what Armacost described as "our major policy challenges in the period ahead." The first was "our growing trade deficit with Asia." In order to reduce this deficit and to prevent it from becoming a serious stumbling block in relations with many Western Pacific nations, notably Japan, he suggested the need for "a new trade round," opening "Japan's market further," and continuing "high-level dialogue" with economic and trade ministers of the ASEAN countries. Then he turned to the challenges ahead in relations with some of the key countries of the Western Pacific. He began with some perplexing problems in U.S.–Philippine relations, and he pledged: "We shall continue to encourage the further democratization of Philippine politics, the opening up of the Philippine economy to the freer interplay of market forces, and the reform of the military." He mentioned two points regarding Japan: (1) "We shall continue to urge Japan to assume a larger responsibility for its own conventional defense while extending the range of its surveillance and patrolling capabilities along its sealanes to the south," without encouraging "Japan's assumption of regional military security responsibilities"; and (2) the United States would "consult with the Japanese on how best to coordinate our growing foreign assistance efforts." Regarding the People's Republic of China, Armacost stated that the United States would "continue to nurture an expanding economic relationship," and would "expand cooperation arrangements in the military field," while remaining "sensitive to the views of our other friends and allies in the region." And in spite of expanding ties with the People's Republic of China, the United States would "maintain our unofficial links with Taiwan." Regarding Korea, surprisingly, the only matter he mentioned was that the United States would "sustain close cooperation with the R.O.K. as it explores the potential for direct North–South talks."

With regard to Southeast Asia he affirmed that the United States wished "to further our close economic cooperation with ASEAN." In Indochina the U.S. objectives included "support of a political settlement" and "support for the noncommunist resistance elements" in Cambodia and across the borders in Thailand. The United States, he pledged, would "continue to work with the nations of Southeast Asia in our efforts to manage the human problem created by the continuing flow of refugees from Indochina," and would contribute to the security of Thailand, as a "front-line state."

Turning to the Southwest Pacific and Oceania, Armacost warned that "if the Lange government in New Zealand continues to challenge nuclear-powered warship visits or insists upon no visits by nuclear-armed ships, the future of our alliance relationship with New Zealand is in jeopardy. The problem with New Zealand," he continued, "underlines the importance of our ties with Australia." Moving far to the northeast, to the North Central Pacific region of Micronesia, he pointed to the little-known progress "in completing the transition to free association with the Federated States of Micronesia and the [Republic of the] Marshall Islands," and the even less-well-known fact that the United States was working "with the elected leadership on Palau as it likewise seeks to work out a future relationship with us under the Compact of Free Association." He noted that "the Northern Mariana Islands have already opted to enter into a commonwealth status with us upon the termination of the trust" (the Trust Territory of the Pacific Islands, a U.S. trust territory under the United Nations trusteeship system).

Unlike most official analyses of U.S. policies and concerns in the Western Pacific, Armacost did not refer to the Soviet military buildup and threat in the region until he had ended his regional survey. His brief comments were, however, quite interesting:

> As for Soviet ambitions in Asia and the Pacific, we need not be obsessed with their prospects in the region. They are playing with a weak hand politically and have regularly displayed the kind of cultural insensitivity which undercuts their prospects for gains. But we cannot ignore their growing military strength and must work to counteract it by maintaining a strong presence of our own and by bolstering mutual defense arrangements with our friends.

These comments by the secretary of state and the under secretary for political affairs demonstrate that the United States has a multitude of interests and concerns in the Asia-Pacific region and that it has an extensive pattern of relations and interactions with the nations of the region. Whether they add up to a series of well-defined policies or to an overall Asia-Pacific policy is largely a matter of interpretation. Certainly they suggest that the Asia-Pacific region, and especially East Asia, should be high up on the American foreign policy and security agenda in the years to come.

If there is continuing uncertainty about U.S. goals, strategies, and policies in this region in the United States and elsewhere there seems to be no doubt about them in the Soviet Union. A typical statement of the Soviet view was given in an article by a leading Soviet specialist on the United States, published in an Indian journal, *The Nonaligned World*, in late 1984:

> The US basic goals in the Asia-Pacific Basin may be outlined as follows: First, they seek to bring the region under the US control. It is true, Washington realizes that, with the current alignment of forces in the world, it would be hard for the US to secure a position of absolute domination in the Asia-Pacific basin. Nevertheless, it hopes that it will be able at least to assume a considerable degree of control over the march of events there, and thus to prevent them from taking a turn unfavorable to itself, or quickly carry any undesirable changes. Washington apparently regards this goal as optimal. Secondly, the US seeks to prepare the ground for further American economic expansion in the region, making it more attractive for American business investment in an area where opportunities have not yet been fully utilized by American firms. Thirdly, they endeavour to intensify pressure on the Soviet Union from the Asian direction in order to force the Soviet Union to divert its strength and resources, and thus increase America's own opportunities in the build-up of a "central" nuclear force, as well as to tilt the balance of forces in Europe in favour of the NATO. Finally, the US seeks to guarantee

the loyalty of its principal allies in the region (Canada, Japan, Australia) and also Mexico, Chile and Argentina and tie them up, for the foreseeable future, to the course of American foreign policy.[16]

According to this Soviet scholar, the United States has developed a variety of strategies for attaining its basic goals. These have ranged from hegemony, which the United States tried to establish throughout the 1950s and 1960s "with the help of military and political pacts, ... and through bilateral security treaties concluded with Japan and other countries," to "a more flexible balancing in the region for which the Nixon Doctrine and Ford's Pacific Doctrine provided the conceptual basis, a temporary and abortive "attempt to break away from such a 'detrimental system' of the multipolar balancing," based on "the so-called Brzezinski doctrine of trilateralism," and "a return to the balance of power policies in the region." The Reagan administration, in the view of this Soviet analyst, hopes "to replace the balance by a more consolidated pro-American association, such as, say, a Pacific Community." It is "trying to accomplish such an association, not on the basis of, say, broad economic interests, but again by using anti-Soviet emotions as a cementing factor."[17]

It is obviously desirable to view American policies from the perspectives of other nations, even including those which operate from very different premises and with whom relations are strained. But it is also important to consider U.S. goals, objectives, policies, and activities in world affairs from the point of view of American national interests, as conceived of by responsible policymakers, with due consideration to their validity and feasibility in the light of existing, and changing, world realities—or "correlation of forces," as the Russians might say—and to the reactions to them, at home and abroad.

As all previous administrations, the Reagan government has been criticized for inadequate attention to the changing situation in the Asia-Pacific region, for an obsession with the Soviet threat in that region, as elsewhere, and with security over all other considerations. A few years before Under Secretary Armacost explained the broad outlines and objectives of U.S. policy toward the region and argued that East Asia was "increasingly important to the security and prosperity of the West," a leading American academic specialist on Asian affairs, Professor Robert Scalapino, suggested that the United States had been unable to choose among three alternative strategies, which he labeled the "withdrawal" strategy, the "united front" strategy, and the "equilibrium" strategy. The conference report, based on Professor Scalapino's analysis, commented on the implications for U.S. policy: "Elements of each of these strategies can be found in U.S. policy in the Asian/Pacific area. While there is nothing necessarily wrong with this ... the resulting composite policy ... does not form a conscious and coherent design. Therefore, U.S. policy appeared to be neither predictable nor wholly credible."[18]

Many Asians living in countries with which the United States had fairly extensive and generally friendly relations obviously entertained doubts about American understanding and appreciation of Asian affairs, about American reliability and credibility, and about what they felt was an overemphasis on security at the expense of more deep-seated interests and priorities. In the late 1970s a distinguished Indonesian diplomat and intellectual, Soedjatmoko, in presenting "An Indonesian Perspective on Security Trends in East Asia," wrote: "I believe it is very important for the United States to accept the limits of its capacity to influence the very deeply rooted social and political processes now transforming various parts of the world and to resist the temptation to use its military power for political purposes in the mode of earlier decades and historical periods."[19]

U.S. MILITARY PRESENCE AND COMMITMENTS IN THE WESTERN PACIFIC

In the Asia-Pacific region the United States has deployed substantial military strength, but because the region is so vast, because the Soviet strength in the region is so great, and because there are so many existing and potential threats to security in the region, the defense planners of the United States are faced with the all-too-familiar dilemma of a great gap between defense capabilities and the missions assigned to them. The missions are obviously multipurpose ones and are global as well as regional in nature. The Asia-Pacific region, as the U.S. Joint Chiefs of Staff pointed out in their FY 1982 *Military Posture Statement*, constitutes a major segment of an interlocking system of "strategic zones," extending from North America through Western Europe to the Western Pacific, and including the Atlantic, Indian, and Pacific Oceans. Therefore, stated the joint chiefs:

> ... it is no longer practical to design autonomous regional strategies, for a threat in one strategic zone will almost certainly have a serious impact on the security of others. ... Under such circumstances, the missions of the U.S. Pacific Command may become integral to fulfilling the new transregional security challenge and, as caretakers for the largest U.S. theater of military operations, its missions in the Asian Pacific have become vital to the dynamics of world power.[20]

Deterrence of the Soviet Union is a major mission of American forces in the Asia-Pacific region, as elsewhere, but these forces have many other missions, relating to diverse threats and challenges. As Richard Solomon has pointed out: "In short, the American military presence in Asia in the 1980s must be responsive to a full range of challenges—from helping to maintain the strategic balance to deterring conventional conflict among great and regional powers in discouraging proxy interventions and enabling allies to deal with insurgent threats."[21]

According to the U.S. Department of Defense, in March 1981 the United States deployed 340,241 military personnel in the Pacific region (excluding the Continental U.S.). Of these, 168,611 were afloat—146,719 in the Third Fleet and 21,892 in the Seventh fleet. Of the land-based personnel, 19,769 were in Hawaii, the same number in Alaska, 46,137 in Japan (including 29,782 in Okinawa), 37,883 in South Korea, and 15,664 in the Philippines. Most of the Navy personnel were afloat, most of the Army units were stationed in South Korea and Hawaii, most of the Marines were on Okinawa, and most of the Air Force personnel were in Alaska, Japan (mostly on Okinawa), South Korea, and the Philippines.[22]

In four of the countries of the Western Pacific—Japan, South Korea, the Philippines, and Australia—the United States, by treaty agreement, maintains significant military installations and/or bases (see maps 2.1 and 2.2). Airfields available for U.S. use in Japan are located on Okinawa and in several places on Honshu. Naval facilities are maintained at Yokosuka and Sasebo. In South Korea the U.S. Army command headquarters is located in the DMZ and major airfields are at Osan, Taegu, and Kunsan. The major U.S. bases and installations in the Philippines are well known—the naval facility at Subic Bay and the major air base at Clark Field (both in nearby locations on Luzon). In Australia the United States has access to ports and other facilities and maintains several bases and communication stations for submarines.[23]

The U.S. Pacific Fleet, which includes the Third and Seventh Fleets, has headquarters at Pearl Harbor. It "has jurisdiction over both the Indian and Pacific Oceans—covering more than 100 million square miles or roughly 70% of the world's ocean surface."[24] The Third Fleet, by far the larger of the two main units of the Pacific Fleet, with headquarters in San Diego, covers much of the Pacific and all of the Indian Ocean. Its average complement is about 175 ships, including four aircraft carriers and one battleship. The Seventh Fleet, with an average complement of about seventy vessels, including two aircraft carriers, is deployed in the Western Pacific. One aircraft carrier, the *Midway*, and several other major combatant ships, plus a number of support ships, are based at Yokosuka in Japan.[25] In addition to military personnel and combatant and support ships "significant quantities of logistics supply are stored in the region and major U.S. naval and aircraft overhaul and maintenance facilities are present."[26] Bases are available for U.S. Pacific Fleet operations in a limited number of places in the Western Pacific, notably Yokosuka, Guam, and Subic Bay. With the possible exception of Diego Garcia, no well-developed naval bases are available for U.S. Fleet operations in the Indian Ocean, although the United States has been given access to some facilities in Australia, Somalia, and Oman.

The responsibilities of the Pacific Fleet are awesome. Naval leaders repeatedly point out that their complement of personnel and ships is quite inadequate for the responsibilities that devolve upon them, even in times of relative peace, and that they would fall far short of needs in the event of a major conflict anywhere in the vast Asia-Pacific—Indian Ocean area. An indication of this deficiency came in the late 1970s, when units of the Seventh

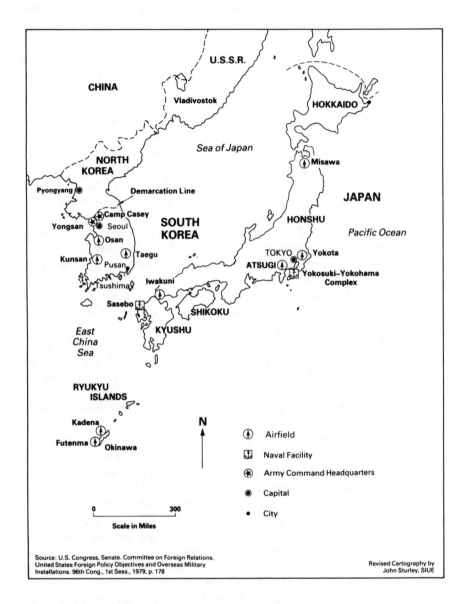

N

- ⊕ Airfield
- ⊞ Naval Facility
- ⊛ Army Command Headquarters
- ⊚ Capital
- • City

0   300

Scale in Miles

Source: U.S. Congress, Senate. Committee on Foreign Relations.
United States Foreign Policy Objectives and Overseas Military
Installations. 96th Cong., 1st Sess., 1979, p. 178

Revised Cartography by
John Sturley, SIUE

Map 2.1. Major U.S. military installations in Japan and Korea

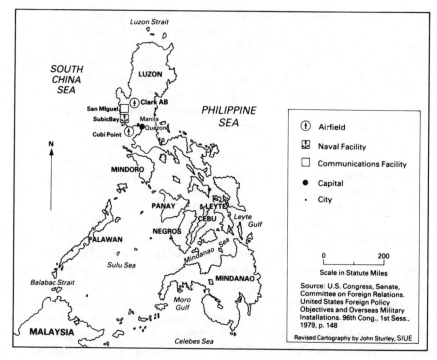

Map 2.2. Major U.S. military installations in the Philippines

Fleet, including the huge aircraft carrier *Midway*, were temporarily detached from the Seventh Fleet and assigned to the Third Fleet to assist in discharging the assignments given the Navy in the Persian Gulf areas. Many commentators, especially in the United States and in some of the countries of the Western Pacific with which the United States is allied, pointed out that such a move created an alarming diminution of U.S. strength in the Western Pacific, which at normal complement was regarded as faced with responsibilities it would be hard put to meet in a time of real crisis in the region.

With four major allies of the Western Pacific the United States is bound by specific security treaties, as well as by other more nebulous and specialized but nevertheless meaningful ties. The security treaties mostly date back to the period of "pactomania" of the 1950s. Three were concluded in 1951—with Japan (later modified in 1960), with Australia and New Zealand (the ANZUS treaty), and with the Philippines. In 1954 a mutual defense treaty between the United States and the Republic of Korea went into effect. In the same year the United States became associated with the Philippines, Thailand, Pakistan, Australia, New Zealand, Britain, and France in SEATO, a major multilateral security arrangement. Although SEATO is now defunct, the United States still has bilateral security arrangements or understandings with most of its former members, and other multilateral security arrangements with Britain and France (especially through NATO), and until recently with Australia and New Zealand (through ANZUS). By mutual agreement the security ties that it had with Thailand during the SEATO period have been reaffirmed. These ties have become particularly significant for both countries because of developments in Indochina and the subsequent added pressures on Thailand.

With its Western Pacific allies the United States has also entered into a large number of agreements of a more specialized nature, relating to mutual security arrangements and military cooperation and facilities. An outstanding example is the bases agreement with the Philippines, first concluded in 1951 and substantially revised in 1983. Because of political and other basically nonmilitary, as well as military, considerations and trends, such agreements are constantly under review and criticism, with varying assessments of their continuing value and utility.

For many years the United States had a security treaty and other security arrangements with the Republic of China on Taiwan, but in 1979 the treaty was abrogated and the United States withdrew its recognition of the R.O.C. as the legitimate government of China, as a part of the price it paid for the new relations with the People's Republic. As a result the United States abandoned its facilities on Taiwan and withdrew its military personnel. It has continued to maintain "unofficial" relations and contacts with Taiwan, including extensive trade and other economic relations. It has even continued to provide some military assistance to Taiwan, although it has agreed, under strong pressure from the Communist regime in Beijing, that it will cease to provide such assistance at an unspecified time in the future. With the People's Republic it has obviously not concluded any formal security treaty or other security arrangements, but it has had some high-level discussions on mutual security interests, especially against the perceived threats from the Soviet Union, and it has even offered to provide the People's Republic with materials and equipment that could be used for military purposes. The Chinese leaders have obviously been reluctant to turn to the United States for military assistance, although a limited amount of such assistance has been requested and promised or provided.

In the Western Pacific doubts about the credibility and reliability of the United States as a source of support against impending dangers, internal or external, are widespread, even in countries with which the United States is formally allied in binding and comprehensive security arrangements. These doubts were particularly manifest after the enunciation of the Nixon Doctrine in 1969, the final withdrawal of U.S. forces from Vietnam under conditions of humiliation and even defeat in 1975, and the announcement by President Carter in 1977 of the intended withdrawal of the bulk of the American forces in Korea within a period of five years. Doubts were enhanced by the mercurial policies of the United States in East Asia, and indeed in the global arena, and by the perceived evidences that the United States really did not assign a high priority to the Western Pacific region and had never formulated a coherent and understandable Asian policy, in general or with regard to security commitments. Asians as well as other peoples have become well aware of the relative decline of American power and influence in the global system, of the widening gap between American commitments and capabilities and of what seem to be withdrawal tendencies on the part of the United States, especially when the hard realities of international life have imposed heavy burdens upon it. They are also well aware of the growing strength and continuing expansionism of the Soviet Union, in East Asia and the Western Pacific as well as in many other parts of the world.

The Nixon Doctrine, in particular, was viewed by Asians as indicating a major U.S. disengagement from Asia. It was of course expounded with particular reference to East and Southeast Asia and to future U.S. security relationships and commitments in Asia. "The Nixon Doctrine was a more limited and discriminating application of U.S. military containment of Communist expansion in Asia, with a determination to avoid American involvement in another Vietnam. The doctrine sought to encourage, via enhanced levels of U.S. security and economic assistance, American allies and client states in Asia to assume the 'primary responsibility of providing the manpower' for their own defense."[27] But in his first enunciation of the doctrine Nixon also emphasized another point, namely that "we will keep our treaty commitments." U.S. insistence on this point was frequently repeated even during the eight years of American retrenchment in Asia that followed, and it has been strongly reasserted by President Reagan.

For some years, the United States has had rather extensive military assistance and sales relations with a number of Western Pacific countries. Between 1950 and 1984, the United States extended major security assistance to three of these countries: South Vietnam ($15.3 billion), South Korea ($9.2 billion), and Taiwan ($4.0 billion). Most of this was in the form of outright grants for military purchases, under the Military Assistance Program (MAP).[28] In the post-Vietnam War years, military assistance has been modest, except for assistance to South Korea and the Philippines. Only Indonesia and the Philippines have received more military support in the form of assistance than of sales. In FY 1980, for example, the United States provided military assistance designated to be worth $227.8 million to South Korea, $95.7 million to the Philippines, $37.9 million to Indonesia, and $26.1 million to Thailand. During the same period, the United States sold military equipment and supplies valued at $1.7 billion to South Korea, $155 million to Australia, $130 million to Thailand, $50 million to the Philippines, $30 million to Indonesia, $10 million each to Malaysia and Singapore, and $5 million to New Zealand.[29] Between 1979 and 1983, arms transfers by the United States to East and Southeast Asian countries were valued at $7.915 billion, with the largest amounts going to Japan ($2.5 billion), South Korea ($1.9 billion), and Taiwan ($1.7 billion). Arms transfers by the Soviet Union to the countries of East and Southeast Asia in the same period were valued at $6.515 billion, almost all of this ($5.3 billion) going to one country, Vietnam.[30]

OVERVIEW AND PREVIEW

Having delineated some of the essential background considerations and traced the overall course of U.S. policy and experience in the Western Pacific, with particular reference to security aspects, commitments, and posture, it is now possible to undertake a more detailed analysis of U.S. security relationships with the nations of the region, within the framework of overall policies and of global as well as regional implications. Since the term *security relationships* embraces far more than alliance relationships, it is essential to deal with the security dimensions of U.S. relations with virtually all of the nations of the region from a broad perspective.

Quite appropriately, one may begin by considering the security dimensions of the U.S. relationship with the Soviet Union, in the Western Pacific and globally. The two superpowers are the major external or intrusive actors in the Western Pacific. In some respects they are internal as well as external actors, for both have long had a significant political, economic, and military presence in the region, and, especially in the case of the Soviet Union, a territorial presence as well. However considered, the interrelationships of the superpowers are clearly a major factor in the entire Western Pacific equation, and therefore must be given very special consideration.

Following a discussion of the United States and Soviet Union in the Western Pacific, this book analyzes U.S. security relations with the two other major actors in the region, Japan and the People's Republic of China. Interrelationships among all four of the major actors is an underlying theme.

Before leaving the East Asian subregion, we must stress the facts of the U.S. security relationships with South Korea. Those relationships are particularly significant and extensive, not only in a bilateral sense, but in terms of the situation in the Korean Peninsula as a whole and of the possible spillover effects of conflict in the Peninsula, including effects on the major regional actors and, more broadly, on the prospects for peace and human survival.

Discussion of the second major subregion, Southeast Asia, focuses on U.S. security relationships with all of the major states of the region, especially Thailand, the Philippines, and Vietnam, and with the region's major regional arrangement, ASEAN. Although ASEAN is not a security arrangement, it has been forced to give greater attention than was envisioned to security considerations, mainly because of the tensions between its member states and Vietnam and Kampuchea. The United States is very much concerned with the ASEAN–Indochinese rifts, and with its developing relationships with ASEAN.

In the context of Western Pacific security, the island nations of the Southwest Pacific and Oceania, including the two major nations of the region, Australia and New Zealand, have a peripheral but still important place. For the United States its security relationships with Australia and New Zealand have both regional and global importance. Three aspects of the changing scene in the Southwest Pacific are of special importance from the point of view of U.S. security and security relationships in the entire Western Pacific region and beyond. They are the increasing contacts of the nations of this subregion with other subregions and states of the Western Pacific, the crisis within ANZUS as a result of recent developments and tensions in U.S.–New Zealand relations, and the emergence of many small island nations in Oceania, in a vast oceanic expanse that is of special importance to the United States for strategic and other reasons.

U.S. relations with the other states of the region are determined largely by its interactions with the other three major actors in the region and on a global scale as well; but it has important security as well as broader kinds of relations with virtually all of the less powerful states. It is important that these relations be conducted through a variety of bilateral and multilateral channels, and not simply within the framework of U.S. global security policies and its interactions with the Soviet Union, China, and Japan. Here we encounter a familiar dilemma for the United States. It can hardly develop satisfactory relations with less powerful states without considering its global interests and policies and the role and policies of other major powers with regard to the same states, but it will create additional complications in its relations with less powerful states if its basic approach and orientation to them are, or are perceived to be, affected too heavily by power-political considerations and by external preoccupations and interests.

The Western Pacific is par excellence an area where the destinies of less powerful states are greatly affected by the policies of major powers. Clearly the interactions of the United States with the other three major powers in the region are of central importance to it and inevitably affect its relations with all of the other nations in the region. But the United States has a broad range of common interests and relations with these less powerful states, and these must be considered apart from, as well as in relation to, U.S. relations with the other major powers of the Western Pacific and U.S. security preoccupations in the region.

In this analysis the focus is on the United States's role in Western Pacific security, in the light of changes in the internal dynamics and external orientation of the countries of the region, and in the regional and international security environment; but the broader approaches and considerations mentioned in this general overview should be constantly borne in mind when the inescapable dimension of security is subjected to special analysis.

Notes

[1] Stephen B. Gibert, "Southeast Asia in American Security Policy," chapter 3 in William T. Tow and William R. Feeney, eds., *U.S. Foreign Policy and Asian–Pacific Security: A Transregional Approach* (Boulder, Colorado: Westview Press, 1982), p. 69.

[2] Ibid.

[3] Ronald Reagan, in the second Reagan-Mondale debate during the American presidential campaign of 1984, October 21, 1984.

[4] "A Forward Look at Foreign Policy," address of Secretary of State Shultz before the Los Angeles World Affairs Council, October 19, 1984; Bureau of Public Affairs, U.S. Department of State, *Current Policy*, no. 625. In an article in *Foreign Affairs*, published a few months later, Secretary of State Shultz incorporated the second paragraph quoted, with only a few minor variations. George Shultz, "New Realities and New Ways of Thinking," *Foreign Affairs* 63 (Spring 1985): 712.

[5] Michael Haas, "Sick Man of the Pacific," *Asia Pacific Community* 21 (Summer 1983): 45–46.

[6] Sheldon Simon, "U.S. Security Interests in Southeast Asia," chapter 5 in Tow and Feeney, eds., *U.S. Foreign Policy, and Asian-Pacific Security*, p. 117.

[7] Norman D. Palmer, "The United States and the Security of Asia," chapter 5 in Sudershan Chawla and D. R. Sardesai, eds., *Changing Patterns of Security and Stability in Asia* (New York: Praeger Publishers, 1980), pp. 118–119.

[8] Jeffrey Record, *Revising U.S. Military Strategy* (Washington, DC: Pergamon-Brassey's International Defense Publishers, 1984), p. 30.

[9] Palmer, "The United States and the Security of Asia," p. 119.

[10] Peter Polomka, "The Security of the Western Pacific: The Price of Burden Sharing," *Survival* 26 (January/February 1984): 8.

[11] Russell H. Fifield, "America's Nonpartisan East Asian Policy," *The Asian Wall Street Journal*, September 25, 1984.

[12] Summarized in Haas, "Sick Man of the Pacific," p. 47.

[13] "The U.S. and East Asia: A Partnership for the Future," address of Secretary of State Shultz before the World Affairs Council of San Francisco, March 5, 1983; Bureau of Public Affairs , U.S. Department of State, *Current Policy*, no. 450 (March 5, 1983).

[14] "NATO and the Challenges Ahead," address by Michael H. Armacost, under secretary of state for political affairs, before the Atlantic Treaty Association, Toronto, October 10, 1984; Bureau of Public Affairs, U.S. Department of State, *Current Policy*, no. 620 (October 10, 1984).

[15] "The Asia-Pacific Region: A Forward Look," address by Michael H. Armacost before the Far East–America Council/Asia Society, New York, January 29, 1985; Bureau of Public Affairs, U.S. Department of State, *Current Policy*, no. 653 (January 29, 1985).

[16] Henry A. Trofimenko, "U.S. Interests in Asia-Pacific Region: A View from Moscow," *The Nonaligned World* (New Delhi) 2 (October–December 1984): 570.

[17] Ibid., p. 572.

[18] Robert A. Scalapino, "Competitive Strategic Perceptions Underlying U.S. Policy in Asia," a paper prepared for a conference on "Pacific Asia and U.S. Policies;" in *Pacific Asia and U.S. Policies: A Political-Economic-Strategic Assessment* (Honolulu: Pacific Forum, 1978), pp. 4–5. For trenchant criticisms of the apparent absence of priorities in American strategic calculations, see Barry R. Posen and Stephen Van Evera, "Defense Policy and the Reagan Administration: Departure from Containment," *International Security* 8 (Summer 1983); Jeffrey Record, "Jousting with Unreality: Reagan's Military Strategy," *International Security* 8 (Winter 1983/84); and Joshua M. Epstein, "Horizontal Escalation: Sour Notes of a Recurrent Theme," *International Security* 8 (Winter 1983/84).

[19] Soedjatmoko, "An Indonesian Perspective on Security Trends in East Asia," chapter 8 in Richard H. Solomon, ed., *Asian Security in the 1980s: Problems and Policies for a Time of Transition* (Cambridge, Mass.: Oelgeschlager, Gunn & Hain, 1980), p. 177.

[20] Quoted in Tow and Feeney, eds., *U.S. Foreign Policy and Asian-Pacific Security*, p. 3.

[21] Richard H. Solomon, "American Defense Planning and Asian Security: Policy Choices for a Time of Transition," chapter 1 in Solomon, ed., *Asian Security in the 1980s*, p. 29.

[22] William R. Feeney, "The Pacific Basing System and U.S. Security," chapter 7 in Tow and Feeney, eds., *U.S. Foreign Policy and Asian-Pacific Security*, pp. 190–191 (Table 7.3, "U.S. Military Personnel Deployments in the Pacific excl. [excluding] Continental, as of March 31, 1981"). Somewhat different and more recent figures are reported by the International Institute for Strategic Studies in *The Military Balance 1985–1986* (London: International Institute of Strategic Studies, 1985). This source lists the number of U.S. forces in the Pacific–Far East as 143,800 (33,600 afloat), including 32,200 Army (29,750 in South Korea), 41,400 Navy (with the Seventh Fleet), 37,500 Air Force (16,600 in Japan, 11,200 in South Korea, and 9,400 in the Philippines), 26,000 Marines (in Japan, mostly in Okinawa), and smaller units at several other locations.

[23] Tow and Feeney, eds., *U.S. Foreign Policy and Asian-Pacific Security*, pp. 172–173 (Figure 7.1, "Major U.S. Military Installations in Japan and Korea," and Figure 7.2, "Major U.S. Military Installations in the Philippines").

[24] Ibid., p. 1981.

[25] Based on information in ibid., p. 191, *The Military Balance 1986–1987* (London: The International Institute for Strategic Studies, 1986), and John M. Collins, *U.S.–Soviet Military Balance 1980–1985* (Washington, D.C.: Pergamon-Brassey's International Defense Publishers, 1985), especially Map 7, "U.S. Naval Deployment," p. 146.

[26] *U.S. Relations with Japan and Korea: Security Issues* (Washington D.C.: U.S. Government Printing Office, 1982), p. 4.

[27] Record, *Revising U.S. Military Strategy*, p. 30.

[28] Harry F. Young, *Atlas of United States Foreign Relations*, 2nd edition, Department of State Publication 9350, December 1985, p. 86.

[29] Tow and Feeney, eds., *U.S. Foreign Policy and Asian-Pacific Security*, p. 53 (Table 2.3, "U.S. Military Assistance and Sales Relations with Asian-Pacific States").

[30] *World Military Expenditures and Arms Transfers 1985*, U.S. Arms Control and Disarmament Agency Publication 123, August 1985, p. 132.

CHAPTER 3

The United States and the Soviet Union in the Western Pacific

Soviet-American rivalry in the Western Pacific must be considered in the light of the larger global confrontation. In fact, as Richard H. Solomon has observed, "it will become increasingly difficult . . . to separate the elements of global Soviet–American competition from those of regional competition in Asia."[1] The course of the overall confrontation will have a profound impact on the relations of the two superpowers in the Asia-Pacific region, and, conversely, the nature of Soviet-American relations in the Asia-Pacific region will have a profound impact on the global confrontation, as well as on the evolving situation in the region itself. "In future efforts to deal with the Soviet Union on a global basis, Northeast Asia must be placed alongside of Europe in the center of the stage."[2]

Already the Asia-Pacific region has become a major theater of Soviet–American confrontation—probably second in importance and in intensity only to the European theater. Both superpowers are becoming increasingly active in the region. Confrontation and tensions between them seem to be growing alarmingly, along with a significant buildup of military forces and capabilities, especially on the part of the Soviet Union. Some commentators insist that the region is, or soon will become, the main focus of the Soviet–American confrontation. Indeed, the distinguished director of the Institute of Oriental Studies of the U.S.S.R. Academy of Sciences has expressed the view that Asia has become "the most dangerous zone of the development of global contradictions."[3] Moreover, "Since World War II Asia has become a region of shifting alignments in the ongoing global rivalry between the Soviet Union and the United States."[4]

Similar views were strongly advanced in 1984 by Peter Polomka, then a visiting fellow in international relations at the Australian National University in Canberra. "That the Pacific region is destined to become the main focus of super-power rivalry," he wrote, "can scarcely be doubted." And the center of rivalry in the Pacific region is East Asia and the Western Pacific. "While in global terms it [the Pacific region] remains in the shadow of Europe . . ., forces are at work shifting the strategic center of gravity slowly towards East Asia." Moreover, as Polomka notes, the Western Pacific region, and especially East

Asia, takes on added significance in the global strategic picture because of the growing roles of Japan and China, in the region and even on a global scale. "It is there that the interests of the super-powers and the two other major Pacific states, China and Japan, directly interact, and the nature of that interaction promises to be critical to security elsewhere."[5]

CONDITIONING FACTORS: GENERAL

The United States and the Soviet Union share at least four objectives, with different implications, in the Western Pacific. First, they seek to prevent the region from coming under the domination of any hostile power or powers, and in this connection each obviously has the other primarily in mind. Second, and as a consequence of the first objective, they are building up their military capabilities in the region, and they are trying to project their influence there through a variety of nonmilitary as well as military "carrot-and-stick" techniques. Third, they are both developing a complicated pattern of interrelations with the countries of the region, especially with China and Japan. In this respect the United States has been more successful in recent years than has the Soviet Union, especially because of the growing rift between the Soviet Union and the People's Republic of China and the development of a new relationship between the United States and China, and because of the continued hard Soviet line toward Japan and the extensive, if often strained, ties between the United States and Japan. And fourth, on a more positive note, each superpower seems to desire to avoid confrontation in the Western Pacific, even though many of the policies and orientations of each and many of the developments and trends in the region seem to place this objective in constant jeopardy.

Clearly the United States regards the Soviet Union as the main security threat in the Western Pacific. This view is an inevitable consequence of its overall assessment of Soviet policies and intentions. Most, and probably all, of the Western Pacific allies of the United States, and some, if not all, of the nonaligned nations in the region as well—notably the ASEAN countries—share American concerns about the Soviet threat, but in almost every case their assessment of the nature and seriousness of the threat is rather different from the American view. Their reluctance to take a strong stand on this issue is reinforced by their dislike of the confrontational policies and tactics of the superpowers, their desire not to get involved in superpower rivalries and conflicts, in their own region or anywhere else, their doubts about American credibility and the reliability of American assurances and commitments, and their acute sense of their own weaknesses and vulnerability. Even the United States realizes that the Soviet threat in the Western Pacific, as elsewhere, is a multifaceted one, and that the threat of a direct Soviet military attack is less imminent than is that of attempted Soviet involvement in the internal affairs and local conflicts of states of the region, either directly or more probably through surrogates, in ways that may have serious spillover effects, with consequent danger of superpower involvement and possible military confrontation. Hence the United States is troubled by the "possibility that local conflicts into which the Soviets or their clients inject themselves will be the major threats to regional security."[6] Many of the states of the region share American apprehensions in this respect, although they are apprehensive of the consequences of direct or indirect American involvement in local conflicts as well.

To a far greater degree than the United States, at least in a geographic sense, the Soviet Union is an Asian power. Its territorial expansion into Siberia dates back several centuries. It now occupies some one-third of the entire Asian continent, constituting the main part of the geopolitical "heartland" of which Sir Halford Mackinder wrote. Wholly apart from the global superpower rivalry and balance of power considerations, its determination to have a say in Asian developments is quite understandable. As one Soviet official explained, "We are only trying to reestablish our rightful historical interests in Asia and the Pacific."[7]

The United States does not question the right of the Soviet Union to pursue and promote its legitimate interests in Asia; but it does believe that Soviet moves in the Western Pacific, as elsewhere, far transcend the needs of legitimate interests. It is alarmed by the Soviet military and naval buildup in the region and by what it regards apprehensively as escalated policies and demands as well as escalated military capabilities.

The Soviet Union, in turn, is alarmed by the formidable military presence, the extensive U.S.-led alliance system, and the overall actions and policies of the United States in the Asia-Pacific region. It believes that the United States should show a greater understanding and acceptance of the legitimate interests and the major role of the Soviet Union in the region. "The United States is expected to deal with the Soviet Union as an equal, to accept the Soviet Union as a major power with legitimate interests throughout Asia and the Pacific, to include the Soviet Union in regional organizations, and to give priority to relations with Moscow over those with Beijing."[8]

Thus in the Western Pacific the United States, a non-Asian power in the territorial sense but with substantial interests in the region, faces a dilemma regarding the proper attitudes and policies toward its major global rival in this vital region. The dilemma was concisely stated by Richard Solomon: "Shall America view the USSR as a legitimate presence in Asian affairs or as a power to be contained and, where possible, excluded from the region? And can the U.S. counter Russian military capabilities while at the same time accepting Moscow's economic and political involvement in regional affairs?"[9]

The Soviet Union seeks to improve its own position in the Western Pacific and to weaken that of the United States. It wishes to break up, or at least to weaken, the elaborate American alliance system, which it regards as anti-

Soviet in nature, and to foster doubts and apprehensions regarding U.S. reliability and credibility among America's Asian and Pacific allies, among nonaligned countries, especially the ASEAN countries, and in the People's Republic of China.

Obviously all of the nations of the Western Pacific in varying ways and degrees are factors in U.S.–Soviet interactions in the region. This is especially true of China, Japan, South Korea, and Vietnam.

Because its own relations with the People's Republic of China have been strained for many years, whereas those of the United States have changed fundamentally from almost complete isolation and hostility to growing contacts and officially friendly relations, pursued with many reservations and hesitations, the Soviet Union seeks to prevent what it regards as an incipient alliance or "quasi-alliance" relationship between the United States and China, directed at the Soviet Union. One of its recurring fears, often expressed, sometimes in a nightmarish sort of way, is that these two major and currently hostile powers will join with Japan, with which the Soviet Union is on continuing bad terms and which has established extensive relations with the People's Republic of China, as well as with the United States, in an anti-Soviet tripartite alliance. It repeatedly warns each of these three countries that it should not trust the other two, and it tries to persuade other nations of the Western Pacific that they cannot trust any of the three. Although it seeks to discredit China among other Asian countries, and even seems to be bent on encircling China, it still insists that sooner or later the Chinese will see the folly of their present ways, will turn away from the "capitalist-imperialist" countries, and will then be ready for improved relations with the Soviet Union.[10]

In addition to raising the specter of a U.S.–China–Japan anti-Soviet alliance, the Soviet Union has consistently criticized Japan for its close associations with the United States. It has been especially critical of the U.S.–Japanese security treaty and Japan's key role in the U.S.-led alliance system in the Western Pacific, of Japan's gradual military buildup, and of what the Soviets allege is the growing militarization of Japan, for which the United States is held to be largely responsible. Soviet spokespersons contend that relations with Japan could be "normalized" and improved if Japan would cut its military ties with the United States and cease to be an agent and supporter of U.S. "imperialist" and "aggressive" policies in the Western Pacific and beyond. It is clear, therefore, that Japan is a major factor in the U.S.–Soviet confrontation in East Asia and the Western Pacific.

Differences over Korea have complicated U.S.–Soviet relations ever since the joint occupation of the Korean Peninsula by the two victorious powers in 1945. Their inability to agree on a formula for the emergence of a unified nation in an area that Japan had controlled for many years led to the "temporary" decision to divide the Peninsula at the Thirty-eighth Parallel, with a demilitarized zone between the two Korean nations that were soon established, one supported by the Soviet Union, the other by the United States. Contrary to the apprehensions of the late 1940s and early 1950s, the Korean Peninsula has not been a theater of direct military confrontation between the superpowers; but it is one of the world's most dangerous conflict zones, and any major escalation of the conflict between North and South Korea could involve the superpowers in a military confrontation. The Soviet Union also has frequently charged that another anti-Soviet alliance, involving the United States, Japan, and South Korea, is in the making;[11] and it sometimes refers to an emerging hostile quadripartite alliance of the United States, Japan, the People's Republic of China and South Korea.

For both the United States and the Soviet Union Southeast Asia is assuming a new strategic importance and is becoming another important area of confrontation. In various ways the involvement in the area of the two superpowers, as well as of China and Japan, has increased significantly in recent years. The center of U.S.–Soviet rivalries and disputes has been Vietnam, where the United States was deeply involved in the 1960s and 1970s and the Soviet Union has been in subsequent years.

The Soviet Union is now closely associated with Vietnam. It is committed to that country's defense, as illustrated by the Treaty of Friendship and Cooperation of 1978, and to the provision of substantial military assistance to Vietnam. It has championed Vietnam in its tensions with China and has supported the Vietnamese occupation of Kampuchea. The United States, in contrast, has refused to extend recognition to the Communist regime in Vietnam, and it is a leading critic of Vietnam's domestic and external policies, actions, and orientation. It is especially critical of Vietnam's relations with the Soviet Union, the move into Kampuchea, and policies toward the ASEAN countries. In the many-faceted Vietnam–ASEAN disagreements the United States is on the side of the ASEAN states.

Regarding Vietnam, the United States and the Soviet Union are obviously poles apart. And the United States is particularly alarmed because the Soviets' close ties with Vietnam have enabled them to develop air and naval facilities in, and to conduct operations from, the important bases of Cam Ranh Bay and Danang in Vietnam. This has already greatly complicated U.S. problems of security in a strategically significant part of the world, and it has larger regional and global implications as well.

At present the Soviet Union is estranged from all of the other major powers in the Western Pacific, whereas the United States has extensive and generally improving relations with virtually all of the noncommunist states of the region, as well as with the world's most populous Communist country. Naturally the Soviet Union is determined to reverse this trend, without abandoning its support of the smaller Communist states of East and Southeast Asia or its rather aggressive political policies and its military and naval buildup in the entire Western Pacific region.

Obviously many factors and trends, in the international system generally as well as in the Western Pacific, will affect the future course of Soviet–American relations in Asia and the Pacific, where so many vital interests are involved and so many present or potential areas of confrontation and possible conflict exist. Professor Donald S. Zagoria has selected nine factors as the most important:[12]

1. The overall nature of Soviet–American relations during the coming decade;
2. The growing role of Japan in the Soviet–American–Japanese triangle;
3. The military balance of power between the two superpowers in Asia;
4. The bitter conflict between Vietnam and China;
5. The conflict between the two halves of still-divided Korea;
6. The Soviet perception of Asia and Asians and Russian experience in Asia during the past several hundred years;
7. The Soviet economic presence in the region;
8. The question of how fast the Russians will seek to develop Siberia and the Soviet Far East and what impact this may have on future Soviet policy in the region; and
9. Soviet worldwide expansion, the Soviet military buildup in Asia, and the evident Soviet dissatisfaction with the present balance of power in the region.

All of these factors, and many others as well, have a bearing on future Soviet–American relations in the Western Pacific, as they are clearly having at the present time. The global and historical factors are certainly deserving of detailed attention. This brief analysis bears these background factors in mind as it focuses on the implications and effects of the Soviet military buildup in the Western Pacific and on a few other contemporary trends and developments.

THE MILITARY BALANCE IN THE WESTERN PACIFIC

The Soviet military buildup in Asia, both quantitatively and qualitatively, in the past two decades has been truly phenomenal (see map 3.1). Ground forces increased from seventeen divisions in 1965, to forty-six in 1980, to more than fifty by the mid-1980s. Most of these are stationed along the Chinese borders. More than 2,000 aircraft, including the latest combat types and Tu-26 Backfire bombers, have been deployed in the Far Eastern Theater of Operations, which was established in 1979 as a major operational theater comprising three military districts: the Far East, Transbaikal, and Siberian. "The Soviet Union maintains about two-fifths of her ICBM force and ballistic-missile-firing submarines, one-third of her strategic bombers and general purpose naval forces in her eastern territories."[13] Japan, Korea, and most of Southeast Asia are within the range of the more than 150 SS-20 IRBMs in the Far Eastern Theater. The more than 400 ICBMs—mostly SS-11s, SS-18s, and SS-19s—in this Theater "are believed to be targeted on the West Coast of the U.S."[14]

The buildup of the Soviet Pacific Fleet has been equally impressive. It is now the largest of the four fleets of the Soviet Navy. Headquartered at Vladivostok, it has at least twice the tonnage of the U.S. Seventh Fleet, which

Map 3.1. Military build-up in the Soviet Far East

is also operating in East Asian waters. It includes over 100 submarines, about one-third of them with ballistic missiles, over 350 surface ships, including more than forty major surface combatants, over 150 amphibious units, and more than 350 aircraft and helicopters.[15] The addition of the Soviet Union's first V/STOL aircraft carrier, the 40,000-ton *Minsk*, and an antisubmarine cruiser, two guided missile vessels, and an amphibious assault ship represent a formidable increment to the offensive capabilities of the Fleet. Solomon recognizes this: "The stationing of the antiship version of the Tu-26 Backfire bomber and MIG-25 Foxbat interceptors in the Soviet Far East heightened the threat of long-range satellite-directed air attack on ships of the U.S. Seventh Fleet and aircraft of the strategic airlift."[16] As the *1983 Asia Yearbook* reported, Tu-95 "Bear" reconnaissance aircraft, based at Vladivostok (with a few at Cam Ranh Bay in Vietnam on a two-month rotation), regularly fly patrols extending into the Western Pacific well east of Japan and over the South China Sea and most of Southeast Asia.[17]

The main Soviet naval bases in the Pacific are on its East Asian littoral, at Vladivostok and Petropavlovsk, with another major base under construction at Korsakov in southern Sakhalin (see map 3.2). The main U.S. naval bases in the region are at San Diego, Pearl Harbor, and Subic Bay, with important facilities on Guam and home-porting facilities at Yokosuka in Japan. Naval rivalry between the superpowers extends over much of the Asia-Pacific–Indian Ocean region, with a concentration in the East and Southeast Asian areas.

The growing reach of the Soviet Pacific Fleet, indicative of its growth from a primarily coastal defense force to one with blue-water capability, is a major new development that is a decisive factor in the changing security environment in the Western Pacific and beyond. So too are the expansion of the U.S. Navy and the deployment of more major naval units in Western Pacific waters—probably in response to the Soviet military buildup worldwide as well as in the Western Pacific region.

The interpretation is no longer valid, if it ever was, that the primary mission of the Soviet Pacific Fleet is coastal defense, not the deployment of offensive capability over vast areas of the Pacific and Indian Oceans, whereas that of the U.S. Pacific fleet is more offensive than defensive. Both fleets have important defensive responsibilities and capabilities, but both are now flexing their muscles and expanding their capabilities and operations in ways that can only be interpreted as indicative of a new emphasis on offensive tactics, strategy, and actions. This is an alarming development between rivals with such frightening destructive potential and with such questionable, and limited, political wisdom and vision.

The North Pacific is becoming "a hot new arena of Soviet–American competition,"[18] where a dangerous cat-and-mouse game is going on constantly, involving major units of both the Soviet and the U.S. Pacific fleets, supplemented by air and land forces at several strategic locations, mainly

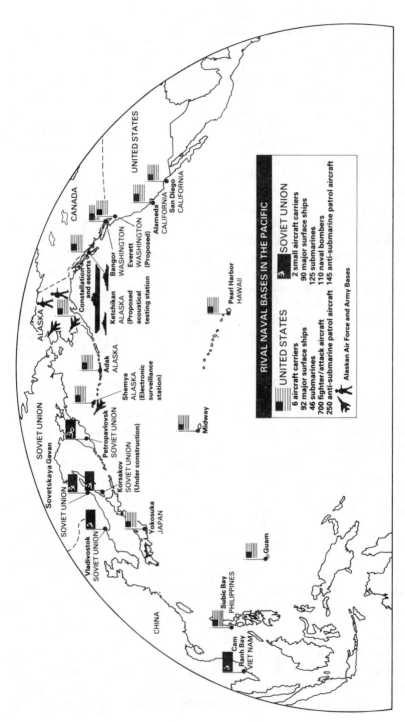

Map 3.2. Rival naval bases in the Pacific

eastern Siberia for the Soviet Union and Alaska for the United States. The military buildup on both sides in the North Pacific is particularly conspicuous and particularly alarming, and so are the techniques and operations that are being used.

Ships of the Soviet Navy and other intelligence-gathering vessels carefully monitor all U.S. fleet movements and exercises and aerial reconnaissance and other operations, and the U.S. Navy is as busy checking on similar Soviet activities. This mutual surveillance goes on constantly, using the most modern electronic devices, satellites, aerial reconnaissance, naval watches, and other means. Soviet surface ships, submarines, and intelligence ships (often disguised as fishing trawlers or other noncombatant vessels) are incessantly on station just off the Western coast of the United States, Hawaii, and Alaska (including the Aleutian Islands). Comparable American vessels are constantly on watch off the coast of Siberia, the Kurile Islands, and Vietnam. "To watch these forces in action is to see a gigantic chess game sprawling across more than 2 million square miles of land and ocean."[19]

Soviet armed forces in the East Asia–Western Pacific region outnumber those of the United States by more than three to one, and the armed forces of Soviet allies in the region (mostly Vietnamese and North Koreans) outnumber those of U.S. allies by more than 500,000 (see Table 3.1). The Soviet–U.S. military balance in the region is obviously affected not only by the size of the armed forces of the two superpowers and their allies, but also by many other factors that include the quality as well as the quantity of the armed forces and the weaponry available to them, the relative capacity to move forces and weapons from outside the region into the region, if needed, and the extent to which the allies of each superpower can, and would, make any decisive difference in the event of a Soviet–American clash in the region. A major factor would be the role of China, if any, in such a clash. With armed forces about as large as the combined total of the American and Soviet forces in the Western Pacific and of all the regional allies (although deficient in organization and modern weaponry), the Chinese role could be significant, if not decisive.

Any efforts by the United States and its Western Pacific allies to counter Soviet military forces in the region might have a better chance of success if noncommunist countries of the region with which the United States is not formally allied—notably Taiwan and Indonesia—joined in the efforts. But until and unless the Soviet-American confrontation in the Western Pacific erupts into open military clashes, the strategic balance in the region will be greatly conditioned by many nonmilitary factors and considerations, as well as by the regional military balance. And the overall regional balance will be affected by the course of U.S.–Soviet rivalry on a global scale, more than regionally, and by many other factors shaping the wider global strategic balance.

Japan has been particularly disturbed by the continued Soviet occupation of the so-called Northern Territories, the southernmost islands of the Kurile

TABLE 3.1
Comparative Military Forces in the Western Pacific

Communist		Noncommunist	
Soviet Union	c. 450,000	United States	143,800
Soviet-allied Communist states		U.S.-allied and other noncommunist	
Kampuchea	c. 35,000	states	
Laos	53,700	Australia	70,731
Mongolia	36,500	Indonesia	278,050
North Korea	838,000	Japan	243,000
Vietnam	1,027,000	Malaysia	110,000
		New Zealand	12,443
		Philippines	114,800
China	3,900,000	Singapore	55,500
		South Korea	598,000
		Thailand	235,300
		Taiwan	444,000

Data obtained from *The Military Balance 1985–1986* (London: The International Institute for Strategic Studies, 1985).

Islands (which the Japanese tend to disassociate from the Kuriles), just north of Hokkaido. This disquiet has been enhanced by the Soviet refusal, until early 1986, to discuss the Japanese claims to these islands, which Japan held until the end of World War II, and by the stationing of large numbers of Soviet forces and the development of airfields and military installations in the islands. "In the summer of 1978, the Soviets began to redeploy Ground Force troops, modern weapons and equipment, and airplanes and helicopters on Etorofu, Kunashiri, and Shikotan. They have also constructed new military bases on these islands. . . . By late 1980, the combined total of Soviet Ground Forces deployed in the northern islands approached the size of a division, i.e., about 6,000 men. . . . In addition, the Soviets have expanded military exercises in the sea surrounding these islands."[20]

The United States and its Western Pacific allies have been increasingly worried by the growing Soviet capacity, and apparently also the growing Soviet intention, to maintain a significant presence and to project significant power in the South China Sea and the Indian Ocean. Soviet naval and air units can operate in these areas from bases in the Soviet Far East and elsewhere in the Soviet Union; and Soviet capabilities for such operations have been significantly increased by the availability of facilities at Danang and Cam Ranh Bay in Vietnam.[21] The Soviets claim that they use these facilities mostly 'for refueling, minor ship repairs, and shore leave;"[22] but American and other analysts, well aware that Danang and Cam Ranh Bay were developed by the United States during the Vietnam War as major air and naval bases, believe that the Soviets are taking full advantage of the facilities, well beyond the limited use they admit they are making of them. As reported in the *1983 Asia Yearbook*:

At least 10 Soviet ships, including one cruise-missile submarine, one major and two minor surface combatants, an oiler, an intelligence gatherer, a buoy tender, a repair ship and a stores vessel currently use the base [Cam Ranh Bay] on what US intelligence sources describe as a continual basis. Units of the Soviet Pacific Fleet heading to and from the Indian Ocean spend up to a month at a time in the South China Sea, taking advantage of Cam Ranh Bay for refuelling, minor shipboard repairs and shore leave. On top of that, four Tu-95 'Bear' reconnaissance aircraft from the Soviet base at Vladivostok are stationed at the coastal facility on a two-month rotation, flying surveillance missions as far south as the Natuna Islands, between east and west Malaysia and ranging north into the Bashi Channel separating Taiwan and the Northern Philippines.[23]

The availability of facilities, and perhaps bases, in Vietnam raises the unwelcome specter of enhanced Soviet threats to the main U.S. naval and air bases in the entire Southeast Asian–Indian Ocean region, at Clark Field and Subic Bay in the Philippines, and constitutes a threat to the vital sea-lanes that pass through the Malacca and other straits in the Southeast Asian region, through which moves so much of the oil and other resources in international commerce en route to Japan and more distant regions. According to an American naval intelligence specialist, "The Soviet fleet presence in the South China Sea is not subtle. It demonstrates Soviet support for Vietnam and gives the Soviet Union the potential in the South China Sea to disrupt a good share of the world's commerce. Our impression is that they have unimpeded access to Cam Ranh Bay with an airfield and logistic capability provided by courtesy of the U.S. taxpayer. That access increases as Vietnam feels more threatened."[24]

The Soviets, haunted by continued feelings of insecurity in a hostile international and Asian environment and by the possibility of a two-front war in Europe and Asia insist that their military and naval buildup, which is regarded by the United States and its Asian allies as well beyond legitimate Soviet defense needs, is wholly for defensive purposes. It is designed to counter the many threats that it perceives in the Western Pacific, especially the challenges posed by the United States and its Western Pacific allies, notably Japan, and by a hostile China. It regards the Western Pacific as a main theater of the global threat from the United States. Some commentators have argued that the Soviet military buildup in East Asia and the Pacific is designed more with this global threat from the United States in mind than with more specifically regional threats, and also to "counter the Oceanic strategy of imperialism," to borrow phraseology commonly used by Soviet analysts.

From the Soviet perspective, as interpreted by two leading American specialists on the Soviet Union,

The steady movement of the economic, political, and military global center of gravity to Asia, the intended development of eastern Siberia, the Chinese military modernization, the important Japanese contribution to American military strength in the Far East, and the continuing American naval and air superiority in the Pacific necessitate a very strong and sustained Soviet military presence in the area. Of fundamental importance is the impact of Pacific concerns on Soviet strategic thinking. A Soviet military official recently alluded to a new position on the Soviet concept of global parity. Just as in the 1970s the Soviets insisted that within their concept of global parity there must also be regional parity in Europe, in the 1980s they will insist on regional parity in the Far East as well.[25]

Richard Solomon has well described the Soviet phobias and objectives in the Asia-Pacific region:

> Moscow faces an increasingly complex security problem in East Asia: The coalition of China, Japan, the United States, and American allies in Southeast Asia and Western Europe constitutes a multifront strategic challenge, and the Soviet Far East is no longer buffered by a friendly China. In Southeast Asia the USSR's Vietnamese allies are caught between Chinese military pressures and the potential opposition of the ASEAN states (two of which—the Philippines and Thailand—are directly allied to the United States): yet Soviet influence in the region is minimal, with its potential for growth limited to Indonesia and Malaysia, that is, the countries that fear Beijing's possible influence over large ethnic minorities. . . .
>
> Using its home-based military capabilities and naval and air facilities in Vietnam, South Yemen, and Ethiopia, Moscow is creating a structure of bases and deployments designed to (1) guard the Soviet Far East against attack and to secure sea-deployed strategic missile forces in the sea of Okhotsk and elsewhere in the Pacific; (2) develop a significant military threat that will inhibit initiatives by China, the United States, Japan, and allied states; (3) deploy a military capability to counter the American Seventh Fleet and U.S. bases in the Pacific; and (4) develop naval and air forces capable to protecting Soviet sea and air transport and challenging the security of sea-lanes communication between the United States and its Asian allies, and from the Middle East and the Persian Gulf to the Western Pacific.[26]

What the Soviet Union regards as a necessary increase in defense capabilities in the East Asia–Pacific region the Chinese describe as proof of Soviet hegemonism and the United States as proof of Soviet offensive and aggressive intentions and policies. In his Annual Report for FY 1981 Secretary of Defense Harold Brown expressed the view that "Soviet forces in the Far East are geographically positioned, exercised, and apparently designed for offensive operations."[27] The extensive American alliance system in the Western Pacific is designed primarily to counter this growing threat. At least, this is the interpretation of the United States. The United States sees the Soviet military buildup in Asia and the Pacific as not only a regional but also a global threat, "in essence part of a worldwide, relentless process transforming the USSR into a truly global power."[28]

IMPLICATIONS OF THE SOVIET ROLE IN THE WESTERN PACIFIC: AN AMERICAN PERSPECTIVE

The U.S. dilemma in dealing with the Soviet Union in the Western Pacific is a part of its overall dilemma of simultaneously pursuing policies of containment and coexistence with the other superpower. As Solomon points out: "The United States is in a period in which it must strengthen its military defenses and alliance relationships while at the same time sustaining efforts to negotiate a framework for coexistence with Moscow. . . . [A] policy of managing the ongoing competitive relationship with the Soviet Union must involve elements of cooperation as well as the expectation of continuing geopolitical rivalry and possible military confrontation."[29]

Whereas both the United States and the Soviet Union profess to seek a reduction of tensions, a substantial reduction of armaments, and a more cooperative relationship—although this will inevitably be within an essentially conflictual framework—they have been allocating far more of their human and physical resources to programs that tend to increase tensions rather than promote cooperation. Each has been developing formidable armaments and defense establishments and bilateral and multilateral security alliances and arrangements primarily directed at the other. This is true of their respective policies and objectives in the Asia-Pacific theater. In Solomon's words, "The ominous worldwide growth of Soviet military power, and particularly its projection into Asia, is the primary factor shaping the emerging pattern of alignments in the region."[30]

But, as has been noted, the United States and the Soviet Union do have some common interests in the Asia-Pacific region, as elsewhere, notably in avoiding a direct military conflict because of confrontationist policies in the region or because of the spillover and escalatory impact of regional conflicts in which they may be involved on opposite sides. Certainly the allies of the United States in this region, though valuing the support of the United States in dealing with security threats with which they cannot cope by themselves, do not wish to be drawn into superpower conflicts or to see their region become a theater for such conflicts. Hence the security and other interests of America's Asian allies, as well as of the United States itself, would seem to dictate a similar course of action, namely, to provide a defensive shield of deterrent strength and cooperative relationships in the region without precipitating a dangerous polarization and heightened tensions.

In the mid-1980s Professor Donald C. Hellmann of the University of Washington expressed the belief that "a situation is developing in which the United States can seek to redefine the political and strategic landscape in Northeast Asia by dealing directly with the Soviet Union while walking hand in hand with our allies and not compromising our overall political-military posture in the region."[31] This possibility should be explored carefully and sincerely by both superpowers, with due attention to their basic national interests and to the interests and concerns of other nations of the Western Pacific.

To turn again to Solomon: "The policy the United States adopts must be designed to prevent an action-reaction cycle of Soviet and American initiatives in Asia (as elsewhere) that would unnecessarily polarize the region and increase the risks of military confrontation."[32] Certainly, he reminds us, "America's Asian policy cannot be exclusively a matter of dealing with the Soviet challenge."[33] This is true even in the security field, and even in the Western Pacific, where the Soviet threat, in the perspective of the United States and to a lesser extent of most of its Asian allies, is a major—perhaps indeed *the* major—threat to the freedom and security of the countries of the region and to the region as a whole.

Taking Solomon's reminder to heart should lead to a broader and more balanced perspective on the problem of security in the Western Pacific and to a greater understanding and recognition of the complex nature of the security threats in the region. It should also lead the United States to place its concerns about and its relations with the Soviet Union in the region in the broader perspective of multifaceted security problems and needs and in the even broader perspective of the many other interests and relationships that the United States has in the region, not all of which can be approached primarily from a "the-Russians-are-coming, the-Russians-are-coming" point of view.

Notes

[1] Richard H. Solomon, "American Defense Planning and American Security: Policy Choices for a Time of Transition," chapter 1 in Richard H. Solomon, ed., *Asian Security in the 1980s: Problems and Policies for a Time of Transition* (Cambridge, Mass.: Oelgeschlager, Gunn & Hain, 1980), p. 10.

[2] "Pacific Forum Northeast Summary Report," an unpublished report to the Pacific Forum, Honolulu, in 1985, p. 15. This is a report of "a study and investigative tour of the Republic of China, the Republic of Korea and Japan . . . made by representatives of the Pacific Forum from September 1 to 15, 1984." Its principal author is Professor Donald C. Hellmann of the University of Washington. The new strategic importance of the Far East and West Pacific to the Soviet Union is clearly delineated by two American specialists in an article published in *Foreign Affairs* in 1986: "In calculating the changing correlation of forces in the 1980s, Soviet leaders continue to regard Europe as the central theater of superpower contention. Yet sufficient evidence suggests that they are receptive to the idea that the center of gravity with regard to superpower economic, political and security concerns is shifting from Europe to the Far East. The accelerating process of Siberian economic development, the construction of the Baikal–Amur Mainline Railroad, the upgrading of Soviet nuclear bases in the Sea of Okhotsk, the priority buildup of the Soviet Pacific Fleet, the attention to continuing American naval and air superiority in the region—all work toward significantly increasing the relative weight of the Far Eastern theater. The emergence of Japan as a major political as well as economic power, the modernization of China, and the dynamism of newly industrializing Asian countries are also fundamental to understanding the new strategic importance of the Far East and West Pacific." Seweryn Bialer and Joan Afferica, "The Genesis of Gorbachev's World," *Foreign Affairs* 64 (1986): 637. This is a special issue on "America and the World 1985."

[3] Quoted in John J. Stephan, "Asia in the Soviet Conception," chapter 2 in Donald S. Zagoria, ed., *Soviet Policy in East Asia* (New Haven: Yale University Press, 1982), p. 39.

[4] Richard H. Solomon, "Coalition Building or Condominium? The Soviet Presence in Asia and American Policy Alternatives," chapter 11 in ibid., p. 283.

[5] Peter Polomka, "The Security of the Western Pacific: The Price of Burden Sharing," *Survival* 26 (January/February 1984): 4.

[6] Solomon, "Coalition Building or Condominium?," p. 33

[7] Quoted in Stephan, "Asia in the Soviet Conception," p. 33.

[8] Ibid., p. 34.

[9] Solomon, "Coalition Building or Condominium?," p. 302.

[10] For representative Soviet views, see M. L. Sladkovsky, "Problems of Peace and Security in Eastern and South-east Asia," a paper presented at the Second Soviet-American Symposium on Problems of Peace and Security in East and Southeast Asia, held in Pushtchino, U.S.S.R., May 1981; "A Policy of Reason Versus Terror and Adventurism," *Far Eastern Affairs* (The Journal of the Institute of the Far East of the U.S.S.R. Academy of Sciences) 1984 (4); and Henry A. Trofimenko, "US Interests in Asia: A View from Moscow," *The Nonaligned World* (New Delhi) 2 (October–December 1984).

[11] See D. Moun, "Japan's Economic Penetration of South Korea," *Far Eastern Affairs* 1985 (3): 68.

[12] Donald S. Zagoria, Preface to Zagoria, ed., *Soviet Policy in East Asia*, pp. ix–xi.

[13] Polomka, "The Security of the Western Pacific," p. 4.

[14] Jong Youl Yoo, *Soviet Military Build-up in the Far East I: A Threat to Regional Peace* (Seoul: The Institute of International Peace Studies, Kyung Hee University, 1984), p. 115.

[15] For details regarding the Soviet Pacific Fleet, see ibid., pp. 16–73; and *The Military Balance*

1985–1986 (London: International Institute for Strategic Studies, 1985), p. 30. The latter source reports eighty-five "principal combatants," including two carriers and fourteen cruisers, and eighty-eight submarines, including many with ballistic missiles.

[16] Solomon, "Coalition Building or Condominium?," p. 291.

[17] "Power Game: The Seas Around Us," *Asia 1983 Yearbook* (Hong Kong: Far Eastern Economic Review, 1983), pp. 22–23. Attention should also be called to the Tu-22M "Backfire" bomber. "Intelligence estimates suggest that as many as 400 TU-22M may be operational by 1985 or later. The TU-22M variable geometry bomber, with a speed of around Mach 2.25 and an unfueled maximum range of about 5,700 km poses a great threat to Japan, the Philippines, Guam, and even Hawaii. With refueling, it can reach major Western parts of the U.S.A. It carries nuclear warheads in its AS-4 air-to-surface missiles." Yoo, *Soviet Military Build-up in the Far East*, p. 105.

[18] Bill Dietrich, "Top Gun in the Pacific," *The Seattle Times*, September 28, 1986. This important article by a staff reporter focuses on the U.S.–Soviet naval buildup and rivalry in the North Pacific, with particular reference to the implications for people in Alaska and the State of Washington; but it also contains an excellent summary of Soviet moves in the entire Pacific region, which "are cited as cause for American military alarm," and of the response of the United States—"a buildup of its own certain to cause equal paranoia on the other side." See also "U.S. Counters Soviets in the Pacific," *The Seattle Times*, August 31, 1986. This dispatch from San Diego, the headquarters of the U.S. Third Fleet, by a correspondent of *The Los Angeles Times*, quotes ex-Secretary of the Navy John F. Lehman, Jr., as saying that "The Soviets were smarter than we were as a government in recognizing the importance of . . . the Northeast Pacific and the Pacific rim," and that "Alaskan waters will become a staging area for regular naval exercises, and the Adak naval base (in the Western Aleutians) will be built up." It also reported: "In what the commander of the U.S. Pacific Fleet calls 'a major shift' in operations, the Navy has for the first time begun a regular deployment of aircraft carrier battle groups in the Northern Pacific to meet a growing Soviet presence in the waters off Alaska." The Pacific Fleet commander-in-chief, Admiral James Lyons, Jr., "admitted that the stepped-up naval and air activities in the North Pacific had a larger purpose: 'We've got a message to send (to the Soviets). And if they take that message back, then we've raised the deterrence equation without firing a shot.'" Obviously what one side regards as necessary deterrence and defensive measures the other side regards as provocative and offensive actions. The result is an alarming increase in naval presence and confrontation.

[19] Dietrich, "Top Gun in the Pacific."

[20] Yoo, *Soviet Military Buildup in the Far East*, pp. 88–90. The Soviet military buildup in these islands seems to be continuing. "According to the Japanese Defense Agency, the islands are well fortified, especially Etorofu, with 10,000 Soviet ground troops, 3,000 border guards and 40 MIG-23 fighter planes." Clyde Haberman, "At Odds for Years, Japan and Soviet Will Test Waters in Moscow Aide's Visit," *The New York Times*, January 14, 1986.

[21] See *Soviet Military Power—1985*, issued by the U.S. Department of Defense (Washington, D.C.: U.S. Government Printing Office, 1985).

[22] "Power Game: The Seas Around Us," p. 22.

[23] Ibid.

[24] Quoted in ibid.

[25] Bialer and Afferica, "The Genesis of Gorbachev's World," p. 639.

[26] Solomon, "Coalition Building or Condominium?, pp. 291–292.

[27] Secretary of Defense, *Annual Report for Fiscal Year 1981* (Washington, D.C.: U.S. Government Printing Office, 1980), p. 4.

[28] Paul F. Langer, "Soviet Military Power in Asia," chapter 10 in Zagoria, ed., *Soviet Policy in East Asia*, p. 256.

[29] Solomon, "Coalition Building or Condominium?," pp. 301–302.

[30] Ibid., p. 284.

[31] "Pacific Forum Northeast Asia Summary Report," p. 14.

[32] Solomon, "Coalition Building or Condominium?," p. 284.

[33] Ibid., p. 326.

CHAPTER 4

The United States and Japan: The Core Relationship

From almost every perspective, the United States considers its relationship with Japan to be "the core relationship" in the Western Pacific. Top spokespersons of the Reagan administration have declared that the United States regards Japan as a "pillar of American policy" in the Asia-Pacific region, with increasingly important global dimensions. The U.S. ambassador to Japan, Mike Mansfield, has described it as "the most important bilateral relationship in the world, bar none." Repeated disagreements with Japan over political and economic as well as security policies and recurring strains in U.S.–Japanese relations have not altered the fundamental U.S. position that Japan is the cornerstone of its relationships in East Asia and the Western Pacific.

This is the view that has prevailed ever since the U.S.–Japanese Security Treaty of 1952 and the reemergence of Japan as an independent nation in the same year. Most Americans would agree with the statement of Edward Neilan, an American specialist on East Asia, who wrote in 1978 that "American policy in Northeast Asia should be fundamentally based on a strong partnership with Japan and even-handed relations with every other nation in the region."[1] Even though the United States has established new and growing ties with the People's Republic of China, most Americans would probably subscribe to Neilan's view that "for the rest of the century—and perhaps beyond—our relationship with Japan will be fundamental to our interests in the region and more significant than our ties with China."[2]

Moreover, the United States has increasingly viewed its relations with Japan as of central importance in global as well as in regional terms. "The American–Japanese alliance," wrote Robert Shaplen in 1976, "remains the linchpin of our Asian policy, and in trilateral terms, of our Euro-Asian policy."[3] As Secretary of State Shultz pointed out in an address to the Shimoda Conference (which he described as "the most important nongovernmental forum for discussions of the Japanese–American relationship") in September 1983, "our relationship has grown beyond the bounds of the bilateral and become global in scope."[4] In March 1982, in a statement before the Subcommittee on Asian and Pacific Affairs of the Committee on Foreign

Affairs of the U.S. House of Representatives, the assistant secretary of state for East Asian and Pacific Affairs, John H. Holdridge, said that "it has become increasingly clear that our relationship with Japan is the bedrock of our Asian policy, and, by extension, an indispensable element in our global diplomacy."[5]

Greater emphasis is being placed on the important role that Japan is playing and on the even more important role it is destined to play on the world stage. More and more Japan is working with the United States and the countries of Western Europe in trilateral relationships and interactions. This is especially true in the economic sphere, but to an increasing degree it is true in the political and security spheres as well. Japan, for example, is a full partner in the Organization for Economic Cooperation and Development (OECD), the economic summit meetings, and other organizations and arrangements in association with the industrially advanced and militarily powerful states of the Western world. In fact, observers have remarked, some critically and some approvingly, that Japan seems to be becoming more of a Western than an Eastern nation. The increasing collaboration is not confined to official circles. The Trilateral Commission, for example, provides a forum for frequent exchanges of ideas and cooperative action on the part of prominent citizens of the United States, Western Europe, and Japan (many of whom, to be sure, have held leading official positions in their own countries). The United States is also involved with Japan in many multilateral regional and international organizations, including the United Nations, its major organs and agencies, its specialized commissions, and its many other branches and affiliates, some of which, like the Economic and Social Commission for Asia and the Pacific (ESCAP) and the Asian Development Bank (ADB), are of a primarily regional nature.

THE "CORE RELATIONSHIP" IN TRANSITION

If official statements and other public pronouncements are taken literally, there can be no question that both Japanese and Americans recognize the importance of the U.S.–Japanese relationship, including its security dimensions, and wish to strengthen and improve their relationship in the light of changing circumstances and abiding national interests. Some differences in perspective, as well as some doubts and suspicions, however, persist. The relationship may in fact be far more fragile than it appears. The Japanese do not doubt the importance of the United States to them, in connection with security, markets, and other needs but they obviously have ambivalent feelings about the United States in general, as well as about the security relationship. They do not want to be as heavily dependent on the United States as they have been in the past. They have continuing doubts about the credibility and reliability of the United States. They feel that the United States has never taken a balanced and informed view of their evolution, traditions, values, culture, and needs. In particular, they feel that the United States has not made the necessary perceptual and policy adaptations to Japan's growing internal strength and to its changing regional and international role and influence and that the United States has not moved from its conception of itself as the patron of Japan to one of genuine partnership and equality.

Americans, in turn, while professing to attach great importance to the relationship with Japan, in fact tend to give higher priority to other countries, and to other problems and issues. Few if any American political leaders have any deep understanding of Japan or of East Asia generally and their main priorities, interests, and concerns lie elsewhere. In foreign affairs their approach is more Eurocentric than Asiacentric and is focused more sharply on the Soviet Union, Western Europe, Latin America, and the Middle East than on the Western Pacific. This Eurocentrism, to the extent that any approach in depth to issues of foreign policy is discernible, is much more apparent on unofficial levels, where the level of knowledge, sustained interest, and understanding with respect to Japan and to Asia generally is still shockingly low. Hence in public perception, as in official relations, there seems to be a considerable asymmetry in the U.S.–Japan relationship. Ambassador Mansfield had this in mind when he wrote in 1981: "The Japanese have no doubts about America's importance to them in many spheres—economics, diplomacy and security, to name a few—but I sometimes think we Americans do not fully appreciate Japan's importance to the United States."[6]

For several years it has been apparent that Japan has been reassessing its position in East Asia, the Asia-Pacific region, and the world, in the light of internal, regional, and international developments and of its changing position in the international system. Politically, it is seeking a new regional and international role, a role more commensurate with its economic power. It is also reassessing its security position and needs, but because it is reluctant to undertake major defense responsibilities and to develop the kind of defense establishment that would be necessary to meet its security needs, it continues to cite the restrictions on rearmament imposed in Article 9 of the "MacArthur Constitution" of 1946 and to rely heavily on the protective shield of the Security Treaty with the United States. There is, however, a growing dissatisfaction with the nature of the alliance and other relationships with the United States, especially among Japanese who do not support the ruling Liberal Democratic Party (LDP), who take a strong anti-nuclear stand, and who want Japan to follow a more independent and a more balanced course in regional and world affairs.

Polls in Japan continue to show a decisive majority of the Japanese people still supporting the security arrangements with the United States, but they also reveal a growing desire for Japan to play a more assertive and more independent role, regionally and internationally, to develop political and security policies that are more in keeping with Japan's position as the world's second economic power, and to avoid the kind of association with the United States that might involve their country in international conflicts, especially in Soviet-American rivalries and confrontations.

The United States, too, is well aware of the changing nature of the "partnership" with Japan, in the light of the significant changes that are under way in both countries, and in regional and international affairs. The United States is encouraging Japan to play a more active regional and international role and to assume a larger share of responsibility for its own defense and, to a more limited degree, for defense of the East Asian and Western Pacific regions. Fundamentally, the main stresses and strains in the U.S.–Japan relationship are due to the great changes that have occurred, and are occurring, on national, regional, and international levels, and to the search by both countries for ways of promoting national as well as common interests. The United States believes that in the long run, as the assistant secretary of state for East Asian and Pacific affairs, John H. Holdridge, stated in March 1982, "The assumption of greater international responsibilities by Japan should benefit the U.S.–Japan relationship;" but the United States also recognizes, as Holdridge noted, that "the adjustment to shifts in our relative power position and influence would also entail a certain amount of friction."[7]

Many of the current problems are in the economic realm, and these have spillover effects that impinge on every aspect of the relationship. As Paul F. Langer wrote in 1979, "The question for the 1980s is whether U.S. and Japanese cooperative efforts can prevent economic issues from spilling over into the more fundamental political and security dimensions of the U.S.–Japan tie."[8] Some observers go even further and insist that the tensions in U.S.–Japan economic relations not only complicate the cooperation of the two countries in political and security fields but constitute a major security threat as well. "Rather than be overexercised by the Soviet threat," wrote Derek Davies, a veteran student of the changing scene in the Western Pacific, in the mid-1980s, "I would argue that the much greater threat to the entire Asia-Pacific region is the emerging Cold War between the United States and Japan."[9]

Certainly economic issues—even more than security issues—have dominated the U.S.–Japan agenda in recent years, and the foremost economic differences have been in the area of trade. "Bilateral trade policies," reported the U.S. deputy secretary of state in February 1981, "require more of our attention than any other area in the U.S.–Japan relationship."[10] Americans are particularly disturbed by the enormous, and growing, deficit in their trade with Japan, which reached $37 billion in 1984, around $50 billion in 1985, and $58.8 billion in 1986, nearly one-third of the total U.S. trade deficit, and by Japanese restrictive trade practices which, Americans insist, make it very difficult for American business businesses to gain access to Japanese markets or to carry on business operations in Japan. They want Japan to alter its long-standing policies in order to reduce the trade imbalance and to open up Japanese markets. If Japan will not take such steps voluntarily, Americans warn, the U.S. Congress will impose retaliatory restrictions on Japanese trade with the United States and on Japanese investment and other business operations in the United States. Japanese, in turn, point out that they are constantly relaxing their restrictions on foreign trade, investment, and business enterprise in their country, and that they are taking a number of "voluntary" measures to restrict their exports to the United States that include leading export items such as automobiles and electronic and other high technology products. Japanese economic leaders also argue that they are not responsible for the marked decline in America's international economic competitiveness, which can only be reversed by sounder American policies, greater industrial efficiency, higher standards of workmanship, and lower costs of production and distribution.

The differences and frictions over trade relations were clearly brought out in a bi-national poll conducted concurrently in late September 1985 by the *Los Angeles Times* and a leading Japanese newspaper, the *Yomiuri Shimbun*, based on telephone interviews with 1967 persons in the United States and 2257 in Japan. American negative feelings on this aspect of U.S.-Japanese relations were strongly substantiated. Over 80 percent of the Americans polled thought that Japan was "completely," "very much," or "somewhat" responsible for the imbalance of trade between the two countries and believed that U.S. trade with Japan (its second largest trading partner) "did more harm than good." Surprisingly, 40 percent of the Japanese who were interviewed expressed the view that their country was being "fairly blamed" for U.S. trade problems; but the great majority were strongly opposed to U.S. trade sanctions against Japan and contended that Japan was at least as fair in trade practices as the United States.[11]

Because of the leading roles of the United States and Japan in the world economy and the relative size of their bilateral trade, differences over trade policies and issues are particularly serious, with major adverse effects both on overall U.S.-Japanese relations, including security relations, and on the international economy generally. The United States and Japan are the world's two largest market-oriented economic powers. Their combined GNP is about 35 percent of the total world GNP, and they account for about one-fourth of the trade of the noncommunist world. Their bilateral trade—which was over $94 billion in 1985—is far greater than that between any other two countries. The United States is Japan's largest overseas market, and U.S. trade with Japan is second only to U.S. trade with Canada; hence, as is often said, Japan is the United States' largest *overseas* trading partner. Marked improvement in trade relations of such gigantic scale would obviously have beneficial effects on the entire U.S.–Japan relationship. These relations could hardly have reached such a level without extensive cooperation and collaboration, both bilaterally and multilaterally.

The two countries often work closely—some external critics believe much too closely—in the international economic arena. In his address to the sixth Shimoda Conference in September 1982, Secretary of State Shultz stressed the importance of Japanese cooperation in the promotion of "an open trading system," "a more stable international monetary system," "the development of the less-developed economies of the world," and "new trade liberalization agreements."[12] But within the framework of extensive international economic cooperation, bilateral trade disputes will continue to plague U.S.– Japanese relations. These differences will complicate the efforts of the two countries to continue to maintain what has been a very successful relationship and to reach agreements on a wide range of issues relating to the second major area of differences, the vital area of security.

U.S.–Japan relations have often been affected by political and personality changes in both countries. Obvious possibilities for changes in both that might adversely affect the overall relationship are, for example, if governments less friendly to the United States than those of the ruling LDP should come to power in Japan, or if future governments in the United States should give less attention to Japan, and be even more Eurocentric, more protectionist, and more critical of Japan's political, security, and economic policies than past governments have been. The main frictions between Japan and the United States will probably continue to be over economic issues, and these frictions may create serious complications in both political and security fields. But in the political and foreign policy spheres the changing relations can probably be accommodated within an essentially cooperative relationship.

In 1979 Professor Langer predicted that "Japanese policies during the decade will . . . continue to emphasize an 'omnidirectional' foreign policy orientation, albeit within the framework of the special relationship with the United States."[13] In the 1980s Japan's foreign policy has become more omnidirectional in some respects and less so in others, reflecting the diverse interests and continuing ambivalence in foreign affairs. This policy has become more omnidirectional because of increasing involvement in regional and international affairs and the desire not to become too heavily involved with or dependent on the United States. The policy has become less omnidirectional because of growing security roles and commitments and because of some alarming changes in the security environment in the East Asia-Western Pacific region. These latter two developments have in some respects identified Japan even more than previously with the United States, but increasingly on the basis of greater equality and interdependence. A strong impetus in the direction of closer association has been provided by a series of Soviet actions, including the military buildup in the Soviet Far East and the Pacific, the invasion of Afghanistan, the support of Vietnam and a Vietnamese move into Kampuchea, the continued occupation and military reinforcement of the Northern Territories, and the KAL-007 incident. These actions have accentuated anti-Soviet feeling and the sense of a Soviet threat in Japan.

Although anti-Soviet feeling has been growing in Japan, the basic attitudes toward the United States seem to have been little affected by continuing differences on trade, security, and perceptual approaches. This conclusion seems to have been substantiated by the binational poll in September 1985. The poll also reveals differences in perception and national character, as well as in perspectives on specific trade issues. Whereas the Americans were far more dissatisfied with existing trade relations than were the Japanese, they were more optimistic about overall relations between the two countries. Only 9 percent of the Americans polled rated U.S.–Japan relations as "unfriendly," compared with 22 percent of the Japanese interviewees. This poll, however, confirmed the findings of all previous polls of its type in the postwar era that both Japanese and Americans regard the basic relations of their countries as "friendly." The fact that this poll, as previous ones, indicates that relatively more Americans than Japanese hold this opinion may be due more to differences in psychology and perception between the two peoples than to the cumulative impact of differences over particular developments or issues. As the president of the Pacific Basin Institute in Santa Barbara, California, observed, "The American tends to be an optimist whereas the Japanese tends to be a pessimist. That difference in attitude almost always influences polls like this." The Japanese consul general in Los Angeles pointed out that the poll "clearly shows that there is a perception gap between Japan and the United States. . . . If confrontation comes to the surface in Japan, that means that the two parties are not so friendly . . . whereas in the U.S. confrontation is commonplace even among friends."[14]

The basic U.S.–Japan security relationship is obviously undergoing major changes, due to changing internal and external conditions and circumstances. One has only to recall the vast changes that have taken place in Japan since the end of World War II—from abject defeat and occupation to reemergence, first as a sovereign state and then as a major power, especially in the economic field—and in the United States—from unquestioned predominance to a lesser but still superpower status in an increasingly pluralistic and interdependent world, and in the entire world situation, to realize that changes in relations between two such important countries would be an inevitable consequence.

In the security field these changes are already quite manifest. Paul Langer has summarized them in a perceptive way. For some three decades Japan was able to follow "a national strategy that proved both effective and cheap." This was made possible by the U.S.–Japan Security Treaty and the assumption of a large part of the responsibility for the defense of Japan by the United States. "Sheltered against external threats by the American military umbrella, Japan has enjoyed the enviable position of controlling the extent and manner of its political and military involvement with the problems and conflicts of other nations." But this condition is changing, with unpredictable impact and consequences. "It would be surprising if the American–Japanese relationship did not demand adjustments reflecting changes in the domestic conditions of the alliance partners, in the correlation of their forces, and in the international context in which the United States and Japan must pursue their policy objectives."[15] Generally speaking, from the Japanese point of view the objective is a more balanced security relationship in which Japan will assume more responsibility for its own defense, determined by its own security perspectives, without incurring excessive new political and financial burdens and commitments. From the American point of view the objective is the assumption by Japan of a larger share of the burden for its own defense and a larger role in the efforts to ensure security in the East Asian and, to some extent, the entire Western Pacific region, without a revival of the militarism that wrought such havoc in the 1930s and 1940s.

The U.S.–Japanese alliance relationship seems to be strongly supported in both countries. In fact, polls indicate that it now has more rather than less support. In a poll conducted for the Prime Minister's Office in 1979, 66 percent of the residents answered yes to the question: "Do you think that the Japan-United States Security Treaty is contributing to the preservation of peace and security of Japan?" Sixty-one percent favored a future defense policy that would "maintain the status quo, namely defend Japan by both (the) Japan–United States Security Treaty and (the) SDF (Self Defense Forces)." Only 8 percent wanted to 'abrogate the Japan–United States Security Treaty and defend Japan by strengthened indigenous defense capability," and even less—5 percent—favored both the abrogation of the Japan–U.S. Security Treaty and the reduction or dissolution of the SDF.[16] As Langer points out, 'Support for extreme pacifist views has steadily eroded in Japan. Today, a limited self-defense effort—vaguely defined as 'minimum necessary defense power'—is accepted by the majority of the Japanese people."[17] Hence the focus is on the "character and mission and geographic scope" of the SDF, rather than on desirability, and on the extent of burden sharing and mutual commitments of the United States and Japan rather than on any desire to remove the U.S. military umbrella altogether. In the United States, of course, the value of the Japanese relationship is repeatedly proclaimed (as has been mentioned, ambassador Mike Mansfield has called it the most important relationship in the world), as are endorsement and support of the U.S.–Japan Security Treaty as "the cornerstone of U.S. security policies in Asia."[18]

Thus the security relationship between Japan and the United States seems to be firmly anchored in both countries. But in its process of transition it could be adversely affected by any number of developments in either country, in the Western Pacific region, or in the global system.

DIFFERENCES IN SECURITY PERSPECTIVES

The relationship is in constant jeopardy because of certain basic differences between the two countries with regard to political, economic, and security policies. At least three major differences in security approaches and perspectives hamper the search for ways to strengthen security cooperation. These are (1) different conceptions of the nature of security itself; (2) different threat perceptions, especially with regard to the Soviet Union; and (3) Japan's concerns about U.S. security policies in the Asia-Pacific region and globally and doubts about the credibility and reliability of U.S. commitments in the event of major threats to Japan's security.

Japan places a much greater emphasis than does the United States on what the Japanese like to call "comprehensive national security."[19] This includes nonmilitary as well as military dimensions of security and often, in fact, tends to minimize or even to erode the military dimensions which the United States seems to regard as central. This comprehensive approach gives greater weight to the political, economic, and psychological aspects of security and to overall national policies and objectives. It even includes Japan's changing images and aspirations regarding its proper internal and external policies generally. This approach dominates security thinking and policies in Japan to a far greater degree than in the United States. "A major question for the 1980s," wrote Richard H. Solomon of the Rand Corporation in 1982, "is how to develop the U.S.–Japan defense relationship so that it reflects a greater balance among Japanese industrial capabilities, security concerns, and new aspirations for leadership in regional and world affairs."[20] Japanese leaders regard all of these matters as important aspects of "comprehensive national security." It will be difficult for those responsible for the formulation and implementation of U.S. political and security policies to reconcile their more technical and military-oriented approach to security with this more comprehensive and more nebulous framework of Japanese security thinking.

Japanese attitudes toward national security have fluctuated widely, at different time periods and among different groups in government, in political parties, and in the public generally. For some time the Japanese seemed to be content to avoid military buildup by citing the restrictions of Article 9 of the 1946 Constitution and by relying on the U.S.–Japan Security Treaty and the American defensive shield. As the nation reemerged and became an important economic power, it faced the desirability—or even the necessity—of developing political and security policies more in keeping with its new economic status and with the changing and increasingly unfavorable regional and international environment. But its ambivalence regarding security policies continued. Gradually support for its SDF mounted, but there was still a reluctance to develop these forces beyond very limited levels, as evidenced by the continuing policy not to allow defense expenditures to exceed 1 percent of GNP and not to remove the ban on regular armed forces imposed in Article 9 of the 1946 Constitution. Moreover, pacifist, neutralist, and anti-nuclear sentiments remain strong among certain groups in Japan, especially younger people and some opposition political parties.

However, if Japan ever was content to enjoy the "free ride" made possible by American troops and bases in Japan and American defense commitments to Japan, that period is clearly coming to an end. The Japanese face the unwelcome necessity of assuming a larger share of responsibility for their own defense and possibly of accepting some regional and international security responsibilities as well, although they have not yet developed agreed-upon security policies or the necessary defense establishment to achieve the new security objectives and policies they have set for themselves. The concept of comprehensive national security is too imprecise and general to constitute a viable defense and security policy, and the measures for security incorporated in the National Defense Program Outline of 1976 and in subsequent reaffirmations and revisions have not yet been implemented in many significant aspects. Thus the security issue is still a major unresolved dilemma for Japan as well as a major irritant in U.S.–Japan relations.

Many Japanese feel that the United States, too, lacks a well-defined and generally supported security policy and strategy for the Western Pacific, an area that U.S. political and security planners seem to regard largely in global rather than regional terms and mainly as a theater of the global U.S.–Soviet conflict. The Japanese also regard U.S. security commitments in the Western Pacific as too mercurial, too unreliable, and too dependent on the fluctuations of opinion and mood among U.S. political leaders and the American public generally. The Japanese believe that U.S. policies and actions in the Western Pacific, and, indeed, in all other parts of the world, are too militarily oriented, too confrontational, and too much concentrated on the Soviet Union. They want the United States to continue to maintain substantial military power in their country and elsewhere in the Western Pacific, but they do not want to be forced into larger defense commitments than they feel they need, nor to be involved in superpower conflicts in the Western Pacific or anywhere else.

The clear lesson that emerges from the differing American and Japanese security perspectives and policies is that there is a growing need for each country to reassess and reformulate its own security concepts and to give greater consideration to each other's views and interests on security matters, to take practical steps to implement the strategic policies that evolve from this new assessment and consultation, and to seek in each country more wide-spread support for and understanding of these strategies and policies.

Differences in threat perceptions of Japan and the United States have led to different perspectives regarding the threat from the Soviet Union. The United States is primarily concerned with the global nature of the Soviet threat, whereas Japan focuses more specially on possible Soviet threats in the Western Pacific region. Both countries, however, are concerned with both regional and global aspects of the threat, even though their main focus and evaluation may differ considerably. This difference has become less marked in recent years. Both countries are perturbed by the rapid Soviet military buildup in East Asia and the Western Pacific. The United States is more disturbed than Japan is by the Soviet Union's involvement in Indochina, its strong support of Vietnam in that country's difficulties with China and military operations in Kampuchea, and by Soviet access to air and naval facilities in Vietnam. Japan is well aware that a strong Soviet presence in Vietnam can add to tensions in East and Southeast Asia, and that Soviet bases in Vietnam raise the unwelcome possibility of an interdiction of the sea-lanes from the Persian Gulf to Japan, through which much of the oil that is essential to Japan's economy and survival must pass. Moreover, the rather unyielding policy that the Soviet Union has been following toward Japan, especially with regard to the continued military occupation of the Northern Territories, has puzzled and alarmed the Japanese, and has led them to proclaim publicly that they now regard the Soviet Union as a major threat. But they do not believe that Japan itself is in much danger of open Soviet aggression, and they are hopeful that their difficulties with that country will not lead to a serious confrontation.

It is still probably true, as Stephen Gibert wrote in 1982, that "the dominant group of Japanese leaders simply do not share Washington's perceptions of the threat posed by the Soviet Union," even though they are increasingly frank in acknowledging that such a threat exists. In keeping with their concept of comprehensive national security, they pay as much attention to political as to purely military factors in their estimates of the Soviet threat. They believe that "American estimates of the Soviet military threat tend to focus on the hardware and physical capabilities that the Soviets are amassing."[21] In their view the United States exaggerates and misconceives the Soviet threat and pursues policies too confrontational toward the Soviet Union. The similarities and differences in their approach to the Soviet Union are well summed up by Franklin Weinstein: "The Japanese clearly share the U.S. concern about the Soviet buildup but less deeply. The Japanese government has publicly identified the Soviet Union as a threat to security, and Tokyo has gradually moved toward acceptance of a limited expansion of its defense role. But growing Japanese awareness of the Soviet threat has been accompanied by the frequent experience of Japanese reservations about a confrontational policy toward the Soviet Union."[22]

Japanese hopes for improved relations with the Soviet Union were raised by a statement of Mikhail Gorbachev, shortly after his summit meeting with President Reagan in November 1985, that improved ties with Japan were necessary, by the official visit to Japan by Soviet Foreign Minister Eduard Shevardnadze in January 1986—the first visit by a Soviet foreign minister in ten years[23]—and by Gorbachev's speech in Vladivostok in July 1986, in which he presented a five-point plan for regional cooperation designed to reduce tensions in the Asia-Pacific region.[24] Several agreements, mostly of an economic nature (regarding plans to step up Soviet–Japanese trade, which had declined dramatically in 1985, and to renew Soviet–Japanese collaboration in the development of Siberia, for example), were signed during Shevardnadze's visit.

The Japanese leaders took advantage of the Soviet foreign minister's presence in Tokyo to raise the touchy issue of the Northern Territories, but they received no indications that the Soviet Union would change its position on this issue. Hence it continues to be the most visible barrier to improved Soviet-Japanese relations. Japan has refused to sign a peace treaty with the Soviet Union until its claims to the Northern Territories are considered and resolved to its satisfaction. For the first time, after Shevardnadze's visit, Japan perceived some indications that the Soviets might at long last be willing to discuss this issue, but few if any signs that they would consider any real change in their unyielding stand on this issue.

The United States has consistently supported the Japanese position on the Northern Territories issue, but its support has generally been low-key and not highly publicized. This is rather surprising, especially in view of the importance that the Japanese attach to this issue and in view of the strategic significance of the Northern Territories with respect to Soviet access from the Sea of Okhotsk to the open waters of the Western Pacific Ocean.

Whether or not Soviet–Japanese relations begin to emerge from the long deep-freeze, U.S.–Japan relations will continue to be close and extensive and to have a major security component. Clearly the Japanese still regard the security treaty with the United States as the sheet-anchor of their security. But they are obviously uneasy about it. For some years they have been engaged in a major internal debate on the proper security policies to follow in the future, a debate that has often been characterized by a high degree of emotionalism. Japan's evolving security perspectives seem to presage a change in the security relationship with the United States, probably without the abrogation of the security treaty.

Their alliance with the United States gives the Japanese both comfort and alarm. They are still dependent on the United States for essential protection against major external threats, for the provision of a wider regional security umbrella, and for nuclear capabilities, in which they are wholly deficient militarily. But the Japanese are uneasy not only about the security treaty and the present relationship with the United States, but also about U.S. policies in the Asia-Pacific region—about the reliability and credibility of America's commitments to Japan in the event of any major aggression in the region. If a nuclear power—presumably meaning the Soviet Union—undertook military operations in the Western Pacific, Japan and other possible targets of military aggression would be heavily dependent on American aid. If such a development occurred, it would probably be a phase of an even larger conflict, and the United States would probably be neither able nor willing to commit a substantial part of its military resources and efforts to the Western Pacific. Japan also shares the apprehensions of the weaker U.S. allies in the region regarding what it views as the overly conflictual and confrontational policies of the United States in the Western Pacific and elsewhere, and the desire not to get involved in superpower conflicts. In short, Japan wants greater assurance that the United States will come to its aid if it gets involved in a conflict with the Soviet Union, or any other major power or powers, but it does not want to become involved itself in conflicts between the military giants if its own security is not directly threatened.

Japan, as most of the Western Pacific allies of the United States, has been particularly concerned about the credibility and reliability of U.S. commitments since the American withdrawal from Vietnam, under circumstances and after an experience that could only raise grave doubts and alarms on the part of America's Western Pacific allies. Japan fears a substantial American disengagement from Asia, both militarily and psychologically. It finds a great deal of evidence of the consequences of this mood, as reflected in such puzzling moves as President Carter's decision to withdraw the bulk of the U.S. ground forces from South Korea (a decision later reversed, as a result of congressional and other pressures in the United States as well as from Japan and other Asian allies). Japan is also troubled by what it regards as the U.S. propensity to make major decisions affecting Japan and other Western Pacific countries without proper consultation or even notification, as happened (for reasons that the United States regarded as impelling) in the case of the "Nixon shocks" of 1971, with respect to both the opening of China and to changes in the international monetary system. Japanese uneasiness about U.S. policies in the Western Pacific and doubts about the reliability and credibility of American commitments in the region help to explain why Japan still wants to maintain a strong security relationship with the United States yet at the same time to follow more independent and "omnidirectional" security policies, as well as economic and political ones.

OTHER WESTERN PACIFIC COUNTRIES AS FACTORS IN THE U.S.–JAPANESE SECURITY RELATIONSHIP

As the "pillar" of U.S. policy in East Asia, Japan plays a central role in U.S. security policies and activities in the region and indeed in the entire Asia-Pacific theater. Thus the U.S.–Japan security relationship is central to the defense of East Asia and the Western Pacific, as well as to the defense of Japan itself. Both Japan and the United States are concerned with any threats to security anywhere in the area, and therefore the other countries of the region are factors in the U.S.-Japan security equation. This is particularly true of the Soviet Union, the People's Republic of China, North and South Korea, and the ASEAN countries and Vietnam.

As has been noted, many of the differences between the United States and Japan in security perspectives and threat perceptions center around the Soviet Union, but these differences have diminished as the Japanese have increasingly come to recognize the Soviet Union as the major external threat to Japan and the Western Pacific region. The Soviet Union is a central factor in much of the security cooperation between the United States and Japan, as both countries publicly acknowledge. The Japanese still have rather different perspectives regarding the nature and magnitude of the Soviet threat and the proper policies to adopt to cope with it. In particular, as has been pointed out, they think that the United States exaggerates the threat from the Soviet Union, particularly the direct military threat, and tends to aggravate, rather than mitigate, the danger of military confrontation. But in both Tokyo and Washington, when security in the Western Pacific is under consideration, the Soviet Union occupies a prominent place in all security discussions. Without this common concern over the Soviets, the problem of Western Pacific security and of the security policies and relationships of the United States and Japan would take on quite different dimensions.

Since the early 1960s, when the Sino–Soviet split became manifest, Japan and the United States have followed many similar policies and approaches toward the People's Republic of China, reflecting an awareness of China's emerging role in East Asian and international relations. Before that time both countries viewed what appeared to be the close association—even a monolithic front—of the two major Communist states with great apprehension. Neither the United States nor Japan was willing to enter into formal diplomatic relations with the People's Republic until the 1970s. Taiwan was a complicating issue for both nations. But Japan was much more concerned about its limited contacts and strained relations with the People's Republic than was the United States. Part of Japan's hesitation to normalize relations with China was occasioned by American attitudes and pressures. As soon as the U.S. opening to China occurred, in the early 1970s, Japan moved much more expeditiously than the United States in normalizing relations with China. It formally recognized the Chinese Communist regime as the legitimate government of China, withdrew recognition of the Republic of China on Taiwan, and established formal diplomatic relations in 1972, whereas the United States did not take these steps until January 1, 1979. In 1978 Japan signed a Treaty of Friendship and Cooperation with the People's Republic of China, a step that the United States has not taken. Japan has more extensive relations with China than the United States on almost every level, official and unofficial. Both countries recognize that they must move slowly and cautiously in their new relationship with the People's Republic of China for many reasons that include uncertainty about China's future political evolution, its future relations with the Soviet Union, and its future military and foreign policies. Soviet spokespersons have repeatedly warned both countries that the People's Republic of China would be a fickle and dangerous ally, and they have often raised the specter of a Sino–American–Japanese alliance directed against the Soviet Union. Thus China has become an important factor in U.S. relations with Japan as well as with the Soviet Union.

South Koreans often look askance at the U.S.–Japan security relationship and are concerned about its implications for them. They still have unpleasant memories of the long years of Japanese control, and their suspicions and dislike of the Japanese are still often manifest. They are also fearful that U.S. policies toward them will be dominated by the U.S.–Japan security relationship. They do not want to become pawns of the two nations on whom they rely most heavily for protection and with whom they have the closest political, economic, and military contacts. Japan has generally supported U.S. policies in South Korea, in both tangible and intangible ways, but it does not want the U.S.–South Korean nexus to become too close, and it does not want its own policies toward South Korea to be influenced unduly by its connections with the United States. Japan is also fearful that the United States will follow too aggressive and militaristic policies in Korea, thereby aggravating the already tense situation in the Korean Peninsula, one of the world's most dangerous conflict zones, in ways that may precipitate armed conflict and involve it as well as the other two major intrusive powers, the Soviet Union and China. Japan has long taken a more flexible and relaxed attitude toward the North Korean regime than has the United States, and it has shown much greater interest in establishing various kinds of direct and indirect contacts with Pyongyang, well short of formal recognition. In many respects the two Koreas, and especially South Korea, have become factors in the U.S.–Japan security relationship.

Southeast Asia and the Southwest Pacific are not as important as factors in the U.S.–Japan relationship, mainly because there are few major differences between the policies and interests of the United States and Japan in these two Western Pacific subregions. These subregions were main theaters of Japanese expansion and control during World War II, and of the long and costly military campaigns that were waged on land, sea, and in the air from the islands of the South and Southwest Pacific and the jungles of Burma through the Philippines, the Marianas, Iwo Jima, and Okinawa, eventually leading to Japan's defeat and surrender. During the long American involvement in Vietnam the Japanese Government permitted the United States to use Japanese bases, especially on Okinawa, in support of the operations in Vietnam, and it profited greatly from the Vietnam War in economic terms. Otherwise Japan gave little more than lukewarm support to the American effort in Vietnam, and it clearly did not want to become too closely associated with the United States in Indochina. Since the American withdrawal from Vietnam, however, Japan has followed policies toward the Communist governments in the Indochinese states that are similar to those of the United States. Japan has not recognized Vietnam or Kampuchea, it has been openly critical of Vietnamese ties to the Soviet Union and the Vietnamese move into Kampuchea, and it has given some support to the Cambodian refugees and the anticommunist Cambodian groups in Thailand.

Japan, as the United States, has developed extensive ties with all of the ASEAN countries. These are mostly of an economic nature. Japan and the United States are the largest trading partners and the major sources of foreign capital and investment of most of these countries, and hence are competitive as well as cooperative actors in the ASEAN area. Japan, as the United States, has taken a special interest in ASEAN and participates with the United States and other "dialogue partners" of ASEAN in the postministerial conferences that are now held annually, following the regular annual meetings of the foreign ministers of the ASEAN countries. Both Japan and the United States are well aware of the reservations and suspicions, stemming from different sources and experiences, of the ASEAN states toward them, and this awareness causes both to be tentative and cautious in their developing relations with the ASEAN countries.

Suspicion of Japan also lingers on in the Southwest Pacific, but Japan has developed rather extensive economic relations with Australia, and it has even participated in some joint air and naval exercises with the ANZUS countries (plus Canada) in the Pacific. The United States, of course, has much closer and much more extensive relations with its ANZUS allies, although in recent months its relations with New Zealand have been subjected to unexpected strains because of the position of the Labor government in New Zealand on visits by nuclear-powered or nuclear-armed warships and U.S. reactions to this limitation on the alliance.

PROBLEMS OF DEFENSE COOPERATION AND BURDEN SHARING

Paradoxically, the United States, which imposed on Japan the Constitution of 1946 with its much-quoted prohibition, in Article 9, of any organized military establishment, has put in recent years a great deal of pressure on Japan to do precisely what the 1946 Constitution forbids. But in spite of changing times and circumstances, until Article 9 is deleted, or at least revised, Japan cannot legally develop standing armed forces. Moreover, the psychological mood in Japan has been uncongenial to any movements to revise the Constitution. In the meantime a formula has been found—the organization of a skeleton military force, the SDF.

The mood in Japan regarding defense needs and policies has been changing markedly in recent years. Defense issues are now discussed publicly, and avidly, in both official and unofficial circles; the strong antinuclear, and even antidefense, movements of former years have lost some of their momentum and support; and there is a growing support for building up the SDF, still within rather narrow limits.[25] Although Japan has been spending less than 1 percent of its GNP on defense, only six or seven other nations in the world have higher defense budgets. The SDF is primarily a force for the defense of Japan itself and its offshore waters, within a rather limited range, but Japan has expressed a willingness to play some role in the defense of its sea-lanes within a range of about 1000 nautical miles from its shores. Japan has also shown a greater willingness to discuss broader security matters, such as the situation in the Persian Gulf and the protection of the sea-lanes from the Gulf to Japan, with the United States and to some extent with other members of both ANZUS and NATO.

Japan is clearly in a process of transition in its security thinking and policies. The trend is definitely toward building up its defense forces, with or without a modification of the restrictions imposed in the 1946 Constitution, and toward greater collaboration in security as in other areas with the United States and with the ASEAN countries (independently or in cooperation with the United States). But constitutional limitations, the psychological mood of the Japanese people, reluctance to breach the 1 percent-of-GNP barrier in defense spending, continuing debate on security policies and directions, and the possibilities of political change within the ruling LDP or of a greater political role of opposition parties less willing than the LDP to embark on even a limited military buildup, will continue to be restraining factors for some time to come.

In U.S.–Japan security relations the question of burden sharing is a thorny one. For some time the United States has been urging Japan to increase its defense expenditures and to some extent its defense commitments, and to bear a greater share of the costs of its own security. This would involve a greater contribution to the costs of maintaining the nearly 40,000 U.S. forces in Japan (more than one-half of them on Okinawa) and more than 100 U.S. bases and facilities on Japanese territory, until such time as Japan feels able to assume a larger share of its own defense. The position of the Reagan administration on this matter is quite clear. As a leading administration spokesperson stated in a public address in January 1985: 'We shall continue to urge Japan to assume a greater responsibility for its own conventional defense while extending the range of its surveillance and patrolling capabilities along its sealanes to the south. We will not, however, encourage Japan's assumption of regional military security responsibilities.'[26]

Undoubtedly, this constant U.S. pressure for what it regards as more equitable burden sharing has been a factor in the slow but steady buildup of Japan's SDF and a cautious broadening of its defense commitments. This pressure has also created a great deal of resentment in Japan and elsewhere and has led to some additional strains in U.S.–Japan relations. Too much American pressure, especially if applied without due consideration of Japan pride and sensitivities, could be counterproductive. "As long as Japanese public opinion remains ambivalent on defense issues, additional U.S. pressure to increase military spending could deepen tensions between Tokyo and Washington. It could also undercut the fragile consensus in Japan in support of a broader Japanese defense role."[27]

Within the broad guidelines laid down in the "Basic Policy for National Defense," adopted as far back as 1957, as reaffirmed and slightly modified in later White Papers of the National Defense Agency and other official reports and pronouncements, Japan has been entering a new era in its defense thinking and policies, in a hesitant and limited way. All of the basic Japanese pronouncements on security reaffirm the importance of the Security Treaty with the United States, as does the document approved in 1978 entitled "Guidelines for U.S.–Japanese Defense Cooperation." The famous Report on Comprehensive National Security of 1980, according to a Japanese analyst, "concluded that Japan would now have to become a more active participant in future Western international security efforts by achieving true self-reliance in defense and by broadening its defense perspectives."[28]

Japanese, American, and West European scholars and officials have participated in a number of conferences and have jointly authored a number of reports on "The Common Security Interests of Japan, the United States, and NATO," to cite the title of the report of a Joint Working Group of the Atlantic Council of the United States and the Research Institute for Peace and Security in Tokyo, published in Washington, D.C., and in Tokyo in 1980. "Japanese recognition that the security interests of Japan and NATO–Europe are inseparable was recorded by Japan's formal endorsement of the formal communiqué of the Williamsburg Summit in May 1983 in which it was stated that 'the security of the participating countries [i.e., the six NATO countries represented at the Summit and Japan] is inseparable.'"[29]

The participation of Japanese military and naval units in joint military exercises with similar units of ANZUS and NATO countries has become more extensive, although still rather rare, in recent years. The outstanding example was probably the participation of Japanese naval and air units, along with those of the United States, Australia, New Zealand, and Canada, in a three-week multilateral training exercise off Hawaii in February and March 1980, known as RIMPAC.[30] "This sort of effort," in the opinion of an American admiral, "must be broadened to encompass all phases of warfare training and planning."[31] The Japanese are not yet ready to coordinate their defense training and planning to such an extent with the United States, but they have already done more along these lines than is generally realized, and, if their economic relations with the United States can be improved, they will almost certainly be willing to cooperate more fully in the military field in the future.

After many years of irresolution and disagreements, the delicate issue of burden sharing seems to be on the way to solution. In any event, the division of security roles and commitments seems now to be relatively clear, at least in general terms. This division was explained by Paul D. Wolfowitz, U.S. assistant secretary of state for East Asian and Pacific Affairs, in an address before the Japan-America Society in Tokyo on September 18, 1985: "We have now divided defense roles and missions between us. The United States provides a nuclear umbrella and, if necessary, a power projection capability; Japan is responsible for the defense of its territorial land, air, and sea, and Japan has undertaken to provide for the defense of sealanes out to 1,000 miles. The division is a logical one, fitting well our respective capabilities and restrictions."[32]

In its security dimensions, as in most other aspects, as Professor Paul Langer perceived at the end of the 1970s, "the American-Japanese partnership is entering a new era."[33] It is broadening in scope, and the relative roles of the partners are changing quite significantly. It must develop into a more genuine partnership, and it must be based on more extensive consultation and on a more solid basis of common agreement and mutual interests. These are agreed-upon goals, at least if public pronouncements by leaders of both countries mean what they say, but they are still far from being realized. As U.S. Congressman Stephen J. Solarz, chairman of the Subcommittee on Asian and Pacific Affairs of the Committee on Foreign Affairs of the House of Representatives, observed in 1981, "A fundamental difficulty in the future will grow out of the changes occurring in the relative power of the two countries."[34] This point, and its implications, was underscored in the final report of the Fourth Regional American Assembly, which was held in Philadelphia a month after Congressman Solarz's article was published, to consider U.S.–Japanese relations: "The structure of the early postwar period, when Japan was so clearly junior partner of an all-powerful American patron, no longer obtains. At the present time, however, a partnership of equals seems difficult to envision, let alone construct. Given this central ambiguity, it will no longer suffice to meet change in this dynamic relationship with repeated prescriptions for greater consultation. ... The new circumstances demand more than tactical shifts in alliance management; the real imperative is for deeper self-examination on both sides."[35]

In the past the relationship, in security and almost all other aspects, has been quite asymmetric, but the underlying conditions have so changed that a more balanced relationship, a more genuine partnership, is essential. This is certainly true in the political and economic fields, and it is becoming true in the security field, where the asymmetry is certain to continue if the security relationship is confined to military capabilities and policies, but will become more balanced when the more comprehensive dimensions of security are factored into the equation. A basic question, as Richard H. Solomon has pointed out, is: "[H]ow can the two countries transform what has thus far been a protectorate relationship into a working alliance between equals?" Certainly the Japanese will settle for nothing less, and Solomon clearly expresses this view: "Public and official attitudes in Japan will no longer tolerate a 'second class' or subordinate status in relations with the U.S., and there will be increasing sensitivity to American actions that imply either a lack of awareness of Japanese interests or unreliability in the U.S. commitment to Japan's defense."[36]

Here again differences in perspectives and are quite apparent. "The fundamental danger facing the U.S.–Japanese relationship over the next five years," said the assistant secretary of state for East Asian and Pacific affairs in 1982, "is the likelihood of a growing disparity between U.S. expectations of Japan in the economic and defense areas and Japan's ability and willingness to meet these expectations."[37] Although U.S.-Japanese relations will continue to be extensive and generally more cooperative than conflictual, it is quite likely, as Admiral Hanks warned in 1981, that future relations are "going to be somewhat less cordial than in the recent past."[38] Continuing differences and disagreements in the economic and security fields will probably make more genuinely cooperative relations in these and other fields more, rather than less, difficult.

Achievements of a more genuine partnership in the security field will call for continuing commitments on the part of the United States and an increase in Japan's burden sharing and commitments in its own defense. It will also call for closer U.S.–Japanese consultation on problems of security in the entire Asia-Pacific region, and to a lesser extent in other parts of the world, especially the Indian Ocean and the Persian Gulf region.

More broadly considered, in Paul Langer's words, "It would be surprising if the American-Japanese alliance relationship did not demand adjustments reflecting changes in the domestic conditions of the alliance partners, in the correlation of their forces, and in the international context in which the United States and Japan must pursue their policy objectives."[39] "Within this global strategic-political setting," as was pointed out in a "Summary of a Transatlantic Dialogue" between a distinguished group of Americans and of Japanese in Tokyo in 1983, "the major aspects of the U.S.–Japanese strategic relationship should be considered."[40]

For both Japan and the United States the security relationship is "the core relationship." For the United States the Security Treaty with Japan is the cornerstone of its security policy in the Western Pacific, and is perhaps its most important bilateral security relationship. There is, indeed, considerable basis for the rather sweeping statement made by Ray Cline, a former high official of the Central Intelligence Agency, now associated with the Center of Strategic and International Studies at Georgetown University, that "[t]he success of U.S. policy in Asia, indeed in the whole world, depends upon the continuance of strong ties with Japan."[41] These ties cannot be taken for granted. They will certainly continue, with various changes and adaptations; but they require constant attention and nurturing.[42]

Notes

[1] Edward Neilan, "American Policy and Northeast Asia," *Policy Review* no. 6 (Fall 1978): 117.

[2] Ibid., p. 106.

[3] Robert Shaplen, "Three Areas of Asia Concern for Carter," *The Philadephia Inquirer*, December 5, 1976.

[4] George Shultz, "Japan and America: International Partnership for the 1980s," address before the sixth Shimoda Conference, Warrenton, Virginia, September 2, 1983; Bureau of Public Affairs, U.S. Department of State, *Current Policy* no. 506, pp. 1, 4.

[5] John H. Holdridge, "Japan and the United States: A Cooperative Relationship," statement before the Subcommittee on Asian and Pacific Affairs of the Committee on Foreign Affairs, U.S. House of Representatives, March 1, 1982; Bureau of Public Affairs, U.S. Department of

State, *Current Policy*, no. 374, p. 2.

6   Mike Mansfield, letter to the World Affairs Council of Philadelphia, June 16, 1981; in *The United States and Japan*, a report by the World Affairs Council of Philadelphia on the Fourth Regional American Assembly, held in Philadelphia, June 18–20, 1981.

7   Holdridge, "Japan and the United States," p. 7.

8   Paul F. Langer, "Changing Japanese Security Perspectives," chapter 4 in Richard H. Solomon, ed., *Asian Security in the 1980s: Problems and Policies for a Time of Transition* (Cambridge, Mass.: Oelgeschlager, Gunn & Hain, 1980), p. 77.

9   Derek Davies, "Signs and Portents of a Future Full of Change," *Asia 1986 Yearbook* (Hong Kong: Far Eastern Economic Review, 1986), p. 14.

10 Kenneth W. Dam, "U.S.–Japan Relations in Perspective," address before the Japan Society, New York, February 6, 1984; Bureau of Public Affairs, U.S. Department of State, *Current Policy*, no. 547, p. 2.

11 "Press Poll Shows Strong Anti-Japanese Bias on Trade Issues Between Japan, U.S.," *The Seattle Times*, October 27, 1985 (reprinted from *The Los Angeles Times*).

12 Shultz, "Japan and America," p. 3.

13 Langer, "Changing Japanese Security Perspectives," p. 69.

14 Quoted in "Press Poll Shows Anti-Japanese Bias, . . ."

15 Langer, "Changing Japanese Security Perspectives," p. 69.

16 *Asian Security Environment, 1980*, report submitted by a Special Study Mission to Asia, January 5–23, 1980, under the auspices of the Subcommittee on Asian and Pacific Affairs of the U.S. House of Representatives (Washington, D.C.: U.S. Government Printing Office, 1980), p. 13.

17 Langer, "Changing Japanese Security Perspectives," p. 71.

18 Franklin B. Weinstein, "The U.S. Role in East and Southeast Asia," chapter 7 in Raymond H. Myers, ed., *A U.S. Foreign Policy for Asia: the 1980s and Beyond* (Stanford, Calif.: Hoover Institution Press, 1982), p. 129.

19 See *Report on Comprehensive National Security*, by The Comprehensive National Security Group (Tokyo, 1980). The Group was established in April 1979 as an advisory body to Prime Minister Ohira. Its report in 1980 attracted a great deal of attention, in Japan and elsewhere, and is often cited as an informed explanation and rationale for Japan's emerging security thinking and policies. See also Robert W. Barnett, *Beyond War: Japan's Concept of Comprehensive National Security* (Washington, D.C.: Pergamon-Brassey's International Defense Publishers, 1984).

20 Richard H. Solomon, "Coalition Building or Condominium? The Soviet Presence in Asia and American Policy Alternatives," chapter 11 in Donald S. Zagoria, ed., *Soviet Policy in East Asia* (New Haven: Yale University Press, 1982), p. 310.

21 Stephen B. Gibert, "Northeast Asia in American Security Policy," chapter 3 in William T. Tow and William R. Feeney, eds., *U.S. Foreign Policy and Asian-Pacific Security: A Transregional Approach* (Boulder, Colorado: Westview Press, 1982), p. 80.

22 Weinstein, "The U.S. Role in East and Southeast Asia," p. 120.

23 Clyde Haberman, "At Odds for Years, Japan and Soviet Will Test Waters in Moscow Aide's Visit," *The New York Times*, January 14, 1986.

24 For a summary of this important address, see *Facts on File 1986*, 46: 579–580.

25 Japanese military expenditure increased from $86 million in 1951 to $13.4 billion in 1985. A new five-year plan for defense spending, approved in September 1985, called for military expenditures of $76 billion in 1986–1990. It is doubtful if this level of expenditure can be maintained without breaching the 1 percent-GNP barrier. See "Japan's Defense Budget for Fiscal 1988 would exceed 1 percent of the Nation's GNP," *The Wall Street Journal*, December 30, 1986. A Soviet commentator, reflecting prevailing views in his country, asserted that this defense spending plan marked "a new stage of militarization" for Japan. A Markov, "Japan: A New Stage of Militarization," *Far Eastern Affairs 1986* (1).

26 Michael H. Armacost, undersecretary of state for political affairs, "The Asia-Pacific Region: A Forward Look," address before the Far East–America Council/Asia Society, New York, January 29, 1985; Bureau of Public Affairs, U.S. Department of State, *Current Policy*, no. 653, p. 3.

27 *The U.S.–Japanese Security Relationship in Transition: Summary of a Trans-Pacific Dialogue* (Cambridge, Mass.: Institute for Foreign Policy Analysis, 1984). This publication

contains a summary of the discussions at a conference in Tokyo in August 1983, co-sponsored by the Institute for Foreign Policy Analysis, Cambridge, Mass. and the Japan Center for the Study of Security Issues, Tokyo.

28 William T. Tow, "U.S. Alliance Policies and Asian-Pacific Security: A Transregional Approach," chapter 2 in Tow and Feeney, *U.S. Foreign Policy and Asian-Pacific Security*, p. 29.

29 *The U.S.–Japanese Security Relationship in Transition*, p. 3.

30 See Ryochi Nishijima, "Participation of Maritime Self-Defense Forces in RIMPAC," *Asian Pacific Community* 7 (Winter 1980).

31 Robert J. Hanks, *The Pacific Far East: Endangered American Strategic Position* (Cambridge, Mass.: Institute for Foreign Policy Analysis, 1981), p. 65. "It is a maxim in joint military operations that combat skills must be perfected in times of peace through realistic training exercises. The best place to possess these well-honed skills, and the worst place to seek to acquire them, is in an approach to battle," ibid., p. 66.

32 Paul D. Wolfowitz, "Japan and the U.S.: A Global Partnership," address before the Japan–American Society, Tokyo, September 18, 1985, Bureau of Public Affairs, U.S. Department of State, *Current Policy*, no. 746, p. 3.

33 Langer, "Changing Japanese Security Perspectives," p. 70.

34 Stephen J. Solarz, "U.S.–Japan Strains Are Inevitable, but Reconcilable," *The Washington Star*, May 14, 1981.

35 *The United States and Japan*, pp. 2–3.

36 Richard H. Solomon, "American Defense Planning and Asian Security: Policy Choices for a Time of Transition," chapter 1 in Solomon, ed., *Asian Security in the 1980s*, p. 27.

37 Holdridge, "Japan and the United States," p. 6.

38 Hanks, *The Pacific Far East*, p. 58.

39 Langer, "Changing Japanese Security Perspectives," p. 69.

40 *The U.S.–Japanese Security Relationship in Transition*, p. 18.

41 Ray S. Cline, "U.S. Foreign Policy for Asia," chapter 1 in Myers, ed., *A U.S. Foreign Policy for Asia*, p. 2.

42 In mid-1985 a Japanese scholar wrote in an American journal: "External tensions and mutual suspicions have swollen like a tidal wave on each side of the Pacific Ocean. The two countries need to act with great caution and to avoid saying and doing foolish things that would hurt them both." Kiyohiko Fukushima, "Japan's Real Trade Policy," *Foreign Policy* 59 (Summer 1985): 39.

CHAPTER 5

Security Dimensions of the New
U.S.–China Relationship

The fundamental changes in the relationship of the People's Republic of China with the Soviet Union, dating at least from the late 1950s and early 1960s, and with the United States, dating from the early 1970s, have been two of the most decisive developments since the end of World War II. They have profoundly affected the global balance of power, as well as the strategic and political environment in the Western Pacific. The future course of China in regional and world affairs, and its future relationships with the superpowers, will have an important bearing on "the shape of things to come." Hence a central theme in international relations in the future, as in the recent past, will be the evolution of relations among the members of the "Great Power Triangle," and the impact of these changing relationships upon other countries and upon the whole world situation.

THE NEW RELATIONSHIP: ITS IMPACT ON THE "GREAT POWER TRIANGLE"

The impending change in U.S.–People's Republic of China relations was signaled in dramatic fashion by President Nixon's announcement from Washington in mid-July 1971 of Dr. Kissinger's secret visit to China and the agreement reached during that visit that Nixon would make an official visit to Beijing in the following year. Nixon's visit in February 1972 may not have been "the week that changed the world," as he described it at the end of his stay in China, but it was certainly a major event, with profound implications for the future—not only the future of Sino–American relations, but also the future course of events in East Asia and in the entire world.

Since the Nixon visit of 1972, and the Shanghai Communiqué that was issued at its conclusion, a complex pattern of new relations has evolved between the previously very hostile nations, in political, economic, cultural, and even military fields. The official visits of Premier Zhao Ziyang to the United States in January 1984 and of President Reagan to the People's Republic of China three months later were the climax of a series of high-level official contacts. Thousands of Americans have visited the People's Republic

74

of China as tourists, diplomatic representatives, businesspersons, scholars, and students, and fewer, but still substantial, numbers of Chinese have come to the United States, mostly as students or on official missions. Each country has developed a great interest amounting almost to an obsession in the other.

One wonders, however, how much real understanding and trust have resulted from these growing encounters. Each country has approached its new relationship with the other hesitantly and diffidently, with obvious apprehensions and reservations, as well as expectations. Most aspects of the new relationship have been deliberately limited and controlled, at least from the Chinese side.

Political relations have been influenced as much by fundamental divergencies in outlook and objectives as by common interests in cooperation and security. Nearly seven years elapsed between the Nixon visit and the Shanghai Communiqué and the establishment of formal diplomatic relations on January 1, 1979. Since then relations have been "normalized," but political relations have remained quite limited, correct but cool. As Professor Robert A. Scalapino observed in 1983, "U.S.–China relations currently have a sweet-sour quality, with sourness increasingly coming to the fore."[1]

Economic relations have not developed as extensively as many Americans had anticipated. Relatively few American businesses have learned how to operate effectively within the constraints of a noncapitalist and still relatively closed economic and political system. Some significant trade has developed, but this has fluctuated considerably, subject to the variables of foreign exchange shortages and national policies.

Cultural and other exchanges have been quite extensive within limited circles. Thousands of Chinese have been sent to the United States for advanced study, mainly in scientific and technical fields. Some American scholars have studied, carried on research, or taught in China, but suitable study programs and research opportunities are limited.[2] Cultural and educational exchanges between Americans and Chinese have seldom been really meaningful. And American tourists who have flocked to China, mainly in organized tours, have seen something of the countryside as well as the main cities and historical and cultural sites, but they have had little contact with the Chinese people and few opportunities to gain real insights into Chinese culture and ways of life.

Security relationships have been even more limited. But security concerns—meaning mainly security against the Russians—were uppermost in the minds of both American and Chinese leaders when they agreed to reverse the long period of almost complete isolation and mutual hostility, and they have been a constant feature of the evolving U.S.–China relationship ever since.

Before the split with the Soviet Union the People's Republic of China regarded the United States as its principal external threat. In the 1960s the Soviet Union also became a threat, rather than a socialist ally, and China was faced with the unpleasant situation of perceiving major threats from both superpowers—from the "capitalist imperialism" of the United States and the "social imperialism" and "hegemonism" of the Soviet Union. Since the early 1970s China has perceived only one, instead of two, major external enemies, but the underlying suspicions of the United States remain, just as underlying suspicions of a communist-controlled China remain in American perceptions. One could argue that China is again resorting to the tactics, familiar to all students of Chinese history, of "using barbarians to control barbarians." From this perspective, as Stephen B. Gibert has pointed out, the Chinese leaders may feel that "China must forge a temporary alliance with its secondary enemy in order to deal with its primary enemy."[3] Quite clearly, the new relationship between China and the United States is a fragile one, which could change drastically, for better or for worse, at any time.

The main Chinese security interests are to develop as effective a defense posture as possible against a variety of possible Soviet threats, ranging all the way from direct attack—nuclear, or conventional, or both—to Soviet penetration of noncommunist countries of the Western Pacific, directly or through surrogates, in ways that would be regarded as detrimental to China's security. For this and other reasons China seeks to modernize and otherwise improve its security establishment and defense capabilities. This objective is one of the "four modernizations" to which the present leaders of China are dedicated; but it should be noted that this is usually cited as the last of the four modernizations—the others being in the areas of agriculture, industry, and science and technology—and seems to be regarded as a derivative or consequence of progress in the other three fields (thus suggesting that China, as Japan, seeks "comprehensive national security," the military aspects being only a part, or a result, of the requisite national security effort). China's leaders seem to believe that the United States can be of some help toward containing the Soviet Union in East Asia as elsewhere, but they do not expect from the United States the kind of assistance they will need to improve the defense-planning process and to make the People's Liberation Army, the second largest (but by no means the second best) in the world, into an effective fighting force against the Soviet Union or any other major adversary.

In recent years leaders of the People's Republic have indicated that, contrary to China's past position, they favor the maintenance of American military strength and commitments in the Western Pacific. They have, however, continued to voice criticisms of U.S. military activities in the region and of the United States in general, and they have occasionally reverted to their previous position of demanding a reduction of these activities.[4] Since the Sino–Japanese Treaty of Friendship and Cooperation of 1978, they have ceased to voice strong objections to the U.S.–Japanese Security Treaty and to the buildup of Japan's SDF. They have muted their criticisms of U.S. policies in the Third World, to which they profess to belong, and they have referred less frequently to their doctrine of the "three worlds" (which they seem, in fact, to have abandoned), but they have by no means changed their basic attitudes on such matters.

The Chinese have approved the U.S. efforts to make NATO a more effective alliance and to improve its deterrent capabilities by stationing Pershing-II and cruise missiles in Germany and a few other West European countries. Apparently the Chinese have been motivated by the hope that if the Soviet Union is faced with formidable power and a working alliance on its western front, this will lessen the threat that it poses to the People's Republic of China in the Asian area. They have also joined the United States and most of the other noncommunist nations of the world in condemning the Soviet invasion of Afghanistan and Soviet ties with Vietnam and Kampuchea. In fact, they often state that Soviet withdrawal from Afghanistan and Soviet noninterference in Indochina, along with a major troop and nuclear withdrawal along the borders of China—their main security concern—are prerequisites for any real improvement in Sino–Soviet relations.

The Chinese do not want to become involved in any U.S.–Soviet conflicts. They would probably view with apprehension any significant improvement in Soviet–American relations, as well as any major military confrontation between the superpowers. They fear the latter more than the former, perhaps because it seems to be a more likely possibility. They have, in fact, sometimes expressed the hope that Soviet–American relations would improve, and they have publicly favored efforts by the two superpowers to reach meaningful understandings in the direction of arms limitation and control. But they have also been very critical of the limited and largely unproductive efforts that have thus far been made.

For some time there has been a vigorous debate in the United States regarding whether it would be in its best interests to encourage continued friction between China and the Soviet Union, or whether an improvement in Sino–Soviet relations would be preferable. If continued friction would be preferred, then the further question arises whether the United States can or should do anything to promote this, by playing the "China card" or by other means. If improvement in Sino–Soviet relations is the preferred choice, what can and should the United States do to further this objective? Would the United States prefer to see some relatively modest improvement in the relations between the two communist giants, or a real *rapprochement* between them? The latter development would perhaps have the desirable consequence of removing a major arena of possible regional or even international conflict, but it might also have the undesirable consequence of a return to the former close relations between China and the Soviet Union, which might raise the old bogey or specter of a Communist monolith pursuing aggressive policies on a global scale and seeking world domination through direct and indirect means.

In spite of the present strains in Sino–Soviet relations, the Soviets, at least, are quite convinced that these relations will improve.[5] In fact, there are already many signs pointing in this direction.[6] A great impetus to increasing contacts and improved relations was given by Mikhail Gorbachev's speech in the Soviet port city of Vladivostok on July 28, 1986. In this highly publicized address the Soviet leader announced that the Soviet Union was considering the withdrawal of a substantial part of its forces in Mongolia and six regiments from Afghanistan. He also proposed a five-point plan for regional cooperation, embracing an Asian-Pacific conference on confidence- and security-building measures, a "radical reduction" of conventional forces and steps to block the proliferation of nuclear weapons in the region, talks designed to seek solutions to political conflicts in the region, and talks on the reduction of naval activities in the Pacific Ocean area.[7] This address was given a great deal of attention in China (the *People's Daily*, the Chinese Communist Party newspaper, ran the full text on the following day); but the Chinese reaction was rather cool, indicating that China's leaders were still hesitant about, though interested in, closer relations with the Soviet Union.

The United States must evolve policies regarding both Communist giants that contemplate significant improvement in Sino–Soviet relations, as well as such other possibilities as continued tensions, further deterioration in relations, and some immediate improvement followed in a few years by renewed strains.[8] In any event, as the summary of a conference on "Asian Security in the 1980s," sponsored by the Rand Corporation, stated, "Despite new possibilities suggested by normalized relations with China, the U.S. does not want an 'imbalance' to develop in the U.S.–U.S.S.R–P.R.C. relationship. This is the single most important issue facing the United States today."[9] One could of course argue that such a strange relationship will always be characterized by imbalances. Certainly that was the case when the Soviet Union and China seemed to present a united front against the United States and American "imperialism." It seems to be the case at the present time, when the United States has developed a new and more positive relationship with the People's Republic of China at a time when its relations with the Soviet Union have been deteriorating. It will almost surely be the case in the future, whatever scenario of the triangular relations may be written. The "Great Power Triangle" will doubtless continue to be a strange and shifting *ménage à trois*, with strained relations and mutual distrust among all three members and with continued apprehensions on the part of other nations whose destinies will be inescapably affected by the interrelationships of the major gladiators.

THE UNITED STATES AND CHINA'S DEFENSE MODERNIZATION

A real modernization of the People's Liberation Army[10] and of China's defense capabilities would be a herculean task, and a very expensive one (former U.S. Secretary of Defense Harold Brown has estimated the costs at between $200 and $400 billion), even if other obstacles to effective defense planning and policies could be overcome. Apparently, in spite of listing defense modernization as one of the "four modernizations," the leaders of China are thinking in more modest terms, mainly in improving China's defense capabilities by effective reorganization and by "modest purchases of selected military equipment and technologies with the aim of eventually reproducing them at home."[11]

Until China can meet its needs for defense modernization by a substantial improvement of its own defense production establishment, it will have to look abroad for arms and military equipment, especially for more sophisticated weapons. It is even more interested in technology transfers. As long as the Soviet Union cannot be turned to as a source of arms and technology, China will inevitably turn to a large extent to the other major world arms supplier, the United States. But there is a widespread reluctance in both China and the United States to enter into an arms-and-technology supply relationship, at least on a large scale.

Even though defense modernization was one of the much-publicized "four modernizations" of the post-Mao Chinese leaders, they placed priorities on other "modernizations," especially economic development. China did not have the resources, especially the foreign exchange, for extensive—and expensive—arms purchases abroad. Even more important, the Chinese leaders did not want to become dependent on other countries in any way, least of all for China's military defense. In recent years, as relations with the Soviet Union have shown definite signs of improvement, China's leaders have wanted to avoid unduly provoking the Soviets by arms purchases from the United States.

As long as the United States was associated with the regime on Taiwan in a mutual security arrangement and was supplying arms and military equipment to that regime, the People's Republic of China would not consider the United States as a source of arms and military supplies. When this situation changed, following the establishment of official diplomatic relations between the United States and the People's Republic of China on January 1, 1979, Chinese leaders began to put out feelers to the United States. In 1979, for example, Deng Xiaoping hinted to a visiting delegation from the Foreign Relations Committee of the U.S. Senate that China would be interested in purchasing advanced fighter aircraft if the United States would agree to provide them. "This was the first time that China expressed its willingness to buy U.S. arms."[12]

The United States, in turn, has been reluctant to become a major arms supplier to China or to any other Communist country. It is still suspicious of China's possible internal evolution and external behavior, especially of China's future relations with the Soviet Union. The United States is also deterred by the strong opposition of its allies and other friendly countries in Asia and is apprehensive that China may transfer U.S.-supplied weapons and advanced technology to those with whom the United States has strained or antagonistic relations.

Throughout most of its tenure, the Carter administration was not interested in providing military assistance to the People's Republic of China, an act expected to seriously hamper its efforts to improve relations with the Soviet Union and complete negotiation for the SALT II agreement. But the Soviet invasion of Afghanistan in late December 1979 led to immediate shifts in policy in both the United States and China, and to the initiation of what has proved to be protracted negotiations regarding military assistance to China. Immediately after the Soviets moved into Afghanistan, President Carter authorized sales of "non-lethal" military equipment to China During his visit to China in January 1980, Secretary of Defense Harold Brown informed Chinese leaders that the United States was prepared to sell to China a ground receiving station for data transmitted by a Landsat-D satellite that could also be provided. He indicated that China could use this sophisticated equipment as it wished. During a visit to the United States by Geng Biao, then a Chinese deputy premier, in May 1980, "the Defense Department announced on May 29 that export licences had been approved for tactical air defense radar sets, transport helicopters, pressure transducers used in testing jet engines, truck tractors, and antenna for an early warning radar set, tactical radar equipment, transport aircraft and passive countermeasure devices."[13] The Guardian revealed that items approved for sale in China also included "seismic sensors, ostensibly for oil exploration but also applicable to submarine detection, an infra-red screening system, intended for land surveys but also capable of reconnaissance use in military aircraft, and navigation equipment for the Boeing 707, which is far in advance of anything now possessed by China, and which has obvious applications to other aircraft."[14]

U.S. willingness to supply military equipment to China became more apparent after Reagan came into power. At the conclusion of a visit to China in June 1981, Secretary of State Alexander Haig announced at a press conference that China would no longer be subjected to restrictions imposed in the munitions control list and that the United States would consider sales of "lethal" weapons to China "on a case by case basis."[15] Negotiations on arms supply were facilitated by the U.S. commitment, in the Sino–American joint communiqué of August 17, 1982, to reduce arms sales to Taiwan. By the end of 1982 the United States had issued some 1700 export licenses for possible sales of advanced technology to China.[16] In May 1982 a presidential decision made it possible for China to purchase American technology, including sophisticated weapons and military equipment, on the same basis as the countries of Western Europe and Japan. During his visit to China in September 1982, Secretary of Defense Caspar Weinberger informed the Chinese leaders that China could purchase fifty-four of sixty-five items of military weaponry and dual-use technology that had been itemized in a 1981 Chinese purchase list. During a return visit to the United States by China's minister of national defense, Zhang Aiping, in June 1984, an accord was signed for "the first major arms package with China," including TOW antitank missiles and Black Hawk antiaircraft missiles. Subsequent arrangements have provided for equipment and technical assistance in modernizing a large-caliber artillery plant,[17] and about $500 million worth of advanced avionics to upgrade Chinese-built F-8 jet fighters.[18] This would be the largest U.S. military sale to China.

According to American security specialist Jeffrey Record, the kinds of "comparatively cheap but effective defense technologies" that the United States would be willing to supply to China—and that it would encourage its NATO allies to supply as well—"might include wire-guided anti-armor missiles, short-range surface-to-air missiles, air defense radars, communications equipment, electronic countermeasures, and transport aircraft and helicopters."[19] In other words, the United States is willing to supply a limited amount of defensive military equipment and support facilities, but it is not willing to make a major contribution to China's overall defense needs. In particular, it is unwilling to supply major weapons systems or provide major nuclear support. In the future there will probably be more emphasis on technology transfers, which the Chinese seem to prefer.

In spite of all the negotiations and agreements, very few arms sales have actually been made—or even requested officially and specifically—and only a limited amount of the technology that the Chinese desire for defense modernization has in fact been provided. The reasons for this are political, technical, financial, and psychological. If overall relations continue to improve, some of the contemplated arms sales and technology transfers may soon be made, but they will continue to be highly limited and intermittent. This is probably as far as the two countries can or should go in this delicate area of their mutual relations.

From the United States perspective an improved Chinese military capability can put China in a better position to meet the threat of the more than fifty Soviet divisions along the Chinese borders, but it cannot give China any real offensive capability against the much more powerful Soviet forces. "Western arms transfers to China can strengthen China's ability to resist a Soviet attack, but they cannot endow Beijing [with] the capacity to hold Soviet forces in the Far East hostage to the threat of a Chinese attack against the Soviet Union."[20] Moreover, "In substance, there is little that the P.R.C. could directly contribute to the military security of the West."[21] So long as major units of the Soviet armed forces, however, are concentrated in the Asian theater, along or near the borders of China, the Soviet threat in Western Europe is somewhat lessened,[22] and the Soviet Union is faced with what it regards as the grim prospect of a two-front war, with the fronts widely separated.

Moreover, as Jeffrey Record points out, "China's puny ability to help the West in the event of war with the Soviet Union changes dramatically . . . with respect to regional conflicts involving other challenges to shared Sino-American strategic interests in Asia. [Indochina is an obvious example.] And it is here that the foundation for a more active Sino–American military relationship can and ought to be laid." Record argues that the United States should seek "a closer strategic engagement" with China, "if not directly against the Soviet Union then against other threats to shared vital interests in the region."[23]

In spite of the long-standing expressed willingness of the United States to provide limited technological and military assistance to China to assist that country in its defense modernization, very little assistance of this kind has in fact been provided.[24] Part of the reason is to be found in the continuing doubts of many influential policymakers regarding the desirability of such assistance, and in the logistical and other difficulties in the way. But the main reason is China's hesitation in accepting military assistance from Western capitalist powers, with unknown consequences in terms of its own independence. It also harbors doubts about the reliability of the United States through changing circumstances and in crisis periods.

The People's Republic of China realizes that it cannot achieve its modernization goals without substantial outside help and associations. Its leaders have shown a remarkable capacity and determination to establish trade, investment, and other economic links with international aid and financial institutions, mainly multilateral institutions such as the World Bank, the International Development Association, the International Monetary Fund, and the Asian Development Bank, and with some capitalist countries, including the United States. They have even modified their exclusivist socialist-oriented policies to the extent of adopting a number of free market—or at least freer market—practices. But China still remains a rigidly controlled political and economic system, and its leaders seem to be determined to make the adaptations necessary to advance their modernization goals without in any way altering their basic controls or compromising their sovereignty and independence. Hence their foreign and security policies will continue to be based on a cautious approach to the outside world, and on a strong reassertion of Chinese nationalism and "anti-hegemonism."

Under these conditioning circumstances the prospects of a "closer strategic engagement" with the United States seem to be quite remote. For a time, to be sure, the leaders of the People's Republic of China were warning the United States and the noncommunist world generally that these countries were not sufficiently aware of the nature of the Soviet threat and that they were in danger of losing out in the inevitable confrontation with the Soviet Union. They seemed to favor a "united front" against Soviet "hegemonism." In 1979 Deng Xiaoping even called on the United States and Japan to "further develop their relationship [with China] in a deepening way" and to "unite" in order to "place curbs on the polar bear."[25] But China's enthusiasm for a "united front," if it ever really existed, soon waned, and more recently their reluctance to enter into even more limited political and security associations with the United States or any other countries has become more evident.

A strong argument can be made for some American military assistance to China, if the Chinese leaders request it and if it can be strictly limited and controlled, but the United States should be under no illusions about the extent of the possible or desirable military, as well as political, links with the People's Republic of China. In an article published in late 1984 Professor Parris H. Chang perceptively outlined the limits of the relationship. "[T]heir highly touted strategic partnership," he wrote, "has not been consummated. Because U.S.–China relations were strained in the past few years, both Beijing and Washington have shifted their foreign policy and have deemphasized the strategic aspect of U.S.–China relations." He called attention to "Beijing's doubts about U.S. ability or determination to cope with the Russians." Because of these doubts, China's determination not to be used as a "card" by the United States in the U.S.-Soviet global confrontation, its own fierce independence and nationalist feelings, and many other factors, "Beijing has sought to pursue an independent foreign policy and deemphasized its strategic cooperation with the U.S. Instead, it has reasserted China's identification with the Third World and renewed rhetorical assaults on U.S. hegemony. Meanwhile, Beijing has also taken a less alarmist view of the Soviet threat and has probed the possibility for detente with Moscow, aiming at enjoying greater leverage and flexibility with both superpowers. . . . With a shift in leadership priority, Beijing has no urgency nor strong incentives to forge an alliance with the United States that could provoke extreme Soviet countermeasures."[26]

Neither the United States nor the People's Republic of China desires to develop close or extensive security relations, much less an alliance. Their security relations will remain a limited but important aspect of their evolving but still tentative overall relationship. Neither wishes to develop a relationship that will unduly alienate the Soviet Union or that will interfere with the promotion of their basic objectives in world affairs.

OTHER FORMS OF SECURITY COOPERATION

In recent years the United States and the People's Republic of China have cooperated in intelligence gathering and exchanges; they have discussed limited forms of naval cooperation, especially port calls; they have engaged in sensitive negotiations regarding certain kinds of peaceful nuclear cooperation, which may have security implications; and they have shared information on Soviet military dispositions, actions, and capabilities, especially in Soviet Asia, Vietnam, Kampuchea, Afghanistan, and the Pacific and Indian Oceans. It is difficult to get precise and reliable information about these forms of security cooperation because, for understandable reasons of security and political risk, both countries have refused to provide relevant information or either to confirm or deny the frequent stories regarding such cooperation. Since 1981, when the story was first made public in a National Broadcasting Corporation report in June, speculation has been rife regarding alleged Sino–American collaboration in intelligence-gathering activities along the Sino–Soviet border. According to the NBC report, "two electronic intelligence-gathering stations on the Xinjiang Uygur autonomous region in northwestern China, operating with American equipment and Chinese personnel, were monitoring Soviet missile tests in Central Asia."[27] "Two key Soviet bases for testing intercontinental ballistic missiles and antiballistic missile systems are 300 to 500 miles from the nearest point on the Chinese border. Intelligence collected by the stations has been shared by the United States and China. CIA representatives have periodically visited the stations to advise the Chinese personnel."[28]

When the United States first proposed cooperation in establishing intelligence-gathering stations in China and offered to provide sophisticated equipment and technical advisers, in 1976, China rejected the proposal; but in the following year, after the United States lost its listening posts in northern Iran, Deng Xiaoping let it be known that China would accept U.S. equipment for operating stations, to be manned by Chinese, and would share with the United States information gathered by these stations. This arrangement was incorporated in a formal agreement in 1979.[29] Apparently the stations or listening posts were set up shortly thereafter and have been operating ever since, although there are rumors that they may be shut down as a concession by China to the Soviet Union. When the NBC report appeared, the Soviet Union used it to support its claim that China had played a "disgraceful role" as "voluntary agents of the imperialist intelligence services."[30]

Whether China will continue to cooperate with the United States in intelligence-gathering activities along the Sino–Soviet border will depend on the future evolution of Sino–American and Sino–Soviet relations. In 1986 a Chinese scholar expressed the view that "China and the United States will no doubt secretly continue their cooperation in this area;" but he also pointed out that "[s]ince the issue of sharing and exchanging intelligence is very sensitive, the United States and China will not be expected to openly admit it."[31]

Cooperation between the navies of the United States and China is another interesting example of expanding, if limited, Sino–American security cooperation. Both countries are concerned about the rapid buildup of the Soviet Pacific Fleet, which has transformed it from a coastal to a blue-water navy, with operations both in the coastal waters along the East Asian littoral and in major parts of the Pacific and Indian Oceans, and with Soviet use of the former American naval base at Cam Ranh Bay in Vietnam.

"The most important result of this cooperation between the two navies," according to the Chinese scholar, "is that China has agreed to let US Navy ships call [at] Chinese ports." This arrangement has obvious advantages to both countries. "Since China's Navy is equipped chiefly with a coastal defense force known to lack the air defense, air cover and supply ships to fight a modern war at sea, it cannot effectively resist the challenge of the Soviet Pacific Fleet. The arrangement of port calls by U.S. Navy ships might at least show Moscow that there was some Sino–American naval cooperation, thereby warning the Soviets that they should pay more attention to American responses if it [sic] wants to provoke China. . . . For the United States, the Navy will expand the sphere of its activities and enhance the ability of flexible response if it can use Chinese ports through visiting activities."[32]

During the visit to China of U.S. secretary of the navy John F. Lehman, Jr. in April 1984, "China agreed in principle to let US Navy ships call at ports along the Chinese coast for the first time since the foundation of the People's Republic of China in 1949."[33] But the first port calls were delayed, by mutual agreement, because of the conflict between China's policy of nonadmission of nuclear-armed warships to its ports and the U.S. policy of refusing to disclose whether its warships are carrying nuclear weapons. This was also the issue that led to the recent estrangement between the United States and New Zealand and the virtual abrogation of the ANZUS alliance.

A way out of this impasse with both China and New Zealand may have been suggested by the agreement between China and Great Britain for a port call by a British warship in July 1986. The British have the same neither-confirm-nor-deny policy regarding nuclear weapons on their warships as the United States, but the port call was nevertheless permitted. "Under the agreement for this visit . . . the two parties took note of each other's policies but China avoided insisting on a specific assurance. This opened the way for a U.S. Navy call, a senior Chinese official hinted, if the US was still interested in the subject."[34] The United States was interested, and in November 1986, three U.S. Navy ships—a cruiser, a destroyer, and a frigate—put in at the port of Qingdao for the first visit of American warships since the Chinese Communists came to power in 1949.

China and the United States have been considering limited cooperation in the nuclear field. This cooperation would be limited to "peaceful uses," but in many respects it would inevitably have some possible security implications. In 1984 the two countries entered into a "peaceful" nuclear cooperation agreement, "the first agreement" that the United States had made "with a nuclear-weapon state since the Nuclear Non-Proliferation Act" of 1978.[35] Strong objections to this agreement immediately developed, in the United States, Taiwan, the Soviet Union, and elsewhere (perhaps even in China). Critics in the U.S. Congress expressed concern over the impact of this agreement on relations with the Soviet Union and other countries, over the refusal of China to adhere to the Nuclear Non-Proliferation Treaty of 1968 or to accept International Atomic Energy safeguards on nuclear facilities, and over the alleged assistance that China had been providing to Pakistan in developing a nuclear-weapon capability, as well as nuclear energy for peaceful purposes,[36] which indicates that China might make nuclear know-how and facilities available to other countries as well.

These are all very sensitive issues. Chinese leaders gave verbal assurances that they were opposed to nuclear proliferation. In January 1984 China joined the International Atomic Energy Agency (IAEA). In the same month, during an official visit to the United States, Premier Zhao Ziyang stated: "China does not advocate nor encourage proliferation. We do not engage in proliferation ourselves, nor do we help other countries develop nuclear weapons." The Chinese Government "has stated that it requires the application of IAEA safeguards to nuclear exports to non-nuclear-weapon states."[37] These assurances did not satisfy most critics. President Reagan did not sign the agreement and send it to the Congress for review until the fall of 1985. Two implementing Acts—the Sino–American Cooperation Act of 1985 and the Sino–American Nuclear Verification Act of 1985—have been the subject of extensive congressional hearings.[38] China may become "a dream market for Western arms makers," as *Business Week* headlined in February 1986, but U.S. nuclear cooperation with China may create more complications than improvements in Sino-American relations and may have more adverse than favorable security consequences.

Elsewhere in Asia, where their policies have to some degree been running along parallel lines, the United States and China have been consulting with each other and exchanging information. This is particularly the case with regard to Vietnam and Afghanistan. Both the United States and China are concerned about the growing Soviet presence and influence in Indochina, the Soviet military and political support of Vietnam, Vietnam's occupation and virtual control of Kampuchea, and the use by the Soviet Navy and Air Force of facilities in Danang and Cam Ranh Bay. The two countries have exchanged views, but they have not made plans for concerted action to counteract Vietnam and the Soviet activities in Indochina, and to deter any Vietnamese military moves, with posible Soviet backing, beyond Indochina.

The position of the United States regarding the Chinese military move into Vietnam in February 1979, shortly after Deng Xiaoping's visit to the United States, is still unclear. Apparently Deng informed President Carter and other top American leaders that China was likely to make such a move, to "teach Vietnam a lesson." Whereas it was reported that the American leaders warned Deng against the danger of Soviet involvement or a Soviet ultimatum to China to withdraw from Vietnam, it seems that they did not object strongly to Deng's contemplated move against Vietnam. When the action occurred, the Carter administration did not express disapproval, at least not publicly. Instead it expressed the hope that the Sino–Vietnamese conflict would be brought to a speedy end and that Chinese forces would promptly withdraw. However, "[a]s China hoped, the United States warned the Soviet Union to restrain from intervention while bringing a number of its ships to the South coast of Vietnam."[39]

The United States and China have also attempted to work out cooperative programs of support for Cambodian resistance forces, and to a lesser degree for refugees from Kampuchea, as well as Vietnam and Laos. "When the Pol Pot regime was nearing collapse in November 1978, Peking emissaries held secret talks in Washington with American representatives to arrange cooperation between Pol Pot's forces and the Khmers Grises created with CIA funds. . . . After the Vietnamese invasion of Kampuchea, the United States adopted the same policy as the Chinese in support of establishing a united resistance front in Kampuchea."[40]

In Afghanistan the United States and China have common interests in opposing the Soviet military occupation, in seeking the withdrawal of the Soviet forces, and in countering any Soviet moves beyond Afghanistan into Pakistan or toward the Persian Gulf or the Indian Ocean. Because of the Soviet presence in Afghanistan, both the United States and China have stepped up their assistance—military, economic, and political—to Pakistan. Both have provided clandestine military assistance to Afghan groups resisting the Soviet occupation, and relief and military training to Afghan refugees in Pakistan.

Because much of the Sino–American cooperation regarding Afghanistan is carried on secretly, the actual nature and extent of this cooperation cannot be accurately determined. There are indications that it has been extensive, although far short of the needs of the Afghan resistance forces and refugees. On the whole the policies of the two countries toward the Soviets in Afghanistan have run along parallel but not integrated lines. Chinese scholar Xu Zhiping believes that the cooperation has indeed been quite extensive. "Pakistan," he writes, "has been used as the main staging ground to train Afghan resistance forces by American and Chinese advisers. There was a rational division of labor between China and the United States to arm Afghan rebels. China provided the Afghans with antiaircraft and antitank weapons and small arms delivered regularly by a ship to Pakistan while the United States sent mortars, jeeps, tanks, and ground-to-air missiles to the rebels through Pakistan."[41]

An important but seldom mentioned example of Sino–American security cooperation in Asia is the growing pattern of consultation regarding the common goal of encouraging the governments of North and South Korea to step up negotiations in an effort to reduce the tensions between them, to promote thereby the immediate goal of preventing the Korean Peninsula from becoming a cockpit of civil war, with dangerous spillover possibilities, and the ultimate goal of a mutually acceptable basis of agreement on the peaceful reunification of the Peninsula. China has close associations with North Korea, the United States with South Korea. China is beginning to establish a number of contacts with South Korea and also seems to be willing to act as a mediator between the United States and North Korea. During his visit to the United States in January 1984, Chinese Premier Zhao Ziyang brought a North Korean proposal for tripartite talks with the United States and South Korea. When President Reagan visited China the following April, he asked

Deng Xiaoping to relay to North Korea a counterproposal for quadripartite talks, with China as the fourth party. While no agreement has been reached for either kind of talks, it seems likely that the United States and China can play a useful cooperative role with regard to the two Koreas. This is a possibility that should be further—and discreetly—explored.

A larger area of possible Sino–American cooperation with major security implications concerns the promotion of mutual interests in Third World countries in Asia, Africa, and elsewhere. In his memoirs former President Jimmy Carter speculated in a suggestive way regarding the value of such cooperation from the point of view of the United States: "One of the more interesting potential benefits of having China as a friend would be its ability to quietly sway some Third World countries with whom it was very difficult for us to communicate. . . . China's credentials among some of the developing nations were excellent. We saw our cooperation with China as a means to promote peace and better understanding between the United States and those countries."[42]

THE TAIWAN ISSUE

Aside from basic political, social, and cultural differences, the United States and China take very different positions on a large number of specific issues. The foremost of these issues, at least in Chinese eyes, is that of Taiwan.[43] It has been a major stumbling block in the path of really satisfactory Sino–American relations, but it has not been the insuperable barrier that the Chinese have sometimes declared it to be.

During the protracted normalization negotiations of the 1970s an interesting formula was devised and agreed upon whereby the Taiwan issue was, in effect, set aside, with each country reiterating its long-standing views and agreeing to disagree with the other, but also agreeing not to let the issue stand in the way of a larger consideration, namely a wholly new Sino–American relationship. In the Shanghai Communiqué, issued at the end of Nixon's visit to China on February 1972, a novel device was employed to present the views of each side on issues on which they continued to disagree. The position of each country on Taiwan was clearly stated in two concise paragraphs in the communiqué:

> The Chinese side reaffirmed its position: the Taiwan question is the crucial question obstructing the normalization of relations between China and the United States; the Government of the People's Republic of China is the sole legal government of China; Taiwan is a province of China which has long been returned to the motherland; the liberation of Taiwan is China's internal affair in which no other country has the right to interfere; and all U.S. forces and military installations must be withdrawn from Taiwan. The Chinese Government firmly opposes any activities which aim at the creation of 'one China, one Taiwan,' 'one China, two governments,' 'two Chinas,' an 'independent Taiwan' or advocate that 'the status of Taiwan remains to be determined.' . . .
>
> The U.S. side declared: the United States acknowledges that all Chinese on either side of the Taiwan Strait maintain that there is but one China and that Taiwan is a part of China. The

United States Government does not challenge that position. It reaffirms its interest in a peaceful settlement of the Taiwan question by the Chinese themselves. With this prospect in mind, it affirms the ultimate objective of the withdrawal of all U.S. forces and military installations from Taiwan. In the meantime, it will progressively reduce its forces and military installations on Taiwan as the tension in the area diminishes.[44]

The brief Joint Communiqué on the Establishment of Diplomatic Relations between the United States of America and the People's Republic of China, issued simultaneously in Washington and Beijing on December 15, 1978, nearly seven years after the Shanghai Communiqué, reiterated what to China were basic points, namely that the United States "acknowledges the Chinese position that there is but one China and Taiwan is part of China," and "recognizes the Government of the People's Republic of China as the sole legal Government of China;" but it also contained the statement that "Within this context the people of the United States will maintain cultural, commercial and other unofficial relations with the people of Taiwan."[45]

On January 1, 1979, the United States and the People's Republic of China established formal diplomatic relations. At the same time the United States severed its official relations with the Republic of China on Taiwan and officially abrogated the 1954 Mutual Defense Treaty with Taiwan. Within a few months it withdrew virtually all of the U.S. military contingent that had been stationed in Taiwan. But, as the Joint Communiqué of December 15, 1978, foretold, it continued to "maintain cultural, commercial, and other unofficial relations with the people of Taiwan." In fact, it continued to maintain a variety of "unofficial official" relations, through the American Institute on Taiwan, provided for in the Taiwan Relations Act of April 1979 and largely staffed by U.S. diplomatic personnel who were technically separated from Government service during the period of their service with the Institute, which replaced the U.S. Embassy in Taipei, and through the Coordination Council for North American Affairs, which replaced the former Embassy of the Republic of China in Washington, D.C.

The change in the relations between the United States and the People's Republic of China was generally welcomed in both countries, and in the world community (with some obvious exceptions); but there were influential groups in both the United States and China who were, for different reasons, dissatisfied with the concessions that their government had made regarding Taiwan. In the U.S. Congress and in influential circles in the American public there was much support for the view that Taiwan had been sacrificed for dubious gains in the new relationship with the People's Republic of China. This feeling was a strong factor in the enactment by Congress, only two months after formal diplomatic relations between the United States and the People's Republic of China had been established, of the Taiwan Relations Act, which laid down the guidelines for continuing "unofficial" relations and contacts between the United States and Taiwan. The Act declared that

It is the policy of the United States—
   (1) to preserve and promote extensive, close, and friendly commercial, cultural, and other

relations between the people of the United States and the people on Taiwan, as well as the people on the Chinese mainland and all other peoples of the Western Pacific area;

(2) to declare that peace and stability in the area are in the political, security, and economic interests of the United States, and are matters of international concern;

(3) to make clear that the United States decision to establish diplomatic relations with the People's Republic of China rests upon the expectation that the future of Taiwan will be determined by peaceful means;

(4) to consider any effort to determine the future of Taiwan by other than peaceful means, including by boycotts or embargoes, a threat to the peace and security of the Western Pacific area and of grave concern to the United States;

(5) to provide Taiwan with arms of a defensive character; and

(6) to maintain the capacity of the United States to resist any resort to force or other forms of coercion that would jeopardize the security, or the social or economic system, of the people on Taiwan.[46]

Leaders of the People's Republic of China strongly objected to the Taiwan Relations Act, which they insisted was a violation of U.S. pledges in the Shanghai Communiqué. They particularly resented the last four planks in the policy statement quoted above, which they regarded as insulting and an unwarranted interference in China's internal affairs. In 1985 a senior Chinese scholar called the Act "the stumbling block for Sino–American relations" and asserted that "[a]ll frictions and crises in Sino–American relations stem from this act."[47]

Shortly before his historic visit to the United States in January 1979, following the establishment of diplomatic relations between the United States and the People's Republic of China, Vice Premier Deng Xiaoping stated that the People's Republic of China was willing to allow Taiwan to have a considerable degree of autonomy—pehaps even including its own armed forces—after reunification with the People's Republic of China.[48] He and other P.R.C. spokespersons have frequently stated that they want to resolve the Taiwan issue peacefully, but they have also adhered to their "right" to use force, if necessary, to resolve the issue in their favor. They have continually reasserted their basic position that the issue is an internal matter to be dealt with by the Chinese themselves, within the framework of "one government for one China," and that no outside interference will be permitted.

The P.R.C. leaders did not welcome the election of Ronald Reagan as president of the United States in 1980. During the presidential campaign Reagan frequently criticized the concessions that the Carter administration had made regarding Taiwan in order to establish official relations with the People's Republic of China. Occasionally he even charged his opponent with "betraying" the Republic of China on Taiwan. He indicated that if elected he would consider the restoration of official relations with the Taiwan regime, and would favor the continued supply of "defensive weaponry" to Taiwan. P.R.C. spokespersons alleged that Reagan intended to "turn back the clock" on the normalization process and to undo all the long and careful negotiations that had led to the new U.S.–China relationship.

Many observers in China as well as in the United States concluded that improved Sino-American relations would be impossible if Reagan was elected president. This did not prove to be the case. Again pragmatism triumphed over ideology. After his election Reagan continued to endorse the Taiwan Relations Act and to promise not to desert America's friends on Taiwan, while at the same time indicating an interest in promoting relations with China. In August 1981 he suggested a broader pattern of contacts with Taiwan, including "meetings between U.S. and Taiwanese representatives in official offices . . ., permission for Taiwan to open more quasi-official branches in this country, and resumption of training of Taiwanese military officers in the United States."[49] Most of these suggestions, however, have not been implemented.

While continuing to express "the abiding interest" of the United States in "the peaceful resolution of the Taiwan question," Reagan also repeatedly expressed his desire to develop the new relationship with China He recognized, as he stated in letters to top Chinese leaders, letters which Vice-President George Bush personally delivered during a visit to Beijing in April 1982, that "there is only one China." In these letters Reagan also wrote: "We will not permit the unofficial relations between the American people and the people of Taiwan to weaken our commitment to this principle."[50] This position was reaffirmed and given more formal recognition in a landmark joint communiqué of the United States and the People's Republic of China issued on August 17, 1982. The communiqué contained the following declaration: "The United States Government attaches great importance to its relations with China, and reiterates that it has no intention of infringing on Chinese sovereignty and territorial integrity, or in interfering in China's internal affairs or pursuing a policy of 'two Chinas,' or 'one China, one Taiwan.'"[51]

Spokespersons of the People's Republic of China were particularly critical of the continuing sales of weapons and military equipment to Taiwan, and they demanded a speedy end to these sales. This the United States was unwilling to promise in the near future, but in the joint communiqué of August 1982, centering on the Taiwan issue, it did pledge to reduce and eventually to cease these sales. The communiqué contained the following statement: "[T]he United States Government states that it does not seek to carry out a long-term policy of arms sales to Taiwan, that its arms sales to Taiwan will not exceed, either in qualitative or quantitative terms, the level of those supplied in recent years since the establishment of diplomatic relations between the United States and China, and that it intends to reduce gradually its sales of arms to Taiwan, leading over a period of time to a final resolution. In so stating, the United States acknowledges China's consistent position regarding the thorough settlement of this issue."[52]

The Taiwan issue has been kept generally on the back burner of U.S.–Chinese relations ever since the opening to China in the 1970s and the interesting formula embodied in the Shanghai Communiqué of February 1972. But, as Richard H. Solomon has warned, "it remains a potentially

explosive issue for both China and the United States." A number of developments relating to Taiwan could jeopardize the fragile U.S.–China relationship. Solomon notes some of these:

> Future American arms sales to the island [of Taiwan] could generate a strong political
> reaction in Peking, especially if unbalanced by U.S. efforts to help China strengthen its
> defenses. And Peking's abandonment of current policies of moderation and restraint toward
> Taiwan could elicit a strong political reaction from the United States, especially from a Reagan
> administration concerned with upholding the credibility of America's support for allies and
> friends. Moreover, political instability on the island, precipitated by a succession struggle to
> the current leadership of Premier Chiang Ching-kuo, or a strong movement for Taiwanese
> independence, could force policy changes in Peking and Washington which would seriously
> strain the U.S.–PRC relationship.[53]

Thus, as Solomon emphasizes, "As the potentially destructive element in the
complex equation of U.S.–PRC relations, the Taiwan issue in the 1980s will
require the most delicate and restrained handling by leaders in Peking and
Washington. What is needed is a sense on both sides of the relative importance of the island in the larger strategic context created by normal U.S.–PRC
relations if the Taiwan issue is not to destroy the foundations of a constructive U.S.–PRC tie built with the diplomacy of the 1970s."[54]

The United States is assisting, in a relatively modest way, in the defense and
security of both Taiwan and the People's Republic of China. This creates
obvious complications in relations with both regimes, especially since
Taiwan wishes to strengthen its defenses against the only major threat that it
perceives, namely from the Communist regime on the Chinese mainland.

By mutual, if tacit, consent, continuing disagreement over the Taiwan issue
has not been allowed to stand in the way of the historic reversal in U.S.–China
relations; but it could become a major stumbling block at any time, and it will
certainly continue to be a major complicating factor in the still-limited and
fragile relations between the United States and the People's Republic.

HOW OTHER WESTERN PACIFIC NATIONS VIEW
THE NEW U.S.–CHINA RELATIONSHIP

Military assistance to the People's Republic of China is clearly designed as
a part of a larger effort to encourage China to liberalize its polity and its
economy, to help it to achieve its "four modernizations," in cooperation with
the United States and other noncommunist countries, and to assist it in
developing a better defensive posture and capability against the Soviet threat.
There is of course always the possibility that such assistance will be used in
ways that are detrimental to freedom and for aggressive rather than defensive
purposes.

The point has already been made that many—probably most—of the other
nations of the Western Pacific, including America's allies, view the prospect
of a militarily strengthened China with considerable apprehension. Hence
they have reservations about any outside assistance in building up China's

military strength, including military assistance from the United States.

The Soviet Union, of course, tries to capitalize on the anti-Chinese feeling—and to some extent the anti-American feeling as well—in the countries of the Western Pacific in order to extend its own influence in the region and to counteract the much greater Chinese and American influence there. It views the Sino-American *rapprochement* with alarm. It intimates that this *rapprochement* will develop, or may have already developed, into an anti-Soviet alliance, or at least a quasi-alliance. It sometimes adds Japan to this scenario. Japan, after all, established diplomatic relations with the People's Republic of China well before the United States did (in 1972), and in 1978 it concluded a comprehensive Treaty of Friendship and Cooperation with the People's Republic of China. It has much more extensive trade and other contacts with China than does the United States. To the Soviet Union the new ties of the United States and Japan with China conjure up the specter of a tripartite U.S.–Japan–China alliance, directed mainly at the Soviet Union. For the Soviets this is perhaps the most worrisome specter of all.

As Strobe Talbott has pointed out, "The strategic implications of the Sino-American relationship apply to other countries besides the USSR. America's allies in Japan and Western Europe, along with the neutral nations of the Third World, have mixed feelings about the motivations and consequences of cooperation between Washington and Peking." With respect to the mixed feelings in Japan, Talbott wrote: "Officials of the Foreign Ministry and Defense Agency in Tokyo were quietly supportive of security cooperation between the U.S. and the P.R.C., although always with the caveat that the U.S. neither sell China offensive arms nor rush to upgrade the current level of its security cooperation."[55] Clearly the Japanese would not like to see the limited U.S.–China rapprochement develop into anything approaching a security alliance. An official of Japan's Foreign Ministry expressed this view quite frankly: "We go along with the current U.S. policy of defining China as a friend and not as an ally. Frankly, if the time came when the power equation were so fragile as to require the U.S. to define China as an ally, that would raise very serious questions in our minds."[56]

In Southeast Asia, where suspicions of China are deeply ingrained and are based on long and unhappy experience, the new relationship between the United States and China is also viewed with mixed feelings. Southeast Asians are well aware of the importance of what Lucian W. Pye, a well-known Asia specialist at the Massachusetts Institute of Technology, has described as "the China factor in Southeast Asia," which they fear may become too dominant and too threatening. They are less fearful but perhaps even more uncertain about the impact of "the American factor," which they suspect may be mercurial and unreliable. The feelings of leaders of the ASEAN countries were well summarized by Pye:

> They welcomed, as did the Japanese, any move that reduced tensions in East Asia, but they were deeply concerned that Washington's focus was almost entirely upon the "triangular"

diplomacy involving Moscow–Peking–Washington and the issue of Taiwan. Washington seemed blind to the issues between Peking and Hanoi and to the prospect that the P.R.C. might use its new relationship with the United States not to challenge the Soviet Union but to expand its influence in Southeast Asia, a region the United States seemed all too anxious to forget.[57]

THE FUTURE OF THE RELATIONSHIP: SECURITY IMPLICATIONS

Experience in recent years has indicated that, despite the high hopes of many Americans, the new relationship with China will continue to be a rather limited one, with numerous ups and downs. It is imperative that the United States handle this relationship with special care, seeking such ties as may be accepted by both countries as mutually beneficial, with a high degree of flexibility and with constant reexamination. Such a cautious approach is particularly called for with respect to security ties, which almost certainly will—and should—remain quite modest and limited. It would be a mistake for the United States to press for really extensive security relationships. Any efforts to do so might boomerang.

Just as the United States does not wish to become too closely involved in the Sino–Soviet dispute, it should recognize that China does not wish to become too closely involved in regional or global Soviet–American conflicts. As Henry Kissinger has warned, "any attempt to manipulate Peking might drive China into detaching itself from us, perhaps to reexamining its options with the Soviet Union, to gain control of its own destiny. Equally, any move by us to play the China card might tempt the Soviets to end their nightmare of hostile powers on two fronts by striking out in one direction before it was too late, probably against China."[58] Either eventuality would create far more security problems for the United States than the present pattern of interactions among the members of the "Great Power Triangle."

There are many signs that Sino–American relations, after progressing from flirtation to normalization in less than a decade, are not developing, and are not likely to develop, into the mature partnership that many informed observers foresaw in the 1980s. Both countries are now showing a more realistic appreciation of both the limitations and the possibilities of the new relationship. James C. Hsiung has observed that despite "the Reagan record of accommodation to Peking ... the Chinese have shown no sign of abandoning their present course of an 'independent' foreign policy, which amounts to putting their relations with the United States on hold while cultivating a more amicable working relationship with the Soviet Union."[59] Even if it so desires, however, the People's Republic of China can hardly put its relations with the United States on hold. These relations are already showing and will doubtless continue to show more movement than the words *on hold* suggest. But China does seem to be seeking a limited and more balanced relationship with both the United States and the Soviet Union, which would involve less momentum in the former relationship and more in the latter. This is a trend that may well be in the best interests of all three members of the "Great Power Triangle."

Strategic aspects of the Sino-American relationship are important and should not be ignored. A Pentagon official stated in early 1982, "Both sides recognize the strategic underpinning of this relationship."[60] Interest in this dimension of the relationship will doubtless remain high in both countries, but it is doubtful that this will lead to a closer strategic engagement with the United States, as some American security analysts have predicted.

The existence of a common major adversary was undoubtedly a major factor in leading the two countries to modify the unmitigated hostility and the absence of any direct official relations that had prevailed ever since the Central People's Government of the People's Republic of China was proclaimed on October 1, 1949, and this same factor has clearly been a main basis for the fairly impressive contacts and relationships that have developed since the early 1970s. But Sino–American relations should not be compressed into an exclusively anti-Soviet mold; nor should security aspects of that relationship predominate, unless security is interpreted in a very comprehensive way. There is wisdom in the observation of an American scholar of Chinese origin, in late 1984: "To underscore a new approach toward China, Washington should no longer treat China as the enemy of our enemy. Instead, China should be viewed as a developing country striving to improve the livelihood of its one billion people."[61]

Viewing U.S. relations with China from an anti-Soviet perspective is not only a "negative or reactive approach," as Solomon has characterized it.[62] It is, to be sure, an important aspect of the developing relations between the United States and the People's Republic of China, and a major ingredient in the cement of common interests between the two countries. But unless it is supplemented, and to some extent sublimated, by other and broader approaches, it could be a flimsy and inadequate basis for the emerging new relationship. Moreover, it could also prove to be not only ill-advised, but actually detrimental to U.S. national interests, especially if it alienates other countries—and not just the Soviet Union—and if it proves to be a major stumbling block in the path of efforts to improve U.S.-Soviet relations. And there is always the possibility that China will reverse its present course of open hostility toward the Soviet Union and of limited *rapprochement* with the United States. There are already some signs of movement in this direction. The United States should be prepared to deal with changes for the worse, as well as for the better, in the constantly evolving relations among members of the "Great Power Triangle."

Security aspects are obviously important, but delicate, elements of the new U.S.-China relationship; but they must be considered within a broader framework, including a broader approach to the whole concept of security and other dimensions of the relationship. These include both bilateral and multilateral dimensions. In an analysis of "The Dynamics of the Sino–

American Relationship" Michael Oksenberg, a China specialist at the University of Michigan who was a member of the staff of the National Security Council from 1977 to 1980, has written: "[I]f the relationship is to acquire durability, it must eventually be rooted in more extensive bilateral ties supported by bureaucratic involvement on both sides." He suggested that "[f]ostering a broad range of economic, cultural, and scientific initiatives seems the best way to bring this about." Moreover, he emphasized, multilateral dimensions of the relationship must constantly be borne in mind. "More importantly," he pointed out, "with a thin bilateral relationship the most important interactions between China and the United States tend to take place in third areas where the tangible interests of both sides are engaged: especially Korea, Taiwan, Indochina, and also Japan, Southeast Asia, and South Asia. From this perspective, the real dynamics of the relationship—what has driven the two apart or pulled them together—are to be found less in the bilateral relationship than in the way that China and the United States have interacted in other localities." It is particularly important to remember, Oksenberg reminds us, that "the status of Soviet–American and Japanese relations has had a decisive impact on the Sino–American relationship. Management of all three relationships must be integrated."[63]

All of these relationships are of special significance from the point of view of U.S. national security and foreign policy. The Sino–American relationship, although of increasing importance, probably still has a lower priority of interest and concern than the Soviet–American and Japanese–American relationships. In any event, Sino–U.S. relations must be considered within a multilateral as well as a bilateral framework. They embrace the interactions of both countries with each other, with the Soviet Union, and with other countries in East Asia and the Western Pacific, in Third World countries, and in the international system generally.[64]

Notes

[1] Robert A. Scalapino, "The Uncertain Future: Asian-Pacific Relations in Trouble," chapter 1 in Charles E. Morrison, ed., *Threats to Security in East Asia–Pacific: National and Regional Perspectives* (Lexington, Mass: Lexington Books, 1983), p. 14.

[2] In 1985 two American political scientists, who "were the first [W]estern political scientists in residence and teaching on a regular basis in mainland Chinese universities in over thirty years," reported that "political science in China is a flower with fragile roots indeed. . . . Whatever scholarship does exist is not open, at least not to foreigners and to a great extent not even to the Chinese." Kent Morrison and Robert Thompson, "Teaching Political Science in China," *News for Teachers of Political Science* (a publication of the American Political Science Association), no. 45 (Spring 1985): 2.

[3] Stephen B. Gibert, "Northeast Asia in American Security Policy," chapter 3 in William T. Tow and William R. Feeney, eds., *U.S. Foreign Policy and Asian-Pacific Security: A Transregional Approach* (Boulder, Colorado: Westview Press, 1982), p. 74.

[4] In a two-week period in June 1985, for example, Chinese spokespersons charged that the Reagan administration was acting like the "world's overlord," and called for the withdrawal of all American forces from South Korea. Dwight Schear, "Conflicting Views on U.S., China," *The Seattle Times*, June 30, 1985.

[5] For a summary of the views of Soviet scholars on this point, as expressed at a symposium of

Soviet and American scholars in Pushtchino, U.S.S.R., in May 1980, see Norman D. Palmer, "Soviet Perspectives on Peace and Security in Asia," *Asian Affairs* 9 (September–October 1981): 8–9.

6 See Alan S. Whiting, "Sino–Soviet Relations: What Next?," *The Annals of the American Academy of Political and Social Science* 476 (November 1984); James C. Hsiung, "Soviet–Chinese Détente," *Current History* 84 (October 1985); and Steven I. Levine, "The End of Sino–Soviet Estrangement," *Current History* 85 (September 1986).

7 The text of this address, in English, was published by Novosti Press Agency Publishing House in Moscow in 1986.

8 See James C. Hsiung, "Reagan's China Policy and the Sino–Soviet Détente," *Asian Affairs* 11 (Summer 1984). In an article published in January 1986 Henry Kissinger envisioned the third possibility: "[T]he ultimate crisis in Sino–Soviet relations will not occur in the immediate future—when in fact an improvement in relations is probable—but at the point where Chinese growth has become irreversible and the Soviet Union must abandon its present hope that the Chinese experiment will collapse. At that point the Soviet Union will consider whether to try to interrupt this process by force. Such a decision is by no means inevitable. But the danger cannot be exorcised by ignoring it." "The New China," *The Seattle Times*, January 26, 1985.

9 Richard G. Solomon, ed., *Asian Security in the 1980s: Problems and Policies for a Time of Transition* (Cambridge, Mass.: Oelgeschlager, Gunn & Hain, 1979), p. 301.

10 The PLA "embraces all communist Chinese arms and services, including strategic nuclear, naval, and air defense components." A. James Gregor, "The Military Potential of the People's Republic of China and Western Security Interests," *Asian Affairs* 11 (Spring 1984): 2. For a detailed analysis of PLA's composition and capabilities, see ibid., pp. 1–24.

11 Jeffrey Record, *Revising U.S. Military Strategy: Tailoring Means to Ends* (Washington, D.C.: Pergamon-Brassey's International Defense Publishers, 1984), p. 76.

12 Zhiping Xu, "Sino–American Security Cooperation," unpublished paper prepared for the annual meeting of the International Studies Association/West (Vancouver, B.C.: October 4, 1986): p. 6.

13 *Keesings Contemporary Archives 1980*, p. 31620.

14 Ibid.

15 Don Oberdorfer, et al., "U.S. Reaches Accord with China on Arms Sales," *The Washington Post*, June 17, 1981.

16 Paul Wolfowitz, "Developing an Enduring Relationship with China," *Department of State Bulletin* (April 1983), p. 64.

17 Richard Halloran, "Weinberger Arrives in China and Gets a Mixed Welcome," *The New York Times*, September 26, 1983.

18 Robert S. Greenberger, "U.S. Arms Sales to China Stirs Questions . . .," *The Wall Street Journal*, May 5, 1986.

19 Record, *Revising U.S. Military Strategy*, p. 76.

20 Ibid., p. 77.

21 Gregor, "The Military Potential of the People's Republic of China and Western Security Interests," p. 20.

22 See Whiting, "Sino–Soviet Relations," pp. 151–152.

23 Record, *Revising U.S. Military Strategy*, pp. 77–78.

24 U.S. military assistance to China, in a direct sense, has been virtually non-existent. In 1986 the Reagan administration asked Congress to approve a decision, which it made only after a year or more of deliberations, to sell to China about $500 million worth of radar and navigation equipment for China's Air Force. If approved, this would be only "the second since the U.S. established diplomatic relations with Peking in 1979. The first was a relatively minor $98 million sale of equipment and a design for China to build a factory" for military and other purposes. The Reagan administration also asked approval of its NATO allies and Japan for this proposed sale. Japan immediately expressed concern and reservations. "U.S. to Sell Fighter Equipment to China" (AP dispatch, Washington, D.C.), *The Seattle Times*, January 25, 1986. See also John Bryan Starr, "Sino–American Relations: Policies in Tandem," *Current History* 85 (September 1986): 278.

25 Deng Xiaoping, interview with *Time*, January 1979; quoted in Parris H. Chang, "U.S.–China Relations: From Hostility to Euphoria to Realism," *The Annals of the American Academy of*

98 Westward Watch

Political and Social Science 476 (November 1984): 163.
26 Ibid., pp. 163–164.
27 *Keesings Contemporary Archives 1982*, p. 31621.
28 Xu, "Sino–American Security Cooperation," pp. 12–13. See also Philip Taubman, "U.S. and Peking Jointly Monitor Russian Missiles," *The New York Times*, June 18, 1981.
29 *Keesings Contemporary Archives 1982*, p. 31631.
30 Robert C. Toth, "U.S., China Jointly Track Firings of Soviet Missiles," *The Los Angeles Times*, June 19, 1981.
31 Xu, "Sino–American Security Cooperation," p. 15.
32 Ibid., pp. 15–16.
33 Ibid., p. 17. See also Michael Weisskopf, "China Said Willing to Open Port to U.S. Navy," *The Washington Post*, August 21, 1984.
34 Xu, "Sino–American Security Cooperation," p. 18.
35 Kenneth L. Adelman, Director of the Arms Control and Disarmament Agency (ACDA), statement before the Committee on Foreign Affairs, U.S. House of Representatives, July 31, 1985; "U.S.–China Nuclear Cooperation Agreement," Bureau of Public Affairs, U.S. Department of State, *Current Policy*, no. 729, p. 1.
36 Dwight Schear, "A Shadow over U.S.–China Ties," *The Seattle Times*, September 2, 1984.
37 Richard T. Kennedy, ambassador at large and special adviser to the secretary of state on non-proliferation policy and nuclear energy affairs, statement before the Committee on Foreign Affairs, U.S. House of Representatives, July 31, 1985; "U.S.–China Nuclear Cooperation Agreement," Bureau of Public Affairs, U.S. Department of State, *Current Policy*, no. 729, p. 4.
38 See, for example, U.S. Senate, Committee on Foreign Relations, *Hearings to Consider Proposed Agreement between the U.S. and China Concerning Peaceful Uses of Nuclear Energy*, October 9, 1985 (Washington, D.C.: U.S. Government Printing Office, 1986).
39 Xu, "Sino–American Security Cooperation," p. 20. See also Zbigniew Brzezinski, *Power and Principle: Memoirs of the National Security Adviser 1977–1981* (New York: Farrar, Straus, Giroux, 1983), pp. 410–412; and Sailen Chaudhuri, *Beijing–Washington–Islamabad Entente* (New Delhi: Sterling Publishers, 1982), p. 82.
40 Xu, "Sino–American Security Cooperation," p. 21.
41 Ibid., pp. 22–23. Xu refers to American sources in support of these statements.
42 Carter, *Keeping Faith: Memories of a President* (New York: Bantam Books, 1983), p. 195.
43 See Richard H. Solomon, "The China Factor in America's Foreign Relations," chapter 1 in Richard H. Solomon, ed., *The China Factor: Sino–American Relations and the Global Scene* (Engelwood Cliffs, N.J.: Prentice-Hall, 1981), pp. 33–46. This section is entitled "The Taiwan Time Bomb."
44 The text of the Shanghai Communiqué may be found in ibid., Appendix 1, pp. 296–300.
45 The text of the Joint Communiqué may be found in ibid., Appendix 2, pp. 300–301.
46 The text of the Taiwan Relations Act may be found in ibid., Appendix 4, pp. 304–314.
47 Jia-lin Zhang, "Assessing United States–Chinese Relations," *Current History* 84 (September 1985): 245.
48 See Solomon, "The China Factor in America's Foreign Relations," pp. 36–37.
49 Don Oberdorfer, "U.S. Course on Taiwan Unchanged," *The Philadephia Inquirer*, March 15, 1981.
50 Quoted in Hsiung, "Reagan's China Policy and the Sino–Soviet Detente," p. 3.
51 The text of the Joint Communiqué may be found in "U.S.–China Joint Communiqué," Bureau of Public Affairs, U.S. Department of State, *Current Policy*, no. 413, p. 2.
52 Ibid.
53 "The China Factor in America's Foreign Relations," p. 7.
54 Ibid., p. 46.
55 "The Strategic Dimensions of the Sino–American Relationship: Enemy of Our Enemy, or True Friend?" chapter 3 in Solomon, ed., *The China Factor*, pp. 88 and 101.
56 Quoted in ibid., pp. 101–102.
57 Lucian W. Pye, "The China Factor in Southeast Asia," chapter 8 in ibid., p. 241.
58 Henry Kissinger, *White House Years* (Boston: Little, Brown, 1979), p. 763. Both Kissinger and President Nixon, whom Kissinger served as national security adviser and secretary of state, have adhered to this view ever since their tenure of office at the apex of the decision-making process ended. In the July 1985 issue of the *American Legion Magazine*, for example,

Nixon wrote: "(W)e should not fear but welcome China's attempts to reduce tensions with the Soviet Union. Those who cynically observe that it would serve our interests for the two Communist giants to fight each other ignore the fact that such a war in the nuclear age would inevitably lead to a world war." Many American conservatives, however, seem to be more concerned about a possible Sino–Soviet *rapprochement* than with the consequences of continued tensions between "the two Communist giants." A study of the Heritage Foundation, a leading conservative think tank released at about the same time Nixon's article in the *American Legion* magazine appeared, written by Professor Harold C. Hinton of George Washington University, warned that China was not a normal Asian power or a reliable partner against the Soviet Union. "It is the only Third World country with the intention and capability of becoming a major industrial and military competitor of the United States in Asia. Further, it is a Communist country, albeit determined not to become subordinate to the Soviet Union, and appears fairly eager to establish some sort of working relationship with Moscow." Professor Hinton and the Heritage Foundation obviously view this trend with alarm, whereas Nixon and Kissinger consider it on the whole to be a desirable development, so long as it does not go too far and become an active and hostile alliance against the United States and the noncommunist world. The passages from Nixon's article and the Heritage Foundation study quoted above are reproduced in Schear, "Conflicting Views on U.S., China."

[59] Hsiung, "Reagan's China Policy and the Sino–Soviet Detente," pp. 4 and 6.

[60] Quoted in Jeffrey Antevil, "A Decade Later, Sino–U.S. Relations Are Still Not Easy," *The Philadelphia Inquirer*, February 28, 1982.

[61] Chang, "U.S.–China Relations," p. 167.

[62] "The China Factor in America's Foreign Relations," p. 21.

[63] Michael Oksenberg, "The Dynamics of the Sino–American Relationship," chapter 2 in Solomon, ed., *The China Factor*, p. 75 and 79.

[64] Strobe Talbott has expressed the view that the "global, strategic dimension" of the U.S.–P.R.C. relationship "has been more important than any strictly bilateral issue. Its unifying influence has overridden a number of extremely divisive problems." "The Strategic Dimension of the Sino-American Relationship," p. 82. Talbott's view may be somewhat exaggerated, but he has called attention to an important, and relatively neglected, aspect of the U.S.–P.R.C. relationship.

CHAPTER 6

The U.S.–South Korean Strategic Relationship

Historically, the Korean Peninsula has occupied a strategic position in East Asia. Since 1945 it has become an international as well as a regional strategic zone. The Korean War of the early 1950s—one of the major conflicts since 1945—began as a struggle between two indigenous regimes that had been created after the division of Korea because the United States and the Soviet Union could not agree on a common arrangement for the entire Peninsula. The war soon assumed larger dimensions when the United Nations forces—mostly American, under American command—came to the aid of South Korea, and when shortly thereafter the Chinese Communists intervened against the United Nations and South Korean forces, with the Soviet Union also siding in a nonmilitary way with North Korea.

Thus Korea became a theater of international and regional as well as local conflict, and the DMZ, a narrow strip between two hostile indigenous regimes, became one of the most dangerous areas of possible great power confrontation in the world (perhaps only the heavily garrisoned dividing lines between East and West Berlin, and East and West Germany, rival it for continued confrontation and potential explosiveness). About 1.5 million troops—some 838,000 North Korean troops and about 600,000 South Korean and 40,000 United States forces[1]—are present and constantly on the alert in the Korean Peninsula.

Many of the U.S. and South Korean military forces are concentrated in or near the DMZ, and major units of the larger North Korean forces, including three new mechanized corps, are deployed just to the north. North Korea is a highly militarized state, under a leadership dedicated to the reunification of the Peninsula by whatever means are necessary. Its formidable military establishment, well-equipped and in a high state of readiness, is a continuing threat to South Korea, and also to the United States because of the American presence in and commitments to the Republic of Korea. The magnitude of this threat can hardly be overestimated.

In recent years, North Korea has shown some signs of willingness to meet with representatives of South Korea and to make some concessions to that regime, but at the same time it has expanded and improved its military establishment and increased its forward deployments. Political trends could also add to the tensions between the two Koreas. The possible convergence of a succession crisis in both in the near future may create a particularly dangerous situation in North Korean–South Korean relations. Larger units of the U.S. military, the vast strength of China, the Soviet Union's Far Eastern commands and the Pacific Fleet, as well as the developing SDF of Japan, surround the Peninsula by land and sea. As Ambassador Richard Sneider has warned, "Any recurrence of open hostilities would potentially involve all four powers."[2]

U.S. INVOLVEMENT IN KOREA AFTER 1945

In this troubled area the United States has been a major actor since the end of World War II. In many respects U.S. relations with South Korea have had a very special character.[3] "Since the end of World War II no Asian nation has been in more intense, sustained, and conflictual relations with the United States than Korea."[4] After the defeat of Japan the United States jointly occupied the Peninsula with the Russians, who entered the war in East Asia shortly before the Japanese surrender. The Russians accepted the surrender of Japanese forces north of the Thirty-eighth Parallel, and the Americans did the same in the south. Since the occupying powers could not agree on arrangements for a single Korean regime for the entire Peninsula, Korea was divided along the Thirty-eighth Parallel, with a Communist regime backed by the Soviet Union in the north and a noncommunist regime backed by the United States in the south, and with a narrow demilitarized zone in between. The Thirty-eighth Parallel was set up as an administrative convenience only, but it soon became a political dividing line.

In 1947, frustrated by inability to reach agreement with the Soviet Union regarding arrangements for a united, independent, and democratic Korea, the United States referred the Korean question to the United Nations. The General Assembly, after extended consideration and debate, recommended that elections be held to enable the people of Korea, on both sides of the Thirty-eighth Parallel, to determine the kind of government—or governments—that they wanted. This recommendation was supported by the United States, but it was never implemented because of Soviet opposition. The two occupying powers then moved to establish very different kinds of regimes—creating in effect two very different kinds of countries—north and south of the Thirty-eighth Parallel. On August 15, 1948, a separate pro-Western government was established in South Korea with Syngman Rhee as President, and three months later, on September 9, the Russians countered with the inauguration of a Communist regime in North Korea headed by Kim Il Sung. The Soviet Union withdrew its troops from North Korea in late 1948, and all U.S. troops in South Korea were withdrawn by the following June.

Uneasy coexistence between two fragile and hostile regimes in the Korean

Peninsula and absence of direct foreign intervention did not last long. In late June 1950 the North Koreans, presumably encouraged or even prompted by the Soviets (there is still considerable controversy on this point), launched a direct military attack on South Korea, and seemed about to conquer and occupy the entire peninsula. The United States took prompt military action to assist South Korea to repel the invasion (action possible because significant American forces were available in the region, especially in Japan). At U.S. initiative, the United Nations Security Council, which the Soviet Union was then boycotting because of the China representation issue, condemned the North Korean attack and called for immediate cessation of hostilities and withdrawal of North Korean forces to the north of the DMZ. When the North Koreans continued their military actions, the Security Council voted to provide military assistance to South Korea, asked the United States, already involved in armed resistance to the invasion of South Korea, to name a supreme UN commander (General Douglas MacArthur, then commanding the American forces in South Korea, was so designated), and called on other member states to provide military and other assistance. Eventually nineteen nations sent some assistance, but this was limited in scope (less than 40,000 non-U.S. foreign troops were involved at any stage of the hostilities). In effect the United Nations operation in Korea was an American operation, although under the UN flag, and the control of that operation rested in Washington rather than in Lake Success, Long Island, where the Security Council then met.

When the United States, ignoring the warning of the Indian ambassador to Beijing (conveyed through diplomatic channels) that such a move would lead to Chinese intervention in the struggle, authorized General MacArthur to launch an attack north of the Thirty-eighth Parallel, the Chinese did intervene in force and, as MacArthur himself stated, thereby precipitated a wholly new war—one that threatened the UN forces with possible disaster and gave even more of the character of an international conflict to the struggle that was going on in the Korean Peninsula. In January 1951 the UN General Assembly, with some significant negative votes and abstentions, condemned the Chinese action and called for immediate Chinese withdrawal, but thereafter the UN role in Korea was even more peripheral in a military sense.

By mid-1951 the fighting in Korea had been reduced to desultory skirmishes, with continued military confrontation. Two more years elapsed before a truce was agreed upon, after the Russians finally expressed a willingness to cooperate. This brought an end to the North Korean military presence south of the DMZ. It also marked the beginning of a long-time American military presence, to assist the South Koreans to develop a more adequate defense against the North Koreans and to ward off any subsequent attacks. No major recurrence of the North Korean military offensive of the early 1950s has occurred, but the truce has been an uneasy one, marked by frequent minor clashes, continuing casualties, and constant tension between the two regimes, always threatening to erupt again into major conflict and to spill over into a larger conflagration involving outside powers and threatening regional and even world peace.

For the United States the Korean War involved a major expenditure of lives and money—about 54,000 Americans killed, and an expenditure of about $67 billion. It also led to a major continuing commitment, again at great cost, to the security of South Korea. Needless to say, for both the North and South Koreans the losses were far greater and the consequences even more enduring.[5]

In October 1953 the U.S. long-term commitment to the defense of South Korea was embodied in a mutual security treaty, which entered into effect in 1954. In the treaty each party recognized that "an armed attack in the Pacific area on either of the parties in territories now under their respective administrative control . . . would be dangerous to its own peace and security and declares that it would act to meet the common danger in accordance with its constitutional processes."[6] This treaty has been an important component of the American system of bilateral and multilateral alliances and other mutual security arrangements in the Western Pacific region, and has been the basis of the security relationship between the United States and South Korea. Since its conclusion, substantial U.S. Army and Air force troops have been stationed in South Korea and in the DMZ, and U.S. military and diplomatic personnel have had a major voice in military planning in South Korea and even in the control of the joint military forces of the two countries in the Korean Peninsula. Differences over the nature and extent of this control have been continuing irritants,[7] but the value of the U.S.–South Korean military and security relationship has been frequently acknowledged by both countries.[8]

At the time of the armistice agreement of July 1953, American troops in South Korea numbered 480,000. This number was reduced to about 60,000 within a few months, and to about 40,000 by the early 1970s. After President Carter, in 1977, announced his decision to withdraw all U.S. ground troops over a period of five years another 10,000 troops were withdrawn, but the American military contingent was soon restored to about 40,000 within two years, after that decision was "postponed indefinitely" and then publicly reversed by President Reagan as soon as he assumed office in 1981.

Korea has remained a divided country—one people with two hostile regimes—with formidable military forces in both North and South, with a continuing military presence of the United States, and with continuing attention by both the Soviet Union and China, whose rivalry over their respective roles in North Korea became even more of a disturbing factor after the Sino–Soviet split.

The continuing American military presence in South Korea and the U.S. commitment to that country in the mutual security treaty of 1954 have been very important, and perhaps even decisive, factors in preventing another

North Korean military effort to reunify the peninsula by force, and perhaps also in preventing more direct and extensive Soviet and Chinese intervention in the Korean Peninsula. Relations between the United States and South Korea have been close and generally good, at least on the official level. On unofficial levels, in both countries—and in the U.S. Congress—there have been frequent criticisms of and demonstrations against the relationship. Some South Koreans believe that this relationship has given too much control to a foreign power and has kept their country in a dependent status. They would like to be more independent.[9] This desire for independence has grown in recent years, as South Korea has emerged as an economically dynamic and growing economy and has become much more active in regional and world affairs. It is particularly marked among those who are most dissatisfied with the authoritarian rule that they have experienced and with the U.S. collaboration with and support of that rule in spite of U.S. professions of a desire for greater freedoms and greater respect for human rights in South Korea. Dissident students, who are increasingly vocal and sometimes violent, and those who support opposition parties and groups are conspicuous adherents to this kind of orientation.[10]

Some Americans have been increasingly critical of the "burden" of the commitment to South Korea, which they regard as no longer essential for security purposes either for South Korea or the United States and as an increasingly unproductive extension of American power. They have been particularly critical of the various regimes in South Korea with which the United States has been inescapably associated, almost all of which have been highly authoritarian in nature. They see little that is mutual in the mutual security treaty, and they fear that by its substantial military presence and its political and military involvement in Korea the United States will be jeopardizing rather than enhancing its security interests.[11]

DIFFERENCES BETWEEN THE UNITED STATES AND SOUTH KOREA

In spite of the officially close and good relations, differences of opinion between the United States and South Korea have been numerous and persistent. Some of these are rooted in deep-seated differences in traditions and values and in cultural perspectives and outlook. Some have been on specific issues, such as alleged efforts of South Koreans to bribe members of the U.S. Congress or the Kim Dae Jung case[12] (in which the United States intervened repeatedly to prevent the South Korean authorities from carrying out a death sentence on a prominent Korean opposition leader, to have him released from prison and permitted to come to the United States for medical treatment, and allowed to return to Korea without being tortured or imprisoned there—or assassinated ă la Aquino in the Philippines). On the whole the American troops in South Korea have behaved well, but there have inevitably been large numbers of incidents that have stirred up resentment or friction. U.S. diplomatic and military officers in Korea have been circumspect in dealing with the South Koreans, but they have often tried to put pressure on South Korea's leaders to take actions that would not otherwise be taken, and they have had a role in South Korea's affairs that is bound to create resentment and criticism.

Political differences have been numerous. South Korea's leaders have resented the continuing criticisms in the United States of their alleged authoritarianism and barely nominal dedication to democracy and their alleged repeated violations of human rights and fundamental freedoms. Some South Koreans charge that the United States is not really interested in them, but is simply trying to use their country as a base for U.S. global interests and rivalries, in ways that are not only demeaning but also dangerous for them. Some Americans, in turn, believe that the United States is serving South Korean but not American interests by its heavy (read *excessive*) commitment and involvement in South Korea.[13]

On the economic front differences are especially numerous and often conspicuous. The United States gave major assistance to the economic recovery and development of South Korea, as it did to Korea's larger and more economically powerful neighbor, Japan, but the remarkable economic growth of South Korea—now apparently following in Japan's footsteps, though on a lesser scale and at a later period—has created problems and resentments in U.S.–South Korean relations, even as the United States professes to welcome South Korea's remarkable economic progress. Trade and business relations between the two countries are very extensive. The United States and Japan are the major trading partners of South Korea, and South Korea is the seventh largest trading partner—and the second largest in Asia—of the United States. But Americans are alarmed by the heavy deficit in trade with South Korea—as with Japan on a much larger scale—and by what they allege to be unfair business practices by the South Koreans, including a great deal of dumping, export subsidies, and counterfeiting of name brands. South Koreans, whose economic "miracle" is heavily dependent on exports, are alarmed at the increasing trends toward protectionism and discrimination in the United States. These trends, plus the slump in the American economy that provoked them, are particularly serious for South Korea. They are major causes for the slowdown in economic growth that South Korea, in common with the other "export-driven economies of the Pacific Basin," is now experiencing, after many years of economic dynamism that gave it some of the highest growth rates of any country in the world.[14]

THE CONTINUING SECURITY COMMITMENT

Despite criticisms and uneasiness in both South Korea and the United States, the military presence and the security commitment have continued and been frequently reaffirmed. Both countries agree that as soon as conditions permit—that is, as soon as the defenses and political stability of South Korea seem to be adequate—American military forces should be withdrawn from South Korea, although presumably a commitment to South Korea's security will remain from a greater physical and political distance. But both countries agree that the time for American military withdrawal is not yet here.

The one period when this withdrawal seemed imminent created great alarm in South Korea and was widely criticized in the United States, Japan, and elsewhere. During his campaign for the presidency in 1976 Jimmy Carter pledged that if elected he would withdraw American ground forces from Korea. In the following year, shortly after he assumed office, he announced that U.S. ground forces, numbering over 30,000, would be withdrawn in three stages over a period of five or six years; but the storm of protest over this move was so great that within two years Carter was forced to reverse this decision—or to suspend it indefinitely, as the face-saving announcement of the reversal decision put it. Carter's withdrawal decision, even though not implemented, caused great damage to U.S.–South Korean relations, as well as to the American image and position in the Western Pacific and perhaps globally. It is still often mentioned by East Asians as a concrete example of the unreliability and lack of will of the United States.[15]

After Ronald Reagan, with his strong commitment to support of allies and to a reassertion of American resolve and leadership, became president, the continuing commitment to South Korea was repeatedly reaffirmed, and there was little effective challenge to this. There was, however, considerable criticism both in the United States and in South Korea of Reagan's allegedly too-close support of the authoritarian regime of President Chun Doo Hwan. The decision to welcome President Chun as the first head of state to visit the United States after Reagan's inauguration was not appreciated in many circles in both countries, nor were some of Reagan's more effusive remarks about President Chun when he made an official visit to South Korea in November 1983. Some members of Congress, in particular, have favored a more detached relationship with the Chun regime, and have expressed skepticism regarding Chun's pledge to institute more democratic practices and to retire at the end of his present term in 1988.

The military leaders of South Korea have often complained about the continuing pressures from U.S. administrations to move more rapidly toward promised democratic reforms and to improve their rather sorry record on human rights. These pressures, they contend, reflect a lack of understanding of the Korean scene and of the difficulties with which the rulers of South Korea have to contend. In their view Ronald Reagan is a vast improvement over Jimmy Carter, who not only wanted to withdraw U.S. ground forces, thereby endangering South Korea's very existence, but also made human rights issues a central touchstone of his policies toward the South Korean government. But South Korea's leaders have also chafed under the pressures of the Reagan administration, partially in response to congressional and public insistence, to improve their performance in the areas of democracy and human rights. On a number of specific issues, particularly the Kim Dae Jung case, the two governments have been far apart.

Outside of government circles in South Korea, however, the main criticism has been not that the United States has been too critical of the Chun Doo Hwan regime but that it has not been critical enough, that it has in fact been too supportive of that regime.

Many South Koreans, especially student militants, have publicly demonstrated against the United States, but it is difficult to determine whether these demonstrations have been evidence of anti-Americanism or a means of voicing their opposition to the Chun Doo Hwan regime.[16] Many Korean students blamed the United States as well as the military regime that had been imposed soon after the assassination of Park Chung Hee for the tragic incidents in Kwangju in May–June 1980, when "a full-scale citizens' insurrection," led mostly by dissident students, was brutally repressed by several thousand troops in what has been described as "the most serious crisis in South Korea since the upheaval that brought down the regime of President Syngman Rhee in 1960 and began 19 years of military domination."[17] Among students and other groups in South Korea the Kwangju incident of 1980 has not been forgotten, and among these groups the conviction of American involvement, if only indirectly, in the repression of the Kwangju dissidents is still strong. This was dramatically demonstrated in May 1985, on the fifth anniversary of the Kwangju "insurrection," when military students took over the American Cultural Center (the United States Information Service building) in downtown Seoul for several days, demanding among other things a confession of U.S. involvement in the Kwangju incident of 1980, an apology for this involvement, and an end to the U.S. support of the Chun Doo Hwan regime. These demands were not met, but the students eventually evacuated the building peacefully. This highly publicized affair was viewed as a reminder of the continuing opposition to the Chun regime and association of the United States with that regime. It was also interpreted as a dramatic evidence of the anti-American feeling that seems to be growing in South Korea.[18]

In American eyes the security of South Korea is linked with the larger considerations of the security of Japan and with defense against the Soviet threat in the entire Western Pacific and globally. Many Koreans do not like this kind of linkage, especially because it seems to indicate that the United States is not so much interested in the defense of South Korea as in Korea's strategic position and vulnerabilities in possible larger conflicts, and because this kind of approach seems to expose Korea to involvement in conflicts with which it cannot cope. Moreover, although South Koreans share to some extent the U.S. perceptions of the Soviet threat, they seem to feel that fundamentally they can do little to meet this threat and that this is more a matter of concern to the United States than to them. To them the threat within their own peninsula is more immediate and more serious, although they recognize that the local tensions are aggravated because of external involvement on opposite sides. At times they seem to be about as uncertain and apprehensive about China and Japan as potential security threats as about the Soviet Union. Their suspicions of their more powerful East Asian neighbors are one reason why they do not like to be linked with any of these neighbors in any kind of anti-Soviet security planning or arrangements.

South Koreans are particularly uneasy about the way many American official planners and security specialists link South Korea with Japan. South Koreans are still suspicious of Japan, for reasons of past history and experience, and they believe that their security should not be dependent on the evolution of Japan's defense planning or on the security relationship between the United States and Japan.[19] The Soviet Union has tried to capitalize on these apprehensions and reactions in South Korea. It has warned the South Koreans against too close military or other associations with the United States, or Japan, or both. It has often expressed concern about a possible U.S.–Japan–South Korea alliance, directed not only against North Korea but also against the Soviet Union, although they are of course even more concerned about an anti-Soviet U.S.–Japan–China alliance.[20]

THE UNITED STATES AND INTRA-KOREAN CONTACTS

One encouraging fact is that all of the major powers that are, or have been, closely involved in the Korean Peninsula in various confrontational ways now seem anxious to avoid a recurrence of military hostilities in the Peninsula and seem to desire to follow a relatively low-key policy in that strategic area. In recent years the Korean Peninsula has not been a major theater of such larger conflicts as those between the United States and the Soviet Union, or of the continuing tensions between the Soviet Union and Japan.

The United States has consistently advocated the resolution of the disputes between North and South Korea through direct peaceful negotiations. It has exerted some pressure on the South Korean regimes, and has tried to exert some pressure, through indirect channels, on the Kim Il Sung regime in North Korea as well, to place intra-Korean relations on a more constructive and less dangerous basis. But it has just as consistently rejected any suggestions, some of which have come from feelers from North Korea, that it negotiate bilaterally with North Korea regarding intra-Korean differences. In his address to the United Nations General Assembly on September 24, 1984, President Reagan expressed his support for a long-standing proposal that the two Koreas try to agree on a series of "confidence-building measures," which might include prior notification of military movements and exercises and invitations to one country to send military observers to military maneuvers in the other. The overall U.S. position on North–South relations in Korea was well expressed by Under Secretary of State for Political Affairs Michael Armacost in an address in New York in late January 1985:

> In Korea, we should sustain close cooperation with the R.O.K. as it explores the potential for direct North–South talks. In the past, the North has sought to ignore the South in order to resolve basic issues with us. We shall resist being drawn into talks with Pyongyang at the South's expense. There can be no durable reduction of tension in the peninsula until North and South Korea resolve through direct negotiations the basic issues which divide them. South Korea consistently has proposed that Pyongyang join in agreeing on various confidence-building measures. This is a sensible strategy and deserves our support. Indeed, all regional powers share a responsibility to do whatever they can to promote stability and ensure peace on the peninsula.[21]

North and South Korea have subjected each other to a bitter and continuing propaganda barrage. There have also been repeated instances of sabotage, espionage, murders, and exchanges of gunfire and other minor military clashes. But there has been little direct communication between them, especially communication of a constructive nature. Two major breaks in this logjam of vitriolic attack and virtually nonexistent direct communication came in the early 1970s and in 1984. In each case the Red Cross in North and South Korea played a leading role.

Negotiations between the branches of the Red Cross in 1971, permitted by the two governments, led to some talks at high official levels and to a joint declaration on July 4, 1972, in which the two sides expressed an interest in working out their differences, in agreeing on the reunification of the country by peaceful means, and in moderating their propaganda war. This declaration raised high hopes that a fundamental change for the better was in the offing, but these hopes were soon dissipated. Talks at various levels were held in 1972, 1973, and 1974, with no significant results. Thereafter North–South relations returned to their hostile and uncommunicative pattern.

For almost a decade this all-too-familiar pattern continued. Animosities were heightened in October 1983 when seventeen South Korean officials, including four Cabinet ministers, were killed in a bomb explosion in Rangoon (President Chun Doo Hwan, who led the high-level delegation to Burma and was doubtless the main target of the attack, escaped). The Burmese government officially blamed the North Korean regime for instigating this incident, and the South Koreans were also convinced that that regime was responsible. This incident, which came in the month following the shooting down of Korean Airlines flight 007 over Soviet Far Eastern territory, has had a lasting impact on South Koreans' attitudes and has increased their feelings of insecurity in a hostile environment in their own peninsula and outside. It was an inauspicious backdrop for the remarkable series of North–South contacts that took place in 1984.

After three rounds of talks in the first part of 1984—centered around possible cooperation in sports events, including the possible fielding of a joint sports team in the Asian Games scheduled to be held in Seoul in 1986, and perhaps even in the Olympic Games in Seoul in 1988—President Chun proposed a series of economic talks between the North and the South. To almost everyone's surprise the North Korean response was favorable, and the opening round of these talks was held in mid-September. They were the first such talks since the outbreak of the Korean War in June 1950. An even more surprising development occurred in September. Early in the month the North Korean Red Cross offered to provide food and medical aid for the victims of a devastating flood in South Korea. Although many in South Korea denounced the offer as insincere, as nothing more than a propaganda ploy, the South Korean government authorized the Red Cross of South Korea to accept the offer. Many still assumed that the North Koreans would never actually deliver the promised aid, and this feeling was accentuated when discussions between the two Red Cross branches broke down because of disagreements regarding the logistics of the proposed deliveries. But in late November truckloads of supplies were in fact delivered at Panmunjom. At about the same time the two regimes reached an agreement to end the eleven-year freeze on talks aimed at reuniting divided Korean families, a matter of much emotional significance in the South. South Koreans claim that some 10 million families have close relatives in North Korea, concerning whom they have been unable to get even minimal information and with whom they have not been permitted to establish any contacts.

These encouraging developments, which the United States applauded, came to an abrupt end in late November 1984, following a gun battle in Panmunjom, in which four soldiers were killed—three North and one South Korean—and an American and at least one North Korean soldier were wounded. The clash erupted when a Soviet citizen in a visiting group on the North Korean side of the DMZ suddenly fled into the DMZ, seeking asylum. The North Korean regime accused the South Koreans and the Americans of conniving in the defection, and promptly called off the second round of economic cooperation talks that had been scheduled for December 5. In January 1985 the North Koreans also canceled scheduled trade and Red Cross talks, allegedly in protest at the plans to hold large-scale joint military exercises—labeled "Team Spirit—1985"—involving more than 200,000 South Korean and American troops, from February 1 through mid-April (these exercises had been held every year, although not always on such a large scale.)[22]

Contacts were resumed a few months later. In late May, in accordance with an agreement of the previous November, representatives of the Red Cross societies of the two Koreas met in Seoul to discuss proposals for the reuniting of separated families—the first time such talks had been held since 1971.[23] A second round of talks on this emotionally charged subject was held in late August, and, on August 15, the fortieth anniversary of the liberation of Korea from Japanese rule, the two Koreas cooperated in staging a symbolic reunion of a few long-separated families. Contacts have continued since that time, with occasional abrupt cancellation of scheduled meetings by the North Korean Government.

TIME FOR NEW U.S. INITIATIVES?

The complex and multifaceted relationship between the United States and South Korea continues, and security aspects continue to be a central and often dominant theme in that relationship. For the South Koreans these ties with the United States are still regarded as vital, although increasing evidences of a growing desire for and a growing capability to maintain a more independent position are becoming evident. For the United States the ties with South Korea arise from past circumstances and commitments, and from continuing security concerns and needs. These ties are of course a part of a larger network of alliances and associations that the United States has developed in East Asia and the Western Pacific and that are linked with other U.S. alliances and associations, with strong security dimensions, in other parts of the region and the world.

Many political leaders and analysts, in East Asia, the United States, and elsewhere, believe that the United States must reappraise its entire position and interests in the Western Pacific in the light of the vast changes under way in the regional and global environment, and that the Korean Peninsula is a place where new, imaginative, and sustained American initiatives might be appropriate and productive at the present time or in the near future. These views are prompted in part by evidences that conditions on the Korean Peninsula, as well as in the Western Pacific and elsewhere, are changing in ways that offer some hope that U.S. initiatives in Korea might not only be helpful in creating a better climate for negotiations and better understanding between North and South Korea but might also provide opportunities for the United States to receive larger payoffs as well, notably in improving its relations with the Soviet Union and with other countries in the Western Pacific and even globally. This line of reasoning was expressed by a well-known American specialist on East Asia, Donald C. Hellmann, after a tour of the area in September 1984:

> What is striking about the current situation in South Korea is the growing importance attached to national and regional concerns and the opportunity that is presented for creative American policy initiatives. The South Korean government is moving boldly ahead to secure its own economic and political place in the world, buoyed by the remarkable economic achievements of recent decades, the symbolic importance of staging the Olympics and, above all, a confidence and commitment to the future which was strikingly evident throughout all of our meetings. South Korea is and will continue to be a close ally of the United States and recent policies have done much to strengthen this bilateral relationship. However, in view of the flexibility shown by the Seoul government in policies toward her neighbors, the intense concern for unification of their country, and the central part that great power politics, especially Soviet–American relations, has in the reunification issue, there is a real possibility for American foreign policy initiative in this area which directly involves U.S.–Soviet relations. The Soviet discomfort in trying to control the policies of Kim Il Sung, the difficulties which will flow from boycotting two Olympics in succession and the intense concern over a future U.S.–

Japan–Seoul military alliance provide an opportunity for policy initiatives by the United States from a position of strength. Because the South Koreans are closely tied to the United States and because both the Chinese and the Japanese have publically [sic] displayed a desire to move on to the issue of Korean unification, a situation is developing in which the United States can seek to refine the political and strategic landscape in Northeast Asia by dealing directly with the Soviet Union while walking hand in hand with our allies and not compromising our overall political-military posture in the region.[24]

These views and proposals deserve careful consideration in official circles in the United States, the Soviet Union, North and South Korea, Japan, and elsewhere. Possibly fresh American initiatives could be helpful in reducing tensions in Korea and the entire Western Pacific, and in Soviet-American relations. They should be formulated carefully, and only after consultations with key persons in many other countries, especially countries most obviously and most directly concerned.

In an era when the United States must seek partnership rather than domination, when so many seemingly imaginative and constructive proposals have never really gotten off the drawing board, and when the will to take the supportive actions and to assume the costs and burdens that would be necessary to pursue such promising ideas seems to be lacking, American initiatives of the type proposed must be taken, if taken at all, with great care and caution. This may have the negative effect of vitiating their appeal and prospects of success instead of the positive effect of translating good ideas into realistic policies that will engender practical acceptance and support, but any other approach would almost certainly be doomed to failure. South Koreans might welcome any initiatives that would help to lessen the tensions in their divided country, but they certainly would be suspicious of any that would involve a larger presence and stronger powers on their own soil.

Americans might welcome imaginative U.S. initiatives to lessen tensions in a strategically important region where they have had continuing military presence and commitments and might seek to explore the possibilities of some kind of limited cooperation with the Soviet Union in a region where both superpowers might be prepared to cooperate, if only to a limited degree, in the pursuit of mutual interests, one hopes with constructive spillover effects on their entire relationship. In the meantime, the U.S. strategic relationship with South Korea will continue, and Korea will remain an area of special interest and concern in the pursuit of American national interests, however overshadowed by U.S. relations with the major nations of the Western Pacific, Japan, China, and the Soviet Union.

Notes

[1] These numbers are taken from *The Military Balance 1985–1986* (London: The International Institute for Strategic Studies, 1985).

[2] Richard L. Sneider, "Prospects for Korean Security," chapter 6 in Richard H. Solomon, ed., *Asian Security in the 1980s: Problems and Policies for a Time of Transition* (Cambridge, Mass.: Oelgeschlager, Gunn & Hain, 1980), p. 112.

[3] For an overview of U.S.–South Korean relations, see Claude A. Buss, *The United States and the Republic of Korea: Background for Policy* (Stanford, Calif.: Hoover Institution Press,

1982). For a concise summary of and commentary on the security aspects of these relations, see Tae-Hwan Kwak and Wayne Patterson, "U.S. Political-Security Policy Toward the Korean Peninsula," in Tae-Hwan Kwak, Wayne Patterson, and Edward A. Olsen, eds., *The Two Koreas in World Politics* (Boulder, Colorado: Westview Press, 1984). Fuller treatments are given in Chae-Jin Lee and Hideo Sato, *U.S. Policy Toward Japan and Korea: A Changing Influence Relationship* (New York: Praeger Publishers, 1982); and Gerald L. Curtis and Sung-Joo Han, eds., *The U.S.–South Korean Alliance: Evolving Patterns in Security Relations* (Lexington, Mass.: Lexington Books, 1983).

4   Bruce Cumings, "Korean-American Relations: A Century of Contact and Thirty-Five Years of Intimacy," in Warren I. Cohen, ed., *New Frontiers in American–East Asian Relations: Essays Presented to Dorothy Borg* (New York: Columbia University Press, 1983), p. 236.

5   "About a million South Korean civilians were killed in the fighting. About 580,000 U.N. and South Korean troops (mostly South Koreans) and about 1,600,000 Communist troops were killed, wounded, taken prisoner or reported missing." "Korea 30 Years Later: 'There Will Be No Withdrawal,'" *The Seattle Times*, February 28, 1983.

6   The text of the treaty is given in Sung-Joo Han, ed., *U.S.–Korea Security Cooperation: Retrospects and Prospects* (Seoul: Asiatic Research Center, Korea University, 1983), pp. 235–237.

7   "Combined Forces Command was formed in November 1978, after South Korea demanded more control over its own forces. The Korean troops had been under American command since the Korean War ended in 1953, technically under the flag of the United Nations. When the command was set up, the United States and South Korea agreed to share costs." Richard Halloran, "Seoul Said to Balk on Payments to U.S.," *The New York Times*, March 17, 1985. Not until 1981 did the two countries agree on the basis of cost-sharing—on a 62:38 ratio— but ever since there have been continuing differences over this sensitive issue.

8   This is true even of most students and other dissidents who have demonstrated against the United States as well as against the Chun Doo Hwan regime. "Radical students have notably omitted any demand that US troops leave Korea." Steven B. Butler, "Anti-American Sentiment Rises in S. Korea," *Christian Science Monitor*, January 28, 1986.

9   For many South Koreans, especially of the younger generation, the cultural threat from the outside, especially from the United States, is regarded as even more serious than the political threat. This was effectively brought out by a staff reporter of the *Korea Times* (Seoul) in a column in September 1984. She cited the case of a twenty-three-year-old student at Korea University who "sums up what he wants for the country in a simple two-part recipe: 'I want Korea to be the strongest country and I want our society free of American influence.' Both desires are a result of Korea's entrance into the world economy and society. The student wants to prove to the rest of the world that no matter how small Korea is or how weak it has been in the past, the country is now strong and capable of standing on its own. He is, at the same time, fearful of the United States because he identifies the social changes wrought by industrialization with American culture. These are, for him, the fundamental problems of his nation at present." Jennifer Jean Robinson, "Culture Resilient in Face of Challenges," *Korea Times*, September 26, 1984.

10 See Butler, "Anti-American Sentiment Rises in S. Korea."

11 In a thought-provoking analysis of U.S.–South Korean relations a well-known American scholar wrote: "Korea has never mattered much to Americans for its intrinsic interest or characteristics, but only as it related to some broader concern. Indeed, one can question whether it is proper to speak of mutuality in this relationship at all, since the influence has been so strongly one way." Cumings, "Korean-American Relations," p. 277. Moreover, Americans' interest generally in Korea has been spasmodic and rather uninformed, except perhaps during the Korean War in the early 1950s, in spite of the continuing crisis in the Korean Peninsula that might flare up into a conflict extending well beyond the Peninsula, the continuing presence of substantial American military forces in South Korea and the DMZ, and more recently the growing economic relations with a booming South Korean economy. On Feb. 28, 1983, in an article prompted by the imminence of the thirtieth anniversary of the signing of the Armistice Agreement in 1953, the staff of a major American newspaper wrote: "The July 27, 1953, truce ended the worst of the fighting, but a permanent peace between North and South Korea has never been signed. And, although the Korean involvement of millions of United States television viewers will end tonight with the showing of the final

episode of M*A*S*H, the United States' involvement will be far from over." *The Seattle Times*, February 28, 1983.

[12] For details see Buss, *The United States and the Republic of Korea*, pp. 126–136, and Lee and Sato, *U.S. Policy Toward Japan and Korea*, pp. 73–93, 157.

[13] Cumings, "Korean–American Relations," p. 277.

[14] "Running out of Steam: The Pacific Basin Countries Feel a Drag from the U.S. Slowdown," *Time*, November 25, 1985, pp. 78–79.

[15] See Lee and Sato, *U.S. Policy Toward Japan and Korea*, pp. 106–127.

[16] In September 1986, while the Asian Games were in progress in Seoul, with almost daily demonstrations against the Chun Doo Hwan government—and often against the United States as well—a Korean scholar wrote in a letter to the author: "In spite of the anti-American slogans of students and radicals, it is not really anti-American. You must understand that they are against the Reagan government which, they believe, is supporting the repressive and undemocratic Korean regime. The overwhelming majority of Koreans are still pro-U.S.A. and they want you [to] stay for military security and economic cooperation."

[17] "South Korea: Season of Spleen," *Time* (June 2, 1980), p. 36. See also "South Korea: Ten Days That Shook Kwangju," *Time* (June 9, 1980), p. 40.

[18] Butler, "Anti-American Sentiment Rises in S. Korea."

[19] See Chong-Sik Lee, *Japan and Korea: The Political Dimension* (Stanford, Calif.: Hoover Institution Press, 1985).

[20] The Soviets sometimes profess to see the possibility of a quadripartite U.S.–Japan–China–South Korea alliance, directed against their country.

[21] Michael H. Armacost, "The Asia-Pacific Region: A Forward Look," address before the Far East–America Council/Asia Society, New York, January 29, 1985; Bureau of Public Affairs, U.S. Department of State, *Current Policy*, no. 653, p. 3.

[22] "Team Spirit—1983," however, which began on February 1, 1983, and lasted until mid-April, took about the same length of time and involved almost as many troops. It was described as "the largest ever held in the noncommunist world," involving "about 188,000 military personnel, including 70,000 U.S. soldiers, sailors, marines, and airmen." "Korea 30 Years Later."

[23] An account of these talks is given in *The New York Times*, May 29, 1985.

[24] Donald C. Hellmann, "Pacific Forum Northeast Asia Summary Report," unpublished report of "a study and investigative tour of the Republic of China, the Republic of Korea and Japan," in September 1984, prepared for the sponsoring agency, the Pacific Forum in Honolulu, pp. 13–14.

CHAPTER 7

U.S. Security Relationships in Southeast Asia

Whereas Northeast Asia is the main focus of U.S. security relationships and concerns in the Western Pacific, Southeast Asia is also becoming of increasing importance in terms of security, as well as of political, economic, and other interests. Indeed, as Peter Polomka has observed, there is "a growing inter-linkage between the security of both Northeast and Southeast Asia."[1]

An important regional arrangement, the Association of Southeast Asian Nations (ASEAN), has emerged in Southeast Asia. It is in fact the most important regional arrangement in the entire Asia-Pacific region. Its member-ship—Brunei, Indonesia, Malaysia, the Philippines, Singapore, and Thai-land—consists of most of the nations of Southeast Asia. With the conspicuous exception of the Philippines, all of these nations are among the group of developing countries, most of which are located in East and Southeast Asia, whose rates of economic growth have been among the highest in the world and whose political self-confidence and assertiveness are increasingly apparent. The great divide in Southeast Asia is between the ASEAN countries and the communist states of Indochina, with Vietnam in a dominant—and domineering—role.

Most of the security concerns of the ASEAN states relate to problems of internal security and stability, to relations with Vietnam and Kampuchea (now occupied by Vietnam), and the role of major powers in the region. ASEAN countries have learned how to cooperate more effectively, in spite of the past record of frequent conflicts and very limited cooperation. Their cooperation is mainly in economic, technological, cultural, and political fields, but in spite of their original intent to eschew security matters, they have been forced to consider problems of mutual security as well.

ASEAN PERSPECTIVES ON RELATIONS WITH THE UNITED STATES

U.S. relationships with a changing Southeast Asia, and particularly with ASEAN, must be viewed within a comprehensive framework, and not exclusively or even primarily from the perspective of American global security concerns. As two perceptive American students of Asian affairs have emphasized, "The issue of how the U.S. relates to the self-confident and mature nationalisms of ASEAN in a sophisticated and nonpressuring manner will become increasingly important."[2] Economic relations have also become increasingly important. The United States is the second largest trading partner of the ASEAN countries—second only to Japan—and the ASEAN states are now the fifth largest trading partner of the United States. American private investment in ASEAN countries is quite substantial. This is especially the case in the Philippines, with which the United states has had special relationships and contacts for several decades, and Indonesia, the largest nation of Southeast Asia. It also has special relations with Thailand, mostly of a security nature (Thailand, like the Philippines, was associated with the United States for many years in the now-defunct multilateral security arrangement, SEATO), and with Singapore, mainly because of that tiny nation's major role in the world of international finance and commerce and because of its generally more favorable orientation than most of the other Southeast Asian nations toward U.S. political and security policies and actions.

ASEAN countries, on the whole, prefer to concentrate on their nonmilitary relations with the United States. The reasons for this preference are obvious. These countries are deeply concerned with the preservation of their independence and with their internal stability and development. They do not want to get involved in the conflicts of more powerful nations, especially in any U.S.–Soviet conflicts, and above all, they do not want their part of the world to become a cockpit for rivalries and conflicts of outside powers. Aside from rather general agreement that internal security threats are the most serious that they face, their threat perceptions differ substantially.

All of the ASEAN states are concerned about developments in Indochina, which from their perspectives have greatly aggravated their security problems. Among the alarming developments are the U.S. withdrawal from Vietnam in the mid-1970s, the Soviet–Vietnamese Treaty of Friendship and Cooperation of 1978, the Soviet–Chinese rivalry in the Indochina area, and the Vietnamese invasion of Kampuchea in late 1978. But Thailand, and to a lesser degree Singapore, express far greater concern about the threat from Indochina than do the other ASEAN countries.

In varying degrees the member states of ASEAN perceive real or potential threats from all of the major intrusive powers. Two of them—Malaysia and Indonesia—give higher priority to the potential threat from China than they do to existing potential threats from Indochina, even with the heavy Soviet involvement in that part of Southeast Asia. All (especially Thailand and Singapore) evince some concern about possible threats from the Soviet Union, but in general they are not as absorbed with the Soviet threat as is the United States. All show apprehension about the growing strength and role of Japan, in East Asia and in the world economy as well as in Southeast Asia. Suspicion of both Japan and China in Southeast Asia because of their growing power and assertiveness is reinforced by memories of bitter historical experience with Japan during World War II and with China for many centuries. Virtually all of the ASEAN states—and this is hard for many Americans to understand—often think of the United States as a threat, as well as a major power with which they have many mutually profitable relationships. The feelings of many Southeast Asians seem to fluctuate with regard to the United States; sometimes they think the United States is part of the solution and sometimes part of the problem. "The United States must understand the forces which determine ASEAN's outlook toward the major powers in order to sustain productive working political and security relationships with current or prospective ASEAN governments. This topic has been neglected in past Western studies of Asia's security problems."[3]

ASEAN feelings about security relationships with the United States are particularly ambivalent. Apparently the leaders of these countries are pulled in two different directions—away from any security associations with the U.S. because of suspicions of American power and intentions, doubts about U.S. credibility and resolve, reluctance to compromise their independence by too close associations with a superpower, and a determination not to allow themselves to be dragged into great power rivalries and conflicts; and toward security associations with the United States as perhaps the most acceptable of the major powers in meeting their pressing needs for external assistance in dealing with internal and regional security threats. They seem to feel that the United States does not give adequate recognition to their importance and their sensitivities, and that it thinks of them more in terms of global security interests and preoccupations than in terms of their own interests and needs. This is an expression of a view that is widespread among developing countries in all parts of the world, namely, that the United States is not really interested in them, but approaches them only with a view to its global priorities—that the United States still views them more as objects than as subjects in the larger international game of power, rivalry, and confrontation.

Unfortunately, there is considerable basis for these reservations of the ASEAN countries when they consider security links with the United States. One has only to refer to innumerable statements by responsible American leaders, reflecting their obsession with the global Soviet threat and their apparent relative lack of interest in or understanding of the perspectives and interests of smaller nations.

Many American students of international affairs have also perceived this global anti-Soviet approach as all-embracing, and some have focused on Southeast Asia in support of their view. In late 1984 one American Asian specialist wrote:

> [T]he administration of President Ronald Reagan, taking up where President Jimmy Carter's administration left off, has viewed Southeast Asia primarily in terms of a global struggle against the Soviet Union. The United States now seeks to polarize the region between pro-Soviet and anti-Soviet blocs, as it sought in the 1960's to polarize it into pro-Chinese and anti-Chinese states. . . . Its primary concern in the region is to insure that the ASEAN states do

nothing to hamper the United States ability to bring its military power to bear in conflicts with the Soviet Union or its allies outside the region.[4]

This is an overly harsh and overly simplistic analysis, but it does reflect the kind of global geopolitical approach that seems to be favored by many capable American analysts as well as by some decisionmakers. Responsible American political leaders, however, would deny that they are seeking "to polarize the region between pro-Soviet and anti-Soviet blocs" and would insist that they have much broader interests than this analysis suggests, even in the security field. But it is the kind of analysis that would fit into the perceptions of many Southeast Asians, as well as of some cold warriors and some of their critics in the United States.

For many reasons the United States is interested in encouraging and assisting the ASEAN countries to develop their own security capabilities, individually, bilaterally, and collectively, in order to deal with their own internal and regional security problems and to cope more effectively with any emerging external threats.

One of the main U.S. strategic aims in Southeast Asia, in the words of a secret five-year defense plan of the U.S. Department of Defense, completed in 1982, is to "foster the strength and cohesion" of the ASEAN countries to enable them to "counter Vietnamese expansionism."[5] This is an aim that the ASEAN countries themselves have increasingly come to share, and to consider in their various meetings, including high-level meetings of ASEAN. As the United States, most ASEAN countries feel that the threat from Vietnam is aggravated by the Soviet support of that country, expressed in the Soviet–Vietnamese Treaty of Friendship and Cooperation of 1978, by the presence of large numbers of Russians in Vietnam, and by the strong Soviet support of the Vietnamese military move into Cambodia (Kampuchea) in late 1978. ASEAN states, and to some extent the United States as well, are also apprehensive about the Chinese role in Indochina. This apprehension increased with the brief Chinese incursion into Vietnam in early 1979, during which several thousands were killed on each side. An underlying concern is that the Soviet support of Vietnam and the Chinese hostility toward that country might lead to Sino–Soviet military confrontation in Indochina, with spillover consequences elsewhere in Southeast Asia and perhaps beyond.

Both the United States and the ASEAN countries strongly protested the Vietnamese invasion of Kampuchea, and they have repeatedly called for a Vietnamese withdrawal. They both refuse to recognize the Heng Samrin regime in Kampuchea, and they support the opposition Cambodian groups, a motley lot of pro- and anticommunists—the Khmer Rouge and the followers of Son Sann and Prince Norodom Sihanouk—which are loosely organized under the leadership of Sihanouk. Most of these groups are now operating from Thailand's territory, or have taken refuge in Thailand after opting out of the military struggle. The United States and China, as the ASEAN countries, support the Cambodians who are trying to continue the struggle against the

Heng Samrin regime, but the Chinese give their support mainly to the Khmer Rouge and the Americans to the noncommunist elements of the resistance movement. The United States, like the ASEAN states, is rather embarrassed to be supporting an opposition front whose largest contingent, the Khmer rouge, consists of supporters of Pol Pot (who has officially retired as head of the Khmer Rouge), whose record of brutalities and repression can hardly be exceeded by the Heng Samrin regime and its Vietnamese masters. Under the circumstances, however, there seems to be no realistic alternative option.

Thailand, of course, is particularly affected by events in the adjoining area of Indochina that have spilled across Thai borders in an alarming way. Its alarm is heightened by the presence of more than 100,000 Vietnamese troops just across the Thai frontier with Kampuchea, and by the frequent clashes—thus far rather minor in nature—between Vietnamese and Thai troops, always presenting the threat of larger clashes or even of a Vietnamese attack. The United States shares Thailand's concern. It has assured Thailand that in the event of a military attack by Vietnam it will honor its commitments to Thailand dating back to SEATO days and reaffirmed in 1979. It has provided some military assistance to enable Thailand to develop its security capabilities to meet any Vietnamese moves. It has also provided considerable assistance to Thailand and to international relief agencies in the form of food, medical and other supplies, medical personnel, and logistic support, for the continuing flow of refugees into Thailand from the Indochina states, especially from Kampuchea, and it has permitted several hundred thousand Indochinese refugees (far more than any other country) to come to the United States.

Gareth Porter has well summarized what he calls the Reagan administration's "actual policy" and its "declaratory policy" regarding Kampuchea and Vietnam:

> The administration's policy toward the conflict over Kampuchea has been to maintain the existing polarization of the region between the Soviet Union and Vietnam, on [the] one hand, and a coalition of states including the United States, China and ASEAN, on the other. This policy does not promise to free Kampuchea from Vietnamese occupation or to reduce the Soviet military presence in Vietnam any time in the near future. But it is a strategic alignment, however loose and contradictory, which is useful, in the administration's view, to its broader anti-Soviet strategy in East Asia. The administration's declaratory policy expresses the desire for a negotiated political settlement, emphasizes support for ASEAN's approach to the problem, and pledges that it will not support the restoration of the Communist Khmer Rouge leader Pol Pot to power in Kampuchea. The declaratory policy further asserts that the United States does not seek "permanent hostility to Vietnam" and would end its economic boycott and reconsider its nonrecognition of the Hanoi regime if Vietnam would withdraw its forces from Kampuchea under an ASEAN-sponsored peace plan. In practice, however, the imperatives of the administration's anti-Soviet strategy have nullified its expressed support for a compromise settlement in Kampuchea.[6]

THE UNITED STATES AND ASEAN: MUTUAL CONCERNS, INCREASING CONTACTS, AND DIFFERING PERSPECTIVES

The United States is particularly disturbed by the Soviet military presence in Vietnam because it gives the Soviets base facilities for operations in the South China Sea and the waters of both the Pacific and Indian Ocean, thus extending significantly the Soviet presence and capabilities in vital areas of these two oceans. From the major air and naval bases in Danang and Cam Ranh Bay—bases built by the Americans during the Vietnam War—Soviet planes and warships can patrol and if necessary carry on combat operations in vast areas of the Pacific and Indian Oceans. It would be more difficult to carry on such operations from more distant bases, such as Vladivostok, the headquarters of the Soviet Pacific Fleet. The Soviets are thus within easy range of the major U.S. air base at Clark Field and the huge naval base at Subic Bay in the Philippines. They insist that they have not developed major bases in Vietnam, that they use the facilities available to them simply for port visits, refueling, repairs, and rest and rehabilitation; but the United States believes that their Vietnamese facilities make it possible to go far beyond such uses. The United States, in fact, believes that a significant Soviet military presence in Vietnam may change the whole strategic balance in Southeast Asia, in its offshore waters, and in the Indian and Pacific Oceans, and that, in particular, it will threaten the major American bases in the Philippines and will put the Soviets in a position to cut off the vital sea-lanes from the Persian Gulf through the Malacca, Sunda, and Lumbok Straits to Japan and into the entire Pacific Ocean.

The ASEAN countries probably understand these offshore concerns of the United States, but they do not seem to view the new situation created by possible Soviet operations from Vietnamese bases with the same sweepingly geopolitical and apocalyptic alarms that the United States has manifested.[7] In any event, they feel that they are incapable of doing much about this. They do not want to get involved in any large-scale Soviet–American confrontation, in their own part of the world or anywhere else. The United States appreciates these positions, but it has repeatedly urged the countries lying athwart the Malacca Strait (Singapore, Malaysia, and especially Indonesia, which also controls the Sunda and Lumbok Straits) to forbid Soviet warships to transit these "choke points" or to interdict the unimpeded transit of noncombatant vessels. In 1981 a spokesman for the U.S. Department of Defense warned a subcommittee of the Senate Foreign Relations Committee that the Soviet Union intended to impose a "potential choking grip" on the sea-lanes running through the waters of Southeast Asia.[8]

Differences in security perspectives and threat perceptions between the United States and the ASEAN countries are quite comprehensible in terms of the differences in geopolitical and military capabilities and orientation between a superpower with global interests and commitments and relatively weak states with more limited regional interests and capabilities. But the differences also have deeper roots: they are historical and cultural as well as political, economic, and military. In view of the great gulfs that separate them, it is all the more impressive that in recent years relations between the ASEAN nations and the United States have become so extensive and on the whole so amicable. The ASEAN states still have doubts about the reliability and credibility of U.S. commitments to them, but they obviously now want to develop more extensive associations with the United States, and they want the United States to maintain a presence and play a positive role in the region. The broad concerns that they seem to share, in varying degrees, about the United States were summarized in a report by two American specialists on Asia after a visit to all of the ASEAN member states except Brunei in the summer of 1984:

> US policy is seen as not being comprehensive in the sense of integrating all aspects of its relations with ASEAN into fulfilling the declared commitment to the region. There is concern that the U.S. only really cares about ASEAN when the region is placed by the U.S. in relation to Soviet security policy. ASEAN elites argue that a U.S. security commitment should be more inclusive of all elements of the international environment. Most keenly felt is what is seen as the contradiction between U.S. political statements about common purposes in development and U.S. economic/commercial policy and practice. The issues are both narrow—textile quotas, GSP [Generalized System of Preferences], commodity dumping, etc.—and general— the impact of U.S. interest rates, for example, on the global economy. . . .
>
> ASEAN states do not differentiate functional areas of American foreign policy in terms of the general U.S. stance towards the region. ASEAN irritations about U.S. economic and commercial policy do have the potential to corrode political ties and the security relationship. The question of the comprehensiveness and the integration of U.S. policy in the region needs to be addressed.[9]

This kind of perceptive analysis serves as a reminder that U.S. security relationships with the ASEAN countries must be considered within the broader framework of overall relations and of a comprehensive approach to the whole question of security.

Differences in the relations and perceptions of the United States and the ASEAN countries with respect to the other major external actors in the region—the Soviet Union, China, and Japan—introduce further complications in U.S.–ASEAN relations. As has been noted, the views of most ASEAN states regarding the Soviet threat, in the region or globally, are rather different from and more relaxed than those of the United States, or at least of official U.S. spokespersons. The same observation may be made with regard to the People's Republic of China, although in this case the views of the United States regarding the present or potential Chinese threat to Southeast Asia or the entire Western Pacific area are considerably more relaxed than those of some of the ASEAN states, notably Indonesia and Malaysia. As the American specialists on Asia who have just been quoted point out: "The depth of ASEAN suspicions about the ultimate regional goals of the PRC and suspicion about any US strategic relationship with the PRC should not be underestimated. This appears to be more than simply a useful lever to wring concessions from the US."[10]

In the United States the new relations with China, beginning in the early 1970s and leading to the establishment of formal diplomatic relations in early 1979 and to extensive contacts after long years of virtually no direct contacts, were generally accepted and were regarded as an important positive step in the furtherance of U.S. national interests. But in the ASEAN countries the new relations between the most populous communist state and the most powerful noncommunist state were viewed with considerable apprehension, partly because of the fear that this might enhance China's strength and encourage expansionist and aggressive actions directed at Southeast Asia, perhaps even with the support of the United States. Southeast Asians tend to be very suspicious of China, and the new relationships between China and the United States have added to their suspicions. They are particularly alarmed by the possibility of U.S. military assistance to China. For this reason, as Gareth Porter has observed, "The [U.S.] administration's decision in mid-1981 to sell lethal military equipment to China sent shock waves through the littoral states."[11] Thus far very little military aid has in fact been given, mainly due to China's hesitancy in becoming dependent upon the major noncommunist power for any significant military assistance, and also due to many logistical and financial difficulties and limitations. But any significant U.S. military assistance to the People's Republic of China would certainly have adverse effects on U.S.–ASEAN relations.

U.S. relations with Japan also introduce complications in the U.S.–ASEAN relationship. Suspicions of Japan in Southeast Asia are still strong. The peoples of the ASEAN countries still remember the Japanese occupation during World War II, and they view with some apprehension Japan's growing strength, influence, and presence. As the United States, however, they seem to want Japan to play an even greater economic role in the region than it is playing at present. Japan is already the main trading partner of most of the ASEAN countries and a main source of technology and investment. Their ambivalent feelings with regard to economic relations with Japan were clearly stated by two American Asia specialists: "The ASEAN countries want greater levels of assistance than Japan is yet prepared to offer. At the same time, they are suspicious of Japan's interest in the region."[12] And they are particularly suspicious of and opposed to any significant expansion of Japanese military strength and any Japanese naval or military operations in or near their region. For this reason they strongly objected to the somewhat reluctant Japanese decision, made under strong U.S. pressure, to develop its capabilities and to assume some major responsibility for the patrol of sea-lanes around Japan, to a distance of 1000 nautical miles.

For many years the United states has had extensive contacts with all of the member states of ASEAN, on both a bilateral and multilateral basis. More recently it has been developing extensive ties with ASEAN itself. A major channel of mutual consultation is the so-called postministerial dialogue that is now held every year, following the annual meeting of ASEAN foreign ministers. In these postministerial consultations the foreign ministers of the ASEAN countries meet with their counterparts in the European Economic Community and in the countries with which they have the most extensive economic and political ties—Japan, the United States, Australia, New Zealand, and Canada. At these meetings a wide range of matters of mutual interest and concern is discussed. High-level dialogues on economic questions—particularly trade and investment—are also now held periodically. Representatives of the United States and ASEAN are in touch at other levels and in other ways, including frequent visits, consultations, and exchanges. To illustrate the nature and scope of the high-level contacts and interchanges between the United States and ASEAN, reference may be made to remarks by Michael H. Armacost, U.S. under secretary of state for political affairs, in an address in New York in January 1985. In this address he called attention to "an intensive round of consultations coming up with ASEAN," and he cited the following examples:

> U.S. Special Trade Representative Bill Brock will meet with ASEAN trade ministers in Malaysia in early February. One focus of his talks will be proposals for a U.S.–ASEAN reciprocal trading agreement, as well as a new multilateral trade negotiating round. We will meet in Washington in late March or early April with ASEAN economic and trade ministers for our periodic high-level dialogue covering both policy and practical trade and investment matters. And Secretary Shultz will again lead our delegation to the ASEAN postministerial consultations to be held this year in mid-July in Kuala Lumpur.[13]

ASEAN came into existence as a nonmilitary organization, and security matters have seldom been placed on its formal agenda; but since the Vietnamese move into Cambodia (Kampuchea) ASEAN states have frequently exchanged views on measures to counter any possible threats to their security resulting from the developments in Indochina and the direct involvement of the Soviet Union and China in that area. At their annual meetings the foreign ministers of the ASEAN states have frequently discussed security problems directly among themselves, although not in formal ASEAN sessions. They have also had exchanges on security problems with their counterparts in the United States, Japan, and other dialogue partners at the annual postministerial consultations.

ASEAN is not being militarized, as the Soviets claim, nor is the United States trying to exert pressure on ASEAN in this direction, as the Soviets also claim; but in spite of the deliberate exclusion of security issues from ASEAN since its inception, these issues have intruded themselves in various ways ever since the organization was founded. In more recent years ASEAN has been increasingly involved in such issues. It has provided a forum for joint consideration of major problems with which its member states are concerned, and in a more indirect way, especially through the postministerial meetings, for consultations on security as well as other matters of mutual interest and concern with its dialogue partners. Apparently there has been some consideration of the possibility of developing "confidence-building measures," conducting joint military exercises and training programs, and working out some programs of joint cooperation against any security threat. Apparently, also, some tentative proposals have been advanced, either by ASEAN countries or from some of the dialogue partners, for possible external military assistance and other forms of military preparation, cooperation, and planning.[14] But ASEAN has been a reluctant participant in, and an infrequent instigator of, such proposals. Hence most U.S. security relationships in Southeast Asia have been developed outside of the ASEAN framework, usually bilaterally with some of ASEAN's member states.

U.S. SECURITY RELATIONSHIPS WITH ASEAN STATES

The Philippines

The oldest and closest political and security ties that the United States has with any of the ASEAN states are of course with the Philippines, with which the United States has had a special relationship since the turn of the century. Since the granting of independence to the Philippines after the end of World War II, the United States has continued to have special ties and relationships with that country, and also special responsibilities and commitments, including guarantees of military assistance and protection. The military bases agreement dates from March 1947. It has been amended and renewed many times, most recently in 1983 (the next review is scheduled for 1988). The mutual security treaty between the United States and the Philippines dates from 1951. The Philippines was one of the two Southeast Asian—and presently ASEAN—countries that were members of the U.S.-sponsored SEATO.

In the Philippines the United States maintains two of its most important military bases outside its own borders—the huge naval base at Subic Bay and the largest air base outside of the United States at nearby Clark Field. These bases have taken on added importance with the enhanced American military presence in the Western Pacific and the Indian Ocean and the buildup of Soviet military power and bases in the same region. The development of Soviet air and naval facilities in Vietnam, mainly at Cam Ranh Bay and Danang, presents a more direct Soviet threat to the U.S. bases in the Philippines and puts the Soviets in a position to disrupt the vital sea-lanes through the narrow straits in Southeast Asia and to support its political and propagandistic efforts to turn ASEAN countries against the United States.

The future of the U.S. bases in the Philippines is imperiled more seriously by the uncertainties about the future political evolution of that country, by the growing anti-U.S. feeling, by the increasing activities and strength of the Communist New People's Army (NPA), and by the serious political and economic crisis in the Philippines. U.S. support of the long-lived but increasingly unpopular Marcos regime, which was less manifest after the assassination of opposition leader Benigno Aquino in August 1983, was widely critized in the Philippines, the United States, and elsewhere. It seemed to be essential if the United States was to be permitted to maintain its military bases in the Philippines. Marcos showed considerable hesitation and drove a hard bargain when the agreement came up for renegotiation in 1982–1983. The new agreement extended the lease on the bases to 1991, but it also called for a commitment of the Reagan administration "to ask Congress for a five-year, $900 million package of security and economic assistance to the Philippines. . . . The United States also agreed that the Philippines should assume greater responsibility for the defense of the seas surrounding the islands."[15]

The impact of the deteriorating political and economic situation in the Philippines upon security and overall U.S.–Philippine relations, and upon U.S. security interests in Southeast Asia and the Western Pacific, was clearly delineated in the report of two American Asia specialists after their visit to the ASEAN countries in mid-1984:

> We cannot overestimate the seriousness of the domestic situation in the Philippines. It is no longer a question of recovery or even stability. It is now a question of survival. This means more than the survival of the incumbent leadership. We mean the survival of the system. Of all the ASEAN states, it is the Philippines that appears most vulnerable to the kind of insecurity, economic collapse, and failure of domestic leadership that theoretically could present opportunities for the Soviet Union. . . .
>
> If the principal strategic objective of the Soviet Union in the Philippines is the termination of U.S. rights in Subic and Clark, then the continuing interacting downward economic, social and political spirals are very relevant. If domestic frustrations and anger are channeled into radical nationalist directions and against external actors (banks, the IMF, the US, capitalism) held responsible for the current crisis, then the fundamental political basis of the US–Philippines partnership on the bases would be at risk. The existing anti-base orientations of the intellectuals and left-opposition . . . could be translated to a wider audience. Aggravating the attack on the strategic partnership is the feeling on the part of even the traditional friends of the US in the Philippines government that the US has not been as helpful in the crisis as it might have.[16]

The Philippines is the only ASEAN state that is experiencing such a serious internal crisis and that has not achieved an impressive rate of economic growth in recent years. It also happens to be the ASEAN state with which, as has been noted, the United States has been and is most closely associated. The internal crisis in the Philippines is already having adverse effects on the U.S.–Philippine relationship, and is casting a cloud over the future of the major U.S. bases at Subic Bay and Clark Field. It is quite clear that from a security as well as a political perspective the United States must follow the course of events in the Philippines very carefully, and must constantly reassess its policies toward its oldest Asian ally.

The traumatic events in the Philippines in February 1986, which led to the abrupt ending of the Marcos era and the accession to power of Corazon ("Cory") Aquino, widow of Benigno Aquino, profoundly changed the political situation in the country. It remains to be seen whether the Aquino regime can maintain its widespread popular support and can arrest the deterioration in the political, economic, and social order. The legitimacy of the regime was greatly strengthened by the overwhelming approval (nearly 80 percent of those voting) of a proposed new constitution in a referendum on February 2, 1987. The constitution in effect recognized Aquino as the winner of the disputed election of 1986 and granted her a six-year term as President. The slogan "A Vote for the Charter is a vote for Cory" was clearly a winning one.

Aquino and other leaders of the new regime have been highly critical of the United States in the past, but they were generally pleased with the position of the United States during and after the February 1986 crisis, including U.S. criticisms of the fraudulent practices of Marcos supporters in the national elections, pressure on Marcos to abandon his fight to remain in power and to leave the country rather than risk a bloody civil war, and the prompt recognition of the new government and substantial tangible and intangible assistance to that government.

Aquino's first official visit to the United States after she became President of the Philippines, in September 1986, was a great personal success. She was warmly received, and she did much to personify and dramatize the problems facing her country and her hopes for the future. She was given assurances of strong support from President Reagan and top leaders in the U.S. Congress— assurances that led to some promises of increased aid, not all of which were subsequently fulfilled. She expressed a deep appreciation for U.S. assistance, both tangible and intangible; but she was also frank in stating that her country needed far more assistance than the United States seemed willing to extend. This assistance, she argued, was not an act of charity on behalf of a distressed ally, but a program that was as important for the United States as for the Philippines. When Senator Robert Dole, majority leader in the U.S. Senate, told her that in her address to a joint session of Congress she had "hit a home run," she promptly quipped: "I hope the bases were loaded." Unfortunately, from her perspective the bases were not loaded, and it is still doubtful whether they will ever be, even if the indomitable "Cory" is able to hit more home runs.

The impact of the change in political direction in the Philippines on U.S.– Philippine relations is still uncertain. It seems to provide new opportunities for improved relations, at least as long as the governments in both countries sincerely desire this, as well as some new problems and sensitivities.

The issue of the U.S. bases in the Philippines will remain a delicate but apparently not an immediately critical one. In spite of Aquino's frequently stated opposition to any foreign bases in her country, she has stated that she will honor the existing bases agreement, which permits the United States to use the bases until 1991, leaving her future options open. The new constitution bans foreign military bases after the lease on U.S. air and naval installations expires in 1991; but it also provides that foreign bases will be permitted after 1991, if permission is incorporated in a bilateral treaty subject to senate approval and, if the Filipino Congress required, a national referendum.

The future of the bases would be imperiled by a reversal of past policy, or by a continued political, economic, and social deterioration in the Philippines that might lead to internal chaos and/or the establishment of an authoritarian regime of the extreme left (i.e., the Communist Party) or the extreme right (i.e., the military). Because of these continuing uncertainties, the United States is considering possible alternatives for the Philippine bases, although any alternative would be far less desirable from a strategic and financial point of view.

In this delicate and uncertain environment the United States must move with particular care and caution, and with particular consideration of the sensitivities of the Philippine people and the realities of the internal scene. The U.S.–Philippine relationship will continue to be extensive, if often strained. It is quite clear that from a security as well as a political perspective the United States must follow the course of events in the Philippines very carefully, and must constantly reassess its policies toward its oldest Asian ally.

Thailand

"Military ties are central to the United States relationship with Thailand," Professor Gareth Porter has asserted. "The United States has a security commitment to Thailand under the Manila Treaty of 1954 and the Rusk-Thanat agreement of 1962."[17] When SEATO was in existence, Thailand often joined with the United States in bilateral and multilateral military exercises, and thousands of Thai military personnel were given advanced training in the United States. During the U.S. military involvement in Vietnam, Thailand permitted the United States to carry on air operations against Vietnam from Thai bases. It has also given the United States special facilities for air surveillance over large areas of the Western Pacific and the Indian Ocean. In the years following the American withdrawal from Vietnam relations between the United States and Thailand were cooler and more limited, but extensive military and other kinds of consultation and collaboration were resumed following the Vietnamese move into Cambodia (Kampuchea) in 1978. "The United States agrees with Thailand that Soviet-backed Vietnam, rather than China, is the major threat to the region. (Indonesia and Malaysia still view China as the main adversary.)"[18]

U.S. military assistance to Thailand has increased substantially since 1979. When Thailand's Prime Minister Prem Tinsulanonda visited Washington in April 1984, the United States "reaffirmed its commitment to Thai national security ... and promised to upgrade Thailand's weaponry."[19] President Reagan even told the prime minister that Thailand's request for a squadron of F-16 jet fighter planes—more sophisticated aircraft than has been made available to any other ASEAN nation—would be favorably considered. His administration, however, "asked the Thais to consider as an alternative the F-20 Tigershark, a lower-cost plane with 'intermediate capabilities' planned specifically for export to non-NATO ... allies,"[20] but the Thai military leadership rejected this suggestion.

Thailand is understandably concerned about the threat from Vietnam, which has the fourth or fifth largest army in the world and is strongly backed by the Soviet Union. The Vietnamese presence in Kampuchea, which has led to a flood of refugees from Kampuchea into Thailand, the operations of Cambodian opposition groups against the Heng Samrin Vietnamese-backed regime from Thai territory, and the presence of some 100,000 Vietnamese troops along the eastern borders of Thailand, are daily reminders of the existing threats. The United States regards Thailand as a "front-line" state—on a front where the Soviet as well as the Vietnamese threat is growing—and it has extended a variety of forms of military and other support to Thailand, without any commitment of American troops. Its close identification with the military-dominated regime in Thailand presents some hazards, both to itself and to Thailand. Some of these hazards are described by two American specialists on Asia:

> Most Thais agree that a strong American military presence is needed in the region to balance the Soviet Union and that the US should avoid any destabilizing actions. American policy in the immediate post-Vietnam period is viewed as opening opportunities for the USSR in a kind of vacuum filling exercise. On the other hand, a discussion of the US–Thai relationship quickly brings to the surface a major internal disagreement within the Thai elite, dividing the civilian section from the leading faction of the military. There is concern that with the prompting of the US in terms of overstating the Soviet threat ammunition has been given to those who would deform economic priorities by using this threat perception to justify a military buildup and skewing budget allocations to further favor the military. ... At this point in Thai political history, acts designed to enhance the domestic authority of the military would be destabilizing and play into the hands of the enemies of Thailand and the US.[21]

Indonesia

During their visit to Indonesia in 1984 the two American observers were impressed with Indonesia's "more active and nationalistic foreign policy," with the many signs of "a cooling of U.S.–Indonesian relations," a "growing disenchantment with the United States," and a feeling "that the U.S. under-values its political relationship with Indonesia" and "does not recognize in deeds the fact that Indonesia has been a responsible agent of stability in Southeast Asia which has promoted US interests." They also found that "the China threat looms large in Indonesian eyes," whereas the Soviet Union "is seen as a countervailing power particularly given the U.S.–Chinese relationship, ... as holding a key to the solution of the Kampuchean crisis," and "as a potential source of new aid and assistance, technology, resources and trade." In Indonesia, they reported, "the notion of the equivalency of the great powers seems to be most deeply entrenched."[22]

This kind of orientation is obviously based on very different perspectives from those of the United States. But the two countries also have many interests in common, and contacts and exchanges between them are growing on many fronts. The United States will have to defer to Indonesia's rather sensitive moods and to Indonesia's quest for greater national independence (or "national resilience," to use a favorite Indonesian term) and for "equidistance" in foreign poicy. The United States must seek to develop a better working relationship with the most populous nation of Southeast Asia, one that plays a central role in ASEAN and in regional affairs generally. Except in the broadest sense of "comprehensive security," the security aspects of U.S.–Indonesian relationships will not be uppermost in the formal interactions between the two states.[23]

Malaysia

Malaysia shares many of the Indonesian perspectives regarding the United States and the Soviet Union, and the nature of security threats. Malaysia and Indonesia have explicitly rejected United States views of the Soviet Union as the major threat to the region; they regard China as the major external threat.[24] Malaysia, like Indonesia, is disturbed by the expanding U.S. relations with China, and especially by any signs of security collaboration between these two countries, limited as this collaboration has actually been.

Datuk Seri Mahathir Muhammad, a dynamic leader who became Prime Minister of Malaysia in July 1981, introduced many new orientations in domestic and foreign policies, designed to give Malaysia greater internal cohesion, independence, and self-reliance. His "Look East" foreign policy—marked by a turn toward Japan, South Korea, and the island nations of the Southwest Pacific and away from the "decadence" of the West—led to a cooling in relations with the United States and the countries of Western Europe; but at the same time the United States and Malaysia continued to maintain generally friendly and fairly extensive relations, especially of an economic nature. Because of the divergence in security interests and perceptions, the security aspects of the relationship have been limited and low-key, although the United States has provided limited military assistance to Malaysia and is in touch with that country on security as on other matters in a number of regional and international forums, especially in the postministerial consultations with ASEAN states.[25]

Singapore

As the world's busiest port and a flourishing entrepot of international commerce, banking, and trade, and as one of the so-called "four little tigers" of Asia, along with South Korea, Taiwan, and Hong Kong, all economically dynamic small polities, Singapore is more obviously linked to the outside world and is less regionally oriented than the other ASEAN states. It has generally taken a more pronounced stand in favor of the military as well as the political and economic presence of major powers in Southeast Asia than have its neighbors. It has not hesitated to cooperate with the United States in many ways, even in certain aspects of security planning. It was also more outspoken about the developments in Vietnam than other ASEAN countries. It insists that its publicly stated views are more reflective of prevailing opinions in other ASEAN states than they would seem to be. But in recent years it "has adopted a lower regional profile," and it has followed policies and taken positions in ASEAN that seem to be more in tune with the official stance of the other members. "After several past embarrassments Singapore certainly does not wish to get too far out of step from their [sic] ASEAN colleagues. Singapore is ASEAN's only NIC [newly industrialized country] but is sensitive to the fact that the other ASEAN states view the region as part of the third world and as such cannot openly embrace the U.S. There will always be a tendency to pull the eagle's beak."[26]

In their report on a visit to the ASEAN countries in 1984 two American Asian specialists asked: "If the Singapore position on the USSR is basically unchanged and of all the ASEAN nations the most attuned to US official perceptions, why is Singapore more reluctant today to vigorously advocate them in ASEAN circles and beyond?" They suggest an answer: "One very important reason is the China factor. Given the political attitudes of its Indonesian and Malaysian neighbors, Singapore does not want to give the impression that its line on the U.S.S.R. is similar to the PRC's."[27]

SOUTHEAST ASIA IN THE U.S. SECURITY PICTURE

For some time after its costly and bitter experience in Vietnam, the United States gave relatively little attention to Southeast Asia, except in the context of its global political and security interests and preoccupations. Even its relations with the Philippines and with its other long-time Southeast Asian partner in SEATO, Thailand, became more distant and seemed to be relegated to a relatively low priority in the pantheon of U.S. priorities and concerns. But even during this period, when the United States was recovering from its unhappy experience in Vietnam, its ties with all of the ASEAN states, but not with Indochina and Burma (which had adopted a policy of relative isolation from the outside world), continued to be much more extensive, especially in the economic field, than was generally realized. More recently the United States has returned, so to speak, to East and Southeast Asia, and again has extensive relations with and a conspicuous role in that part of the world.

U.S. security interests and ties in Southeast Asia are overshadowed by other dimensions of the relationship. Many of these are still more closely related to its global security concerns, especially with relation to the Soviet threat wherever it is manifest, than to its security concerns in the region. This is the case of such dominating interests as the independence, stability, and development of the noncommunist nations of Southeast Asia, the protection of these nations against any threats emanating from the Soviet Union or from

Vietnam (which is supported by the Soviet Union), the protection of sea-lanes, unimpeded access through the vital straits of Southeast Asia, and the maintenance and protection of the major U.S. bases in the Philippines. U.S. security concerns in the region seem to grow or decline in accordance with the growth or decline of Soviet presence and power in the region, and to a lesser extent in accordance with the evolution and activities of the Communist regime in Vietnam. Southeast Asia is given much less attention than East Asia in U.S. security policies and planning. But it is receiving greater attention even in this respect than it has received for many years, and there is a growing recognition in the United States that the security of East and Southeast Asia, and of the Pacific and Indian Oceans, both of which extend to Southeast Asia, is inextricably interlinked.

Security considerations certainly account in part for the growing U.S. interest in ASEAN, but of course the main links with ASEAN are not primarily of a security nature. There is a growing feeling in the United States that it should pay more attention to ASEAN, for many reasons. Its record to date in this respect has been rather spotty. The need to give ASEAN a higher priority is well brought out by Donald S. Zagoria:

> [A]fter strengthening its alliance with Japan and consolidating its relations with China, the United States needs to expand its relations with ASEAN. .... Together the five [now six] ASEAN countries account for about one-quarter of total U.S. trade with the Pacific. .... Strategically, a unified ASEAN serves as a barrier to the further expansion of Soviet influence in the region. ... In the recent past several American administrations have tended to take this region for granted as they concentrated on relations with the major powers. The Reagan administration seems to have reversed this unhealthy trend. But a great deal of work remains to be done to convince the region that the United States is a reliable, long-term ally, that it is not going to 'farm out' the region to Japanese or Chinese protection, and that it seeks a genuine partnership.[28]

In Southeast Asia, perhaps more than in any other part of the Western Pacific, doubts about American credibility and reliability are particularly pervasive. This important aspect of the views of Southeast Asians toward the United States was clearly perceived by the two American specialists who visited the ASEAN countries in 1984:

> The credibility of the American commitment to ASEAN remains in doubt. Although the rhetorical reemphasis of the US–ASEAN link is acknowledged and appreciated, and the fact of the enhancement of US naval capabilities is understood as a stabilizing element in the new power dynamic of the region, nevertheless, the political significance of these symbols of commitment is diminished by three factors which, although independent in origin, have a cumulative impact: (a) Recent historical memories of American policy in the region have not been overcome ..., (b) U.S. policy is seen as not being comprehensive in the sense of integrating all aspects of its relations with ASEAN into fulfilling the declared commitment to the region ..., (c) ASEAN leaderships continue to be concerned about US ultimate purposes in the fostering of its strategic relations with the PRC and Japan.[29]

In spite of these reservations in ASEAN countries and in spite of continued U.S. ambivalence about ASEAN and the nature and extent of U.S. security and other interests in Southeast Asia, any serious consideration of U.S. security relationships and concerns in the Western Pacific must give more attention to Southeast Asia than it has in the past. Quite understandably, the focus of U.S. security relationships in the entire area will continue to be on East Asia, and especially on its interactions with the Soviet Union, Japan, and China in that subregion. But Southeast Asia should have an important place in the overall security picture, and the United States should recognize and adjust to this rather neglected reality.

Notes

[1] Peter Polomka, "The Security of the Western Pacific: The Price of Burden Sharing," *Survival* 26 (January/February 1984): 7.

[2] Unpublished report of "a two-man team of the Pacific Forum"—Lloyd R. Vasey, president and executive director of the Pacific Forum, and Donald E. Weatherbee, professor of political science at the University of South Carolina—that "travelled through the ASEAN region" in July and August 1984 "as a followup to the Forum's May 1984 Core Study Group Conference on 'Soviet Policies in the Asian Pacific Region,'" p. 17. (Hereafter referred to as the Vasey-Weatherbee Report).

[3] William T. Tow and William R. Feeney, eds., *U.S. Foreign Policy and Asian-Pacific Security: A Transregional Approach* (Boulder, Colorado: Westview Press, 1982), p. 12.

[4] Gareth Porter, "The United States and Southeast Asia," *Current History* 83 (December 1984): 402.

[5] Quoted in ibid. The defense plan also mentioned a second major aim, namely to develop "further the capacity of member countries to support the projection of United States power from the Western Pacific to the Indian Ocean and . . . the Gulf."

[6] Ibid., p. 437.

[7] As Gareth Porter has pointed out: "Malaysia and Indonesia have explicitly rejected United States views of the Soviet Union and Vietnam as threats to the region. Both believe that the Reagan administration is obsessed with the Soviet threat in general and that the United States has exaggerated the danger of the Soviet military presence in Southeast Asia. They do not believe that the Soviet naval presence in the region is aimed at disrupting maritime traffic through the Straits of Malacca or the South China Sea; they see it as an effort to achieve equal status as a superpower with the United States. They also note that the Soviet naval presence in Vietnam is no match for the United States presence at Subic Bay in the Philippines." Ibid., pp. 403–404.

[8] Richard L. Armitage, deputy assistant secretary of defense, *U.S. Policy in Southeast Asia*, Hearings before the Subcommittee on East Asian and Pacific Affairs, Committee on Foreign Relations of the U.S. Senate, 1981, p. 34.

[9] Vasey-Weatherbee Report, pp. 6 and 16.

[10] Ibid., p. 16.

[11] "The United States and Southeast Asia," p. 404.

[12] Donald S. Zagoria and Sheldon W. Simon, "Soviet Policy in Southeast Asia," chapter 16 in Donald S. Zagoria, ed., *Soviet Policy in East Asia* (New Haven: Yale University Press, 1982), p. 173.

[13] "The Asia-Pacific Region: A Forward Look," address before the Far East–America Council/ Asia Society, New York, Jan. 29, 1985; Bureau of Public Affairs, U.S. Department of State, *Current Policy*, no. 653, pp. 2–3. .

[14] See Sheldon W. Simon, *The ASEAN States and Regional Security* (Stanford, Calif.: Hoover Institution Press, 1982), pp. 113–119. It should be emphasized, however, that the post-ministerials are designed to provide a forum for an exchange of views among the foreign ministers of the ASEAN states and their counterparts in their dialogue partners on a wide variety of subjects. In his welcoming remarks at the postministerial meeting in Jakarta in July 1984, the foreign minister of Indonesia, Mochtar Kusumaatmadja, singled out for special mention the agreement of ASEAN and its dialogue partners that "there is a need for more concerted economic policies to achieve sustained world economic recovery," and the support of the dialogue partners for an ASEAN program for human resources development, which he described as "a concrete scheme covering a broad spectrum dealing with economic, social and political fields." Security problems were not mentioned by the foreign minister. See "ASEAN

Ministerial Conference with the Dialogue Partners in Jakarta," *Indonesian News and Views* 4 (July 20, 1984): 2–3.

[15] Porter, "The United States and Southeast Asia," p. 402.

[16] Vasey-Weatherbee Report, pp. 7 and 9.

[17] Porter, "The United States and Southeast Asia," p. 404.

[18] Clark D. Neher, "Political Forces in Thailand," *Current History* 83 (December 1984): 436. See also Porter, "The United States and Southeast Asia," pp. 403–404.

[19] Neher, "Political Forces in Thailand," p. 436.

[20] Porter, "The United States and Southeast Asia," p. 437.

[21] Vasey-Weatherbee Report, pp. 10–11.

[22] Ibid., pp. 13–14.

[23] This is true of U.S. relations with both Indonesia and Malaysia. "Neither Malaysia nor Indonesia depends on United States military power for regional security. So the Reagan administration must rely on bilateral ties to secure both countries' cooperation with United States global military strategy. The United States sells arms to both countries and pays for the training of their military officers in the United States. (Between 250 and 300 Indonesian officers will be trained in the United States in FY 1985.) But these links, while welcomed, are not the crucial factors that determine the Malay states' attitude toward the United States." Porter, "The United States and Southeast Asia," p. 404.

[24] Ibid., pp. 403–404.

[25] See Hans H. Indorf, "A Hobson's Choice for Malaysia," *Current History* 82 (April 1983); Diane K. Mauzy and R. S. Milne, "The Mahathir Administration in Malaysia: Discipline Through Islam," *Pacific Affairs* 56 (1983–1984); and R. S. Milne and Diane K. Mauzy, "Malaysia's Policies and Leadership," *Current History* 83 (December 1984).

[26] Vasey-Weatherbee Report, p. 15.

[27] Ibid.

[28] Donald S. Zagoria, "The Strategic Environment in Asia," chapter 1 in Zagoria, ed., *Soviet Policy in East Asia*, p. 27.

[29] Vasey-Weatherbee Report, pp. 5–6.

CHAPTER 8

The United States and Security in the Southwest Pacific and Oceania

In the Southwest Pacific, as in East and Southeast Asia, the strategic environment has undergone significant changes, and the United States must adjust its security thinking and policies to take these changes into account. The most obvious change is the development of serious strains within ANZUS and at least the temporary breakup of this security pact, which the United States concluded in 1951 with Australia and New Zealand (the two main actors in the Southwest Pacific) and which until the mid-1980s seemed to be one of the most stable security relationships in the world.

DIFFERING THREAT PERCEPTIONS

Far removed from the central theaters of superpower conflict, America's ANZUS partners (or former partners) have always been less concerned with the Soviet threat than has the United States; and they have rather different conceptions of the nature and seriousness of that threat. Moreover, as a two-person team representing the Pacific Forum in Honolulu, which visited Australia and New Zealand in October and November 1984, reported, "the salience of a Soviet threat has in recent years receded in Australia and New Zealand. ... We ... found opinion in both countries becoming very complacent about the Soviet Union."[1] The prevailing views in terms of capability analysis *vis-à-vis* the Soviet Union that they discerned were particularly interesting:

> Among those who study the subject closely, the consensus is that the U.S. and allied resources are presently at least a match; that despite the advantages generated by their naval and air basing privileges in Vietnam, the Soviets are not nearly as uniformly well-placed throughout the Pacific basin as are the combined assets of countervailing powers. . . . [T]here is a growing view that, while not illusory, Soviet power is nevertheless not the power of a fully developed superpower. The Soviets are an incomplete superpower, burdened at home with seemingly intractable socio-economic weaknesses. In the Pacific basin area, they are seen as quite unable to project political or economic influence of any consequence, even when they attempt to influence by flexing military strength. The Soviets are described as unable to displace unliked regimes, to change the foreign and defense policies of regional nations, to entangle those nations in elaborate economic dependence on Moscow. If anything, the Soviets have succeeded in alienating much of opinion in Asia and the Pacific. Present circumstances in

Vietnam are not seen as a real exception to this rule. The tenor of those who are especially keen on this view is that the Soviet "threat" has been oversold, since it is essentially unidimensional (i.e., military), and not as fearsome as others would insist.[2]

Clearly the United States would be prominent among the "others" in this analysis. Since many in Australia and New Zealand seem to be more concerned with the danger of involvement in great power conflicts than with unilateral threats from the Soviet Union, the United States is sometimes perceived as in some respects a possible source of threat as well as of assistance in the event of a Soviet effort to project power and influence in the Western Pacific by the use of its growing military capabilities in the region for aggressive purposes. As the members of the Pacific Forum team observed:

> Threat perceptions in New Zealand and Australia have also been taking on disheartening features that, implicitly or explicitly, indict the United States as well as the Soviet Union. These views enjoy some currency within moderate political circles, but they are especially common-place among the left wings of the two labor parties, among small but vocal political parties, and among dissident groups. They enjoy a wider following among mass New Zealand than among mass Australian opinion.[3]

Australia and New Zealand, in short, are fearful of the possible repercussions upon them of continuing superpower confrontation and above all of an all-out nuclear conflict beween the superpowers.

EXTRAREGIONAL TIES AND ACTIVITIES OF AUSTRALIA AND NEW ZEALAND

Nevertheless, Australia and New Zealand have many links—political, economic, security, and psychological—with the Western democracies, especially with Britain and the United States. Their orientation is heavily and admittedly toward the West. It is almost inconceivable that they could or would turn away from the West, or isolate themselves from the outside world, let alone establish ties closer to the Soviet Union than to the Western democracies or adopt a pro-Soviet stance in regional or world affairs. In military as well as in political and economic relationships they have shown a willingness to become involved, to a limited degree at least, well beyond the confines of the Southwest Pacific.

Australia, in particular, is an Indian Ocean as well as a Southwest Pacific nation, and it has been continually concerned with the changing geopolitics of the entire Indian Ocean area. It has allowed the United States to establish a large number of naval and air facilities and communication and monitoring stations on Australian soil, and it has engaged in continuing consultations with the United States, in ANZUS and bilaterally, about Indian Ocean developments and interests.[4] It has also been particularly concerned about developments in Southeast Asia, an adjoining region. Its relations with Southeast Asian countries have been both conflictual and cooperative. With Malaysia and Singapore, fellow commonwealth countries, it has maintained special ties, mainly cooperative. With Indonesia, the Southeast Asian nation whose territories extend over vast reaches of the Indian and Pacific Oceans just to the north, its relations have often been more conflictual than cooperative, but whatever their nature they have been quite extensive. Criticism of Australia is quite frequently voiced in Indonesia, and Australians are often critical of Indonesian policies, many of which they regard as inimical to Australia's national interests and security.

New Zealand is less active than Australia in extraregional affairs, but it too is involved in the Commonwealth, the United Nations and its organs and agencies, and many other multilateral relationships and associations beyond its region.

Australia and New Zealand, together with the United Kingdom, are associated with Malaysia and Singapore in the so-called Five-Power Defense Pact (FPDP), and both antipodean nations still maintain some air and ground forces in these two Southeast Asian countries. Both sent small military and other contingents to assist the U.S. military effort in Vietnam, not so much because of any special interest in the struggle in Vietnam as because a small-scale contribution to the struggle in Vietnam was perceived as a means of demonstrating their support of the United States, their ANZUS ally.

With Japan, Australia and New Zealand have been developing some military ties, as well as quite extensive economic relations. Naval and other units of Japan's SDF have participated in joint exercises with the ANZUS countries and Canada, beginning with the large-scale RIMPAC Pacific Rim exercise in 1980. There has even been some speculation about a possible formal association of Japan with ANZUS, which would have broadened the scope of that security arrangement and turned it into what some have described as JANZUS.[5]

The extraregional ties and roles of Australia and New Zealand are still extensive, but recent trends in both nations provide clear signals that, like many other nations in the Western Pacific, their policies and actions will reflect their growing nationalistic assertiveness and determination to function as more independent actors on the world scene. These new trends will doubtless have an impact on their international posture and foreign policies—in fact, there are many evidences that this is already happening—without necessarily leading to a lessening in their international roles or in their general pro-Western orientation. But the implications of these new trends, as well as of the prevailing threat perceptions and perspectives on the Soviet Union, should not be overlooked, especially in the United States. The new dimensions of the external orientation of Australia and New Zealand were thus diagnosed by members of the Pacific Forum team:

> The gradual trend toward less agitated Australian and New Zealand perceptions of the Soviet threats, direct or indirect, may seem somewhat unusual, since both countries for generations have construed their security interests as lying far ashore. They have willingly contributed their military assets in support of powerful friends and allies such as Britain and later the United States, in part because of their felt vulnerability that seemed countervailable only through reliance on a great power. But ... both New Zealand and Australia have in

recent years thought themselves more mature and self-confident, and perhaps wiser. Lessons purportedly learned from their support of the costly, and many would say, mistaken American effort in Vietnam have added their weight to this feeling. One consequence has been something of a historical distancing from the sense of what had traditionally been broadcast about threats from one malevolent source or another. The emerging view is that successive postwar Australian and New Zealand governments, as well as the United States itself, had simply oversold Soviet and Chinese threats.[6]

UNITED STATES AND AUSTRALIA AND NEW ZEALAND: NEED FOR REASSESSMENT

Another notable recent trend in both antipodean nations, and especially in New Zealand, has been the increasing popular support of antinuclear and generally pacifist movements. Since the advent of Labor governments in both countries, this trend has had an increasing impact on governmental policies and orientation. It has already created complications in U.S. relations with both of its ANZUS allies, including a crisis in relations with New Zealand, and has raised disturbing questions about the future of U.S. relations and policies in the Southwest Pacific and especially about the future, if any, of the ANZUS alliance.

In spite of these worrisome complications, the United States continues to attach special importance to its relations with Australia and New Zealand. It recognizes that these two nations have a central role in the Southwest Pacific and are important factors in the security of the entire Western Pacific area. This point was emphasized in the 1984 report of the Pacific Forum team:

> It . . . is well to remember that despite their relatively small populations, Australia and New Zealand are disproportionately significant to the overall course of political, economic, and defense-related developments both in and outside their immediate strategic environments. This is exemplified by their participation in ANZUS and in the Five-Power Defense Arrangements; their special access to and influence especially in the South Pacific, throughout important sections of Southeast Asia and Commonwealth of Nations relationships; by their proximity to, and interest and activity in Antarctica; by the quality and professionalism of their armed forces; by the position of Australia in particular as the site of joint defense facility operations with the U.S. and for American naval and air transit privileges; and for Australia's uncommon abundance of natural resources. Features such as these invest Australia and New Zealand with exceptional importance; what they are and what they do substantially shapes Pacific region security outcomes.[7]

In spite of some recent frictions in their relations with the United States, and the growing evidences of a determination to distance themselves somewhat from their much more powerful American ally, the Labor governments in both Australia and New Zealand insist that they wish to continue the friendly and extensive relations that their two countries have long had with the United States and to remain associated with the United States in the ANZUS alliance, whatever may be the difficulties created by differences in threat perceptions, policy orientation, and attitudes on nuclear issues. Australia and New Zealand profess to attach great importance to their relationship with the United States and hope that their more powerful ally will continue to have the same feeling toward its relations with them. If they have had any major complaint in the past, it has been that the United States has tended to neglect them and has not attached sufficient importance to ANZUS, not that the United States has been assiduous in trying to persuade them to take a more active role in the overall alliance system.

All of these trends and perceptions underline the importance of reassessing U.S. relations with its Southwest Pacific allies. Such a reassessment is clearly under way in both Australia and New Zealand and is as sorely needed in the United States. It will probably lead to rather different relationships among the ANZUS partners without reversing the long-established pattern of widespread cooperation in a variety of fields.

U.S. security and other ties with Australia, the major nation in the Southwest Pacific, have been particularly close and extensive. Australia has cooperated with the United States in various ways in developing a more adequate security posture to meet possible threats in the Indian Ocean and Pacific areas, well beyond the Southwest Pacific. In this larger dimension of joint security preparation and planning, the Soviet threat, both regional and extraregional, has been clearly in mind.

The Soviets have often criticized Australia for this kind of cooperation with the United States and have often called attention to the extensive military facilities that Australia has allowed the United States to develop on Australian territory. A lead article on "Imperialist War Preparations in East Asia and Soviet Policy" in *Far Eastern Affairs*, the journal of the prestigious Institute of the Far East of the U.S.S.R. Academy of Sciences, featured the following comments on the U.S.–Australian security cooperation:

> There are about 40 American bases and other military installations on Australian territory. U.S. nuclear submarines call at the harbours of Freemantle and Cockbern [*sic*] Sound. In 1981, the Pentagon was granted the right to use Australian airfields in Darwin, Perth, and Learmond for strategic B-52 bombers. The Australian military potential is also being built up. Washington and Canberra have reached an understanding on sharing the commitments to 'defend' the region of Asia and the Pacific and step up Australia's military operations in the Indian Ocean.[8]

THE CRISIS IN ANZUS AND U.S.–NEW ZEALAND RELATIONS

For more than a generation the U.S.–Australian–New Zealand tripartite alliance (ANZUS) had been the main forum for exchanges of views and for planning collaborative policies and actions for dealing with mutual security concerns in the Southwest Pacific region and beyond. At the annual meetings of the ANZUS Council, the foreign ministers of the member states had consulted on a wide variety of issues of mutual concern, especially on those with important security dimensions. On logistic levels contacts ranged from large-scale military exercises and extensive training programs in the United States for Australian and New Zealand military personnel to frequent courtesy calls of naval vessels of the member states (especially of American warships to Australian and New Zealand ports) and contacts between military officials from an ANZUS state and their counterparts in the other member states.[9] It was apparently a solid working alliance and had widespread support in all of the member countries. From the U.S. perspective, at least, ANZUS had been one of the most satisfactory and most reliable of the many bilateral and multilateral security arrangements concluded under American leadership during the era of "pactomania" in the 1950s.

In the 1980s, however, ANZUS became an alliance in crisis because of New Zealand's refusal to allow any warships to enter its ports, even ships of ANZUS allies, unless it was assured that these warships were not carrying nuclear weapons. The United States reacted strongly to this new policy, and when no compromise could be reached officially notified both Australia and New Zealand, in April 1986, that it was scrapping the ANZUS treaty. Two months later the U.S. secretary of state, George Shultz, told New Zealand's prime minister, David Lange, that the United States no longer considered itself bound to come to New Zealand's defense under the terms of the ANZUS treaty. With Australia, however, the United States is continuing its alliance commitments, under bilateral agreements and arrangements.

The immediate crisis was precipitated by the new strains in U.S.–New Zealand relations, but the roots of the crisis go much deeper. For some time various groups in both of America's Southwest Pacific allies have voiced criticisms of ANZUS, mainly on the ground that it was an asymmetrical military relationship that made their countries' security position more precarious rather than stronger. These critics argued that the alliance did not meet their regional security needs and, by linking their countries with one of the superpowers, might bring them threats, mainly from the Soviet Union, that they were not prepared to meet by involving them in larger confrontations that they could otherwise evade. In short, they argued that the costs of the alliance outweighed the benefits and that as time went on the imbalance in the wrong direction would become all the greater.[10]

Criticisms of this kind were fueled by the antinuclear sentiment that has been growing in recent years in both Australia and New Zealand and has been given added momentum and significance by the coming to power of Labor governments in both countries. The sentiment is also strong in the newly emergent island nations of the South Pacific, nations particularly concerned about nuclear testing by the French, plans to deposit nuclear waste in the region, and U.S. plans to launch MX test missiles from California with targeted splashdown in the Tasman Sea between Australia and New Zealand.

The South Pacific Forum, a little-known but increasingly important association of South Pacific island states, including Australia and New Zealand, has taken a leading role in voicing antinuclear sentiments and protests and in championing the proposal for declaring the South Pacific a nuclear-weapons-free zone. In August 1984 the fourteen members of the Forum called "for a ban on depositing nuclear waste, nuclear testing, and manufacture and possession of nuclear weapons in the region." The Australian prime minister, Robert Hawke, "negotiated a year's postponement during which he would chair a committee to draw up a proposed nuclear-free-zone treaty to deal with these issues."[11] A year later such a treaty was approved by the members of the South Pacific Forum.

Antinuclear sentiment in both Australia and New Zealand became an important political factor, with possible diminution of support for the ANZUS alliance, with the election of Labor governments in both countries— in Australia in March 1983 and in New Zealand in July 1984. Prime Minister Robert Hawke of Australia won considerable popularity in his country and region by his strong support of a nuclear weapons free zone in the South Pacific, and he often expressed his aversion to nuclear weapons and nuclear diplomacy; but his government remained on good terms with the United States, the nuclear superpower ally, continued to permit the United States to use facilities in Australia, and strongly supported the ANZUS alliance. The Labor government in New Zealand took a more adamant antinuclear position, which caused estrangement with Australia as well as the United States. Its position made New Zealand a virtually noncooperating member of ANZUS. This raised serious doubts about the future of ANZUS[12] and in 1986 led the United States to withdraw from the alliance.

In the election campaign in New Zealand in mid-1984, the Labour Party promised that, if elected, it would ban all visits by any warships, even of New Zealand's ANZUS partners, which were nuclear-powered or nuclear-armed, or both. It asserted that "nuclear defense" in its region was unnecessary and dangerous, and that New Zealand should get completely away from "things nuclear." After the Labour Party won a narrow victory in July 1984, its government, headed by David Lange, an ardent proponent of the antinuclear cause, immediately announced that Labour's antinuclear pledge would be strictly fulfilled. It also stated that it intended to remain within the ANZUS alliance and to observe its alliance commitments. In the 1984 ANZUS Council meeting, held after the Labour government came to power in New Zealand, the foreign minister of that country joined with his counterparts in Australia and the United States in endorsing a joint communiqué which contained the following statement: "Access by allied aircraft and ships to the airfields and ports of the ANZUS members was reaffirmed as essential to the continuing effectiveness of the alliance."[13] But apparently the Labor government of New Zealand did not regard this statement as inconsistent with its stand on port calls by nuclear-powered or nuclear-armed warships.

On this issue the United States and New Zealand were clearly on a collision course, unless some face-saving compromise could be worked out. New Zealand would not permit visits by warships unless it was assured formally that these ships were neither nuclear-powered nor carried nuclear weapons. Its democratically elected government maintained that it had a mandate from the New Zealand voters from which it would not, and could not, deviate. The

United States had a long-standing "neither-confirm-nor-deny" policy. As one high-level spokesman explained: "[I]t would be irresponsible and would weaken the deterrent value of our forces to advertise to potential adversaries when they are or are not carrying nuclear weapons."[14]

For several months representatives of the United States and Australia negotiated with New Zealand officials in an effort to reach an acceptable compromise, but without success. During this period the United States deferred any requests for permission for American warships to make the usual port calls. But in January 1985, just before a regularly scheduled joint ANZUS military and naval exercise, it decided to precipitate the issue by requesting New Zealand's permission for the conventionally powered destroyer *Buchanan* to stop at a New Zealand port. When the Labor government of New Zealand failed to get an explicit U.S. guarantee that the *Buchanan* was not carrying nuclear weapons, it banned the proposed visit.[15] This decision precipitated the crisis in ANZUS that had long been brewing. There were demands in the United States—including in Congress—for strong measures, such as economic sanctions or a total cutoff of military and security as well as other forms of cooperation, against New Zealand.

The U.S. government resisted what a spokesman called "petulant reactions," but it made its displeasure strongly manifest. It canceled its participation in the ANZUS military exercises, "Sea Eagle," scheduled for March. It declared that proponents of antinuclear movements seeking to "diminish defense cooperation" should know "that the course these movements advocate will not be cost-free in terms of security relationships with the United States."[16] U.S. leaders charged that New Zealand was behaving in a way inconsistent with its professed loyalty to ANZUS, and they warned that unless this position was changed in some mutually acceptable way ANZUS itself would be in jeopardy. A typical statement was that of the U.S. assistant secretary of state for East Asian and Pacific Affairs in March 1985: "With words New Zealand assures us that it remains committed to ANZUS; but by its deeds New Zealand has effectively curtailed its operational role in ANZUS. A military alliance has little meaning without military cooperation. New Zealand can't have it both ways."[17] In the previous month President Reagan had said: "We deeply regret the decision by the New Zealand Government to deny port access to our ships. . . . It's our deepest hope that New Zealand will restore the traditional cooperation that has existed between our two countries."[18]

Although opinion in New Zealand was divided on the wisdom of the Labor government's adamant position, there was widespread resentment against what was regarded as strong-armed tactics by the United States. Charging that the United States was trying to "bully" his country, Prime Minister Lange declared: "I regard it as unacceptable that another country should by threat or coercion try to change a policy that has been embraced by the New Zealand people."[19]

In March 1985 the U.S. assistant secretary of state for East Asian and Pacific affairs stated: "[W]e are reluctant at this time to dismantle the [ANZUS] treaty or fall back from our commitment to it;" but he warned that "unless our alliance partners bear a commensurate share of military cooperation essential to the alliance, our partnership cannot be sustained practically or politically."[20] A year later the Reagan administration, believing that New Zealand's unyielding position had made the continuing of ANZUS relationships and commitments impossible, in effect terminated the alliance.

Australia was placed in a particularly embarrassing position by the impasse between its two ANZUS allies. It had special ties and interests in its main Southwest Pacific neighbor. Many Australians shared the antinuclear sentiment that was so strongly demonstrated in New Zealand. This feeling, as has been noted, was especially prevalent in the ruling Labor government in each country. Prime Minister Hawke and other officials in the Labor government of Australia tried to persuade New Zealand's Labor government, as well as the U.S. government, to work out some acceptable compromise and to resume their normal cooperative relationships. They were concerned, quite understandably, with the effects of the quarrel upon ANZUS itself. They continued to allow the United States to use Australian facilities for operations in the Indian Ocean and elsewhere, and they also agreed, rather reluctantly, to enter into a series of new bilateral agreements with the United States for the continuance of some types of military and other kinds of cooperation that were no longer possible within the ANZUS framework. But Australian policy also showed some signs of growing estrangement from U.S. security positions, especially on nuclear matters, and of growing reluctance to permit further use of its territory for any testing of nuclear weapons or long-range missiles. In 1985 Prime Minister Hawke felt compelled by pressures within Australia to retreat from a previous agreement to permit the United States to conduct limited test firings of the new MX missiles from Australian soil, and he also expressed Australia's concern over the proposed test firings of these missiles from launching sites in California into the Tasman Sea.[21]

Existing security arrangements between the United States and Australia will probably continue, but the United States should recognize that these arrangements have been placed in jeopardy by a number of trends in mood and orientation in Australia and by the concern and ambivalence in Australia regarding the impasse between the United States and New Zealand that has led to the virtual abrogation of the ANZUS alliance. In August 1986 the Washington correspondent of The Australian, in a dispatch in The Wall Street Journal, raised the rather alarming question, "Will Australia Become the Final Break in the ANZUS Chain?," and commented: "The U.S. needs to look carefully at the current direction of Australian defense policy, making sure the New Zealand episode isn't repeated. Some official candor might well stop the rot."[22]

The unwelcome change in U.S. security and overall relations with New Zealand, and to some extent with Australia as well, and the serious strains and stresses that led to the breakup of what had been one of the oldest and most solidly based alliances in the entire U.S. alliance system, raised major security concerns for the United States that went far beyond its concerns for the future of its relations with its ANZUS partners, with ANZUS itself, and with the security of the Southwest Pacific. As an article in *Business Week* in October 1984 stated, this new turn of events in the Southwest Pacific

> ... is bringing into question the entire American strategy in the Western Pacific. The New Zealand action is more than just the idiosyncracy of a small South Pacific nation. It is a manifestation of a worldwide phenomenon variously called "Hollanditis" or "the Greek disease"—a widespread and growing pacifist nationalism that is strongly influenced by anti-Americanism and that can be found on both the left and the right in some of the U.S.'s oldest allies. ... An even greater concern for Washington as a result of the New Zealand decision is the possible increase of antinuclear sentiment in Japan and the Philippines. Japanese and Filipino bases are essential for a U.S. naval strategy that requires a strong presence in the Indian Ocean and Persian Gulf. ... This potential hazard to the present U.S. world strategy comes at a time when Soviet military power and presence in the Western Pacific continue to grow.[23]

Thus from the U.S. perspective the security environment in the Southwest Pacific has taken an unexpected turn for the worse, in a region where the past environment has seemed to be unusually favorable, and the possible spillover effects of this great change could be quite serious. Under these circumstances the United States is being forced to reexamine its entire security position and policies, not only in the Southwest Pacific but also in the Western Pacific and indeed in the entire world. Out of a relatively remote and hitherto relatively stable region have come new reminders of the impact of domestic as well as of external developments on the overall security and balance of power picture.

THE SECURITY OF OCEANIA

Australia and New Zealand, the most important states of the Southwest Pacific, have special interests in and special ties with the nine other islands (or island groups) of the Southwestern, South, and West Central Pacific that have become independent nations since the end of World War II. In the order of their emergence into independence these island nations are: Western Samoa (1962); Nauru (1968); Tonga (1970); Fiji (1970); Papua New Guinea, covering the eastern half of the island of New Guinea—the western half is the Indonesian province of Irian Jaya, which was administered by Australia for more than a quarter of a century after World War II—(1975); the Solomon Islands (1978); Tuvalu, formerly the Ellice Islands, with an area of ten square miles and a population of less than 10,000 (1978); Kiribati, formerly the Gilbert Islands (1979); and Vanuatu, formerly the New Hebrides (1980). The Cook Islands became a self-governing state freely associated with New Zealand in 1965, and neighboring Niue was given the same status in 1972. In the same general part of the South Pacific New Zealand has special jurisdiction over Wallis and Futuna and the Tokelau islands.

In the South Pacific, France still has control over New Caledonia and French Polynesia, consisting of over 300 islands (the best-known of them is

Tahiti) scattered over a vast area, and Pitcairn Island in the adjoining region to the east is still a British dependency.

Far to the northwest, in the vast reaches of the Central and West Central Pacific, the United States administered a large number of islands that it captured from the Japanese during World War II as the Trust Territory of the Pacific Islands under the United Nations Trusteeship System; but all of these islands, grouped into four clusters—the Northern Marianas, the Federated States of Micronesia, Palau, and the Marshall Islands—are now in various stages of self-government, either with continued but more autonomous connection with the United States or as emerging independent states.

This vast area, often referred to as Oceania, covers over one-sixth of the earth's surface. In it are thousands of islands, including the nine independent countries that have emerged since World War II, the two "freely associated states," and a much larger number of dependencies of the United States, France, Britain, and New Zealand. On geographic, ethnic, and cultural grounds Oceania is divided into three major subregions: (1) Micronesia, including Guam, Nauru, Kiribati, the Federated States of Micronesia, the Republic of the Marshall Islands, the Republic of Palau, and the Northern Marianas; (2) Melanesia, including Papua New Guinea, the Solomon Islands, New Caledonia, Vanuatu, and part of Fiji; and (3) Polynesia, including Tuvalu, Tonga, Western Samoa, the Cook Islands, Niue, part of Fiji, French Polynesia, and the Pitcairn Dependency.

Among Western countries, the United States, Britain, France, and Canada have the most extensive special interests and roles in the region. For obvious reasons the nations of East and Southeast Asia are also especially interested in this vast region, embracing so much of the Pacific Basin in which their destinies are shaped, and in recent years the Soviet Union has been taking a special interest and seeking an increasing voice in the affairs of Oceania, much to the distress of the United States and other Pacific Basin states.

Cooperation in the South Pacific Forum

All of the eleven independent island nations of the South, Southwest, and West Central Pacific, including Australia and New Zealand, plus Niue and the Cook Islands, are members of the South Pacific Forum, an intergovernmental organization (IGO) not to be confused with the Pacific Forum, a non-governmental organization with headquarters in Honolulu. Established in 1971, with headquarters in Suva, Fiji, it has been a central agency for political, economic, and other forms of cooperation among its members, and for the promotion of their mutual interests regionally and globally.

Nuclear concerns have figured prominently in the discussions and programs of the South Pacific Forum ever since its inception. These concerns relate primarily to nuclear testing, the dumping of nuclear waste, and the

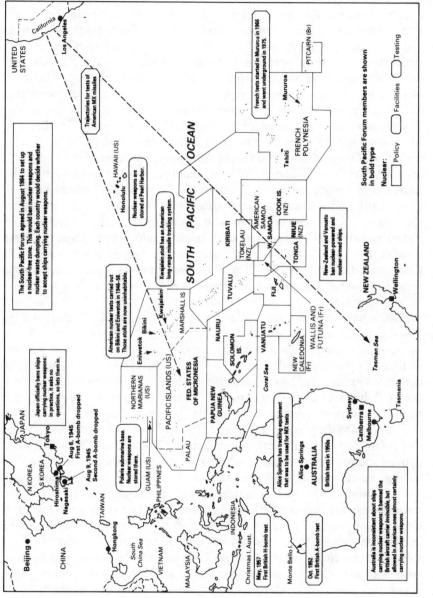

Map 8.1. Did You Say Pacific?

presence of nuclear weapons and nuclear-powered and nuclear-armed warships in the region (see map 8.1). In nuclear testing the United States and France have been the chief offenders. Between 1946 and 1958 the United States carried out a large number of nuclear tests in the vicinity of Eniwetok and Bikini atolls in the Marshall Islands, with disastrous effects on the local inhabitants (who were, of course, removed from the vicinity of the tests) and on the physical environment. More recently the countries and peoples of Oceania have been disturbed by reports that the United States may soon test MX missiles, launched from California with planned splashdown in the Tasman Sea and in the waters of the Trust Territory of the Pacific Islands in Micronesia not far from the former Japanese island fortress of Truk. The nations of Oceania have also voiced strong protests against the numerous French nuclear tests in French Polynesia that began in 1966 in the vicinity of Mururoa in French Polynesia and since 1975 have been conducted underground. Britain has also conducted nuclear tests in the Indian Ocean, just to the west of Oceania and not far from the western and northwestern parts of Australia. Britain's first atomic bomb test was conducted just off the western coast of Australia in October 1952 and its first hydrogen bomb test near Christmas Island in May 1957. These tests were of course conducted with the permission of the Australian government, well before antinuclear sentiment became so strong.

France has been the main offender in the dumping of nuclear waste, although the United States has also been considering various parts of Oceania as possible dumping sites. No real answer has yet been found for the increasingly serious problem of nuclear waste disposal that threatens dangerous radiation effects for centuries to come. Certainly the inhabitants of French Polynesia and of other islands of Oceania strongly oppose steps by the nuclear powers to remove a serious danger from their own citizens by transfering it to the peoples of Oceania. This is obviously a sensitive issue that can complicate relations of the United States, France, and Britain with the nations and peoples of Oceania, where antinuclear as well as anti-imperialist feelings, based on past experience and present weaknesses, are already strong.

The nations of Oceania and the Southwest Pacific are acutely aware that nuclear weapons are stored in a number of surrounding areas from Hawaii to Okinawa, in the Soviet Far East, in China, in the Philippines, and in Guam, and that nuclear-powered and nuclear-armed ships, mainly American warships, traverse their region regularly. They deplore the presence of nuclear weapons and nuclear vessels anywhere in the world, but they cannot do much about this except to voice repeated protests. They are trying to gain acceptance for their desires to keep all such weapons and vessels out of their region. In these efforts the South Pacific Forum has taken the lead. As has been noted, high-ranking representatives of all of the member states of the Forum meeting in Tuvalu in August 1985, approved a resolution to declare their entire region a nuclear-free zone and to ban all nuclear weapons and nuclear waste dumping anywhere in the region. There was considerable support for the position of the Labor government of New Zealand to ban visits by nuclear-powered and nuclear-armed warships of any country, but the resolution merely stipulated that each country should decide whether to permit visits of ships carrying nuclear weapons.[24] This resolution seems to reflect a general desire of the member states of the South Pacific Forum, but it remains to be seen to what extent they will agree on practical measures to promote the objectives stated in the resolution and to what extent other countries, especially the United States and other nuclear powers, will cooperate in these efforts.

The United States and Oceania

The United States has already expressed reservations about this resolution, although it professes to support the broad objectives and the motivations that prompted its adoption. Concern about the future of U.S. relations with Australia and New Zealand, and also with the island nations of Oceania, has taken on added significance and has encountered new complications and problems as a result of the recent developments in the region and elsewhere.

Oceania was a central theater of the war in the Pacific during World War II. Now the Pacific Basin is becoming for the first time a major center of international affairs. Contacts within the region are becoming increasingly extensive and significant, and there is increasing talk of the coming Pacific era, marked by an emerging "Pacific Community," whose outlines and prospects are still not clear. A State Department release in 1985 called attention to the importance of the region for the United States:

> The U.S. has a long history of contact with the islanders, dating back to the vigorous pursuit of dollars and souls by 19th century traders, whalers, and missionaries. During World War II, we suffered almost 300,000 casualties (killed and wounded) in the region—nearly 30% of our worldwide losses. The Pacific islands assume an importance to the U.S. belying their small size because their location commands our lines of communication with Australia, New Zealand, and Southeast Asia (and obviously also with the countries of East Asia). The State of Hawaii, the territories of Guam and American Samoa, and our close relationship with the states emerging from the U.S.-administered Trust Territory also give us a stake in the region's future.[25]

For the United States the security of Oceania is essential to its own security, and is closely related to its security concerns in the Western Pacific. "Our main strategic concern in Oceania," according to the State Department release, "is denial of its use for military purposes by any hostile outside power." This release also stated that "in pursuit of this goal [and, one hopes, in pursuit of other desirable objectives as well—objectives more closely related to the welfare of the inhabitants of Oceania and to the promotion of international cooperation and world peace] we have attempted to maintain good relations with the region by dealing with its concerns." A number of examples were cited:

Separate treaties of friendship between us and Tokelau, Tuvalu, Kiribati, and the Cook Islands, renouncing weak and outdated U.S. claims to uninhabited islands, were ratified in 1983. The U.S. is seeking to negotiate a regional fisheries agreement that would resolve legal differences over tuna fishing by American-owned tunaboats within the islands' exclusive economic zone. Negotiations also are in progress on an environmental protection convention for the region to protect its fragile ecological system from pollution. This convention would address the issue of disposal of low-level radioactive waste, a matter of great concern to the islanders.

The Agency for International Development's (AID) South Pacific Regional Program assists 10 island nations: Fiji, Papua New Guinea, Solomons, Vanuatu, Kiribati, Tonga, Tuvalu, Western Samoa, Cook Islands and Niue. The objectives are to assist national development and support regionalism. The program administers assistance through private and voluntary organizations, regional projects (to which all countries have access), and the Accelerated Impact Program, which implements small grants with the aid of Peace Corps Volunteers and local government officials and organizations. Future AID programs will focus on agriculture, training, and health.

In addition, a modest bilateral assistance program for Fiji is under consideration for fiscal year 1986. About 450 Peace Corps Volunteers, many of whom focus on rural development, are serving in the region. Four countries (Fiji, Papua New Guinea, Solomons, and Tonga) participate in small international military education and training programs. At the request of regional governments, the U.S., Australia, and New Zealand finance a program of oceanographic research. U.S. contributions to international organizations such as the Asian Development Bank also benefit Oceania.[26]

For some years the Soviet Union has been warning Australia and New Zealand of the dire consequences for them of continued association with the United States, especially in ANZUS, and recently it has applauded the growth of antinuclear and antiwar sentiments in both countries. The Soviet Union went out of its way to commend New Zealand for its stand on nuclear issues, and especially for its decision to ban all nuclear-equipped warships from its ports, and has approved similar trends in some of the island nations of Oceania. It has been highly critical of American policies and activities in Oceania, charging that they threaten to turn the entire region into a conflict zone. Quite naturally, the Soviets praised the antinuclear resolution adopted by the South Pacific Forum in 1985.

A standard object of Soviet criticism has been the U.S. administration of the Trust Territory of the Pacific Islands. It has consistently alleged that the United States was not living up to its obligations to the inhabitants of the Trust Territory under its mandate from the United Nations, and that the United States was ignoring inhabitants' wishes and turning the Trust Territory into a fortified area. In 1983 the United States sought to ascertain the wishes of the inhabitants regarding their future political status through a plebiscite in each of the four parts of the Trust Territory. As a result the Federated States of Micronesia, the Republic of the Marshall Islands, and the Republic of Palau are in the process of becoming self-governing states associated with the United States—with complete independence a possibility in the future—and the Marianas have become the Commonwealth of the Northern Marianas Islands, with a status similar to that of Puerto Rico. Far from welcoming these changes, the Soviet Union returned to its standard attack, as illustrated in an article in a 1984 issue of *Far Eastern Affairs*: "A component of U.S. war preparations in the Pacific and East Asia is the conversion of Palau, Micronesia, and the Marshall Islands into 'associated states' as a result of the farcical plebiscite conducted by the U.S. administration on February 10, June 27 and September 7, 1983, respectively, in violation of the U.N. Charter. The United States now runs the islands as if they were U.S. reservations, using them as naval and air bases."[27] In addition to a propaganda barrage against U.S. policies and activities in Oceania, the Soviet Union has been trying in various ways to expand its contacts and its influence in the independent nations of the region. Some observers have professed to see even larger objectives and ambitions, including the establishment of "politico-military footholds in some of the islands."[28]

In 1985 the Soviet Union scored a major success by concluding a fishing agreement with the Central Pacific island nation of Kiribati. This was "a deal that sent shock waves of concern throughout the Pacific. The fishing pact gives the Soviets their first foothold in an area that until now has been dominated exclusively by Western interests."[29] Although it has allowed this pact to lapse, the Soviet Union has also entered into negotiations with several other Pacific island nations with a view toward concluding similar fishing agreements, developing economic and diplomatic relations, and capitalizing on the trends in these young nations to turn away from their pro-Western and especially pro-United States orientation in the direction of greater pragmatism and independence. Several of these nations seem particularly receptive to the Soviet approaches. Vanuatu is a leading example. The young prime minister of Vanuatu, Walter Lini, "unquestionably the most outspoken critic of the West among all Pacific leaders,"[30] has agreed to establish diplomatic relations with the Soviet Union (announced on June 30, 1986), as he had done previously with Cuba, Libya, Nicaragua, and Vietnam. A similar agreement was reached with the United States only after this decision was announced. Soviet presence and influence in Oceania are obviously growing rapidly, but they are still relatively insignificant as compared with the continuing influence and the extensive ties of the United States, Britain, and France in the region.

The main lesson for the United States and its Western allies is not that Oceania is in danger of extensive Soviet penetration, but that this vast region is undergoing profound changes and cannot be taken for granted as the West historically has tended to do. The United States must show more awareness and concern for the interests and sensitivities of the island peoples, and it must adjust its economic, political and military policies in major ways.[31] This readjustment in policies should embrace important new directions in its approach to the region, ranging all the way from revised policies regarding fishing agreements to a greater awareness and concern. "The first step the United States should take in solidifying its ties with the Pacific,"wrote David Knibb, a seasoned observer, in December 1985, "is to conclude the regional fishing agreement that the U.S. has been negotiating with several Pacific nations since 1963."[32] The need for greater recognition of trade and other interests in Oceania was voiced by one of America's best friends among the leaders of the Pacific island nations, Ratu Sir Kamisese Mara, prime minister of Fiji, during an official visit to the United States in late 1985. As Knibb reported, the prime minister warned "that while the pro-Western disposition of the Pacific helped over the years to keep the Soviets in check, the region is now undergoing profound changes" and he complained that the "South Pacific is little known in Washington." His remarks were a needed reminder that "[i]n realizing a broader understanding with Pacific nations, recognition may be the greatest challenge of all."[33]

THE SOUTHWEST PACIFIC AND OCEANIA AND WESTERN PACIFIC SECURITY

The title of the cited article in the Soviet journal *Far Eastern Affairs* is "Imperialist War Preparations in East Asia and Soviet Policy." The authors, editorial writers for this prestigious journal, reflect Soviet attitudes and interpretations and obviously regard the situation in at least the Micronesian part of Oceania as highly relevant to that in East Asia. In this respect one may agree with their approach. For, as has been pointed out frequently, the security of Oceania is related to the security of the Western Pacific. Even more significantly, the security of the Southwest Pacific is related to the security of the other major regions or subregions of the Western Pacific, namely, East Asia and Southeast Asia. These other regions, quite justifiably, are given more attention than is given to Australia and New Zealand and the island nations of Oceania. The major nations of the Western Pacific, China and Japan, and the Soviet Far East are located in East Asia, although their interests and strategic reach extend to Southeast Asia and the Southwest Pacific—and far beyond—as well. The same observation could be made of the interests and strategic reach of the major intrusive power in the Western Pacific, the United States.

After East Asia, Southeast Asia, again for quite understandable reasons, ranks next among the regions of the Western Pacific in strategic importance and priority. But the Southwest Pacific, and to a lesser but still important extent the island nations of Oceania, are also important factors in the whole strategic equation in the Western Pacific, and even in the global strategic context. This point should be borne in mind by anyone concerned with the security of the Western Pacific. The United States, as the indigenous nations of the region, is well aware of this important point, but it sometimes does not seem to be giving it the attention that it deserves to have. Recent events in the Southwest Pacific and Oceania, and in the Western Pacific generally, as well as elsewhere in the world, seem to be giving the United States the necessary push and incentive to undertake a searching reassessment of its policies and roles in the entire Western Pacific region, from which the Southwest Pacific and Oceania cannot be excluded.

Notes

1 *Pacific Forum: Australia–New Zealand Trip Report* (Honolulu: Pacific Forum, 1985), pp. 5, 1. (Hereafter referred to as Pacific Forum Report.) The representatives of the Pacific Forum who made the Australia–New Zealand trip and submitted the Report were Lloyd R. Vasey, president and executive director of the Pacific Forum, and Henry S. Albinski, professor of political science and director of Australian studies at the Pennsylvania State University.

2 Ibid., p. 5.

3 Ibid., p. 6.

4 See Henry S. Albinski, "The U.S. Security Alliance System in the Southwest Pacific," chapter 6 in William T. Tow and William R. Feeney, eds., *U.S. Foreign Policy and Asian-Pacific Security: A Transregional Approach* (Boulder, Colorado: Westview Press, 1982); and Desmond Ball, *A Suitable Piece of Real Estate: American Installations in Australia* (Sydney Hale and Ironmonger, 1980).

5 See William T. Tow, "The JANZUS Option: A Key to Asian Pacific Security," *Asian Survey* 18 (December 1978).

6 Pacific Forum Report, p. 6.

7 Ibid., p. 2.

8 "Imperialist War Preparations in East Asia and Soviet Policy," *Far Eastern Affairs* (Moscow), 1984 (3): 9.

9 See "The ANZUS Alliance," *Gist*, Bureau of Public Affairs, U.S. Department of State, June 1985.

10 See ibid; and "Alliances: Big Flap Down Under," *Time*, February 18, 1985, pp. 48–49.

11 "Rising Nuclear Opposition Threatens U.S. Strategy in the Pacific," *Business Week* (Oct. 22, 1984), p. 58.

12 "Alliances: Big Flap Down Under," pp. 48–49.

13 Quoted in ibid., p. 48.

14 Paul Wolfowitz, assistant secretary of state for East Asian and Pacific affairs, statement before the Subcommittee of Asian and Pacific Affairs, Foreign Affairs Committee of the U.S. House of Representatives, March 18, 1985; reprinted in "The ANZUS Alliance," Bureau of Public Affairs, U.S. Department of State, *Current Policy*, no. 674, March 18, 1985.

15 See "Alliances: Big Flap Down Under," pp. 48–49.

16 Ibid.

17 Paul Wolfowitz, statement before the Subcommittee, March 18, 1985.

18 Statement of February 7, 1985; quoted by Wolfowitz in ibid.

19 Quoted in "Alliances: Big Flap Down Under," p. 49. "New Zealanders are divided in the current national debate. Recent polls show that while 58% of the New Zealand population of 3.2 million opposes visits by nuclear-armed warships, 59% would not be troubled by calls by ships that were merely nuclear-powered and 60% would like their country to remain in ANZUS. But since Lange has the general support of 70% of his countrymen, the U.S. might have a lot to lose by trying to turn the screws too tightly." Ibid.

20 Paul Wolfowitz, statement before the Subcommittee, March 18, 1985.

21 "Alliances: Big Flap Down Under," p. 49.

22 Peter Samuel, "Will Australia Become the Final Break in the ANZUS Chain?," *The Wall Street Journal*, August 25, 1986.

23 "Rising Nuclear Opposition Threatens U.S. Strategy in the Pacific," *Business Week* (October 22, 1984), p. 58.

24 See "Rising Nuclear Opposition Threatens U.S. Strategy in the Pacific," p. 58.

25 "The U.S. and Oceania," *Gist*, Bureau of Public Affairs, U.S. Department of State, March 1985.

26 Ibid.

27 "Imperialist War Preparations in East Asia and Soviet Policy," p. 9.

28 Robert J. Hanks, *The Pacific Far East: Endangered American Strategic Position* (Cambridge, Mass.: Institute for Foreign Policy Analysis, 1981), p. 54. Admiral Hanks offers an interesting example to support his contention: . . . [I]n the 1970s Moscow made overtures to newly independent Tonga. As they had earlier done with respect to Mauritius in the Indian Ocean, the USSR offered to ease the island's acute food supply problem by providing processed catches from Soviet fishing fleets at attractive prices. Follow-up offers to build

modern harbor and airfield facilities suggested that Soviet military forces—air and naval—as has been the case elsewhere, would not be far behind. In the event the ruler of this struggling new country resisted the siren call and Moscow ultimately came away empty-handed." Ibid.

[29] David Knibb, dispatch from Port Moresby, Papua New Guinea, *The Wall Street Journal*, December 3, 1985.

[30] Ibid.

[31] These points were emphasized in a perceptive column in *The Seattle Times* in October 1986: "All the newly independent countries in the Pacific Ocean believe they have long been friends with the United States, but that they have been ignored and taken for granted. But now the bear has been trying to make friends with the ants, and the elephant has suddenly awakened. The Soviet Union has been courting Pacific island countries, and the United States sees the potential strategic harm the Soviets could cause if they could establish a base in the South Pacific, or stir up trouble there against American interests. . . . For the Soviets to make significant inroads in the region would require a reversal of years of American influence and good will. The island countries have little in common with the Soviet Union, and they may be playing the Soviet threat to get attention from the United States." "Tiny Pacific Nations Play the Red Card," *The Seattle Times*, Oct. 19, 1986.

It is a commentary on the obtuseness of its policies and actions in Oceania that the United States did not "suddenly" awaken to the importance of the Pacific island nations in terms of its strategic and other interests, and to the need for showing greater attention, concern, and sensitivity to these island nations and peoples until the Soviets began "fishing" in these waters, in more than a commercial sense. For a good overall work on the United States and Oceania, see John C. Dorrance, *Oceania and the United States: An Analysis of U.S. Interests and Policy in the South Pacific*, National Security Affairs Monograph Series 80-6, National Defense University (Washington, D.C.: U.S. Government Printing Office, 1984).

[32] Knibb, dispatch in *The Wall Street Journal*, December 3, 1985.

[33] Ibid.

CHAPTER 9

Conclusion: Westward Watch in "A Radically Different Era"

In seeking to reassess and reorient its policies and relationships in the Western Pacific, the United States should constantly bear in mind three major considerations. The first is that the region is an increasingly important international actor and is becoming a major center of economic, political, and military power. Hence it is assuming increasing importance for the United States, in terms of global interests and concerns. Second, the Western Pacific is also becoming of increasing importance for the United States in terms of America's regional interests and concerns. Although the United States has at times given a relatively low priority to the Asia-Pacific region and has occasionally shown some definite withdrawal tendencies with reference to the region, it has long been a Pacific and Asian power. It has recovered to a considerable degree from the withdrawal syndrome that it exhibited following the end of the Vietnam War, and from such post-Vietnam withdrawal symptoms as President Carter's decision—soon reversed—to withdraw U.S. ground forces from South Korea. It has renewed its basic regional commitments and is developing a widening pattern of relationships with most of the nations of this vast region. There can no longer be much question about the determination of the United States to "remain a Pacific power," as Secretary of State George Shultz pledged in March 1983.[1] Third, while maintaining a growing interest and presence in the region, the United States will continue to promote its regional interests within the framework of its global interests. This is true in the security as well as in other fields. As the U.S. under secretary of state for political affairs stated in October 1984, "We have no choice but to view our strategic interests from a global perspective."[2]

A LACK OF UNDERSTANDING AND EMPATHY?

The changing political, economic, and strategic environment in the Western Pacific, a consequence of a variety of complex external, regional, and national factors, dictates that the United States should thoroughly review and reassess its policies and interests in the region. Judging from their official pronouncements, official U.S. spokespersons are well aware of at least some

of the major changes under way in the Western Pacific and of the need to
rethink U.S. policies in the light of these changes, but one can question
whether rethinking is really going on, and if so, whether it will lead to any
basic reorientations in U.S. policies and approaches. Certainly many responsible leaders in the region doubt it. And the evidence that exists is conflicting.
There seems to be a dichotomy between declaratory policy and actual policy,
and a tendency to find refuge in established lines of policy. This may be a
result of an understandable desire not to make changes in policies and actions
that might jeopardize what is in general, from the American perspective, a
relatively stable and satisfactory security situation in the region. On the other
hand, this tendency may be a result of a lack of understanding of the nature
and implications of the changes that are under way, or simply of bureaucratic
caution and inertia. "The hallmark of our approach," said Under Secretary of
State for Political Affairs Michael Armacost, in January 1985, "is the patient
tending of policy lines that have already been well laid down. This is an
approach that is more akin to gardening than to architecture." He made this
remark after stating that he had "avoided any grand design for American
policy in the next 4 years."[3]

It is difficult to interpret what Armacost's metaphors, mixed or otherwise,
really mean, and whether they have any real relevance to the actual course of
U.S. policy in the Western Pacific. It would be helpful to know what "the
policy lines that have already been well laid down" actually are, and to what
extent they are being developed to meet changing circumstances. It would
also be comforting to have more concrete evidence that whatever the policies
are, they are being developed and carried out within the framework of some
more recognizable design—which will undoubtedly be much less than
"grand." If the United States is to meet its avowed goal of playing an
enhanced role in a region that is of increasing importance to it and that is
emerging as a significant actor in the international system, it will need more
than gardeners who can nurture the seeds that have already been sown. It will
need creative and skillful architects and planners and many more responsible
leaders who have a deeper understanding of the changing scene in a major
world region and of the opportunities and pitfalls that exist for the promotion
of genuine U.S. interests. It will need more people with vision, understanding,
and empathy as well as those who are capable of making eloquent speeches.
Fortunately, as in the case of Armacost, these two qualities are not necessarily
incompatible.

According to many commentators, American, Asian, and others, the U.S.
relationship with Asia has been notable for its lack of understanding,
empathy, and vision. A usual criticism has been that Americans have not even
tried to see things as Asians see them and instead have tried to project their
own Western-centered views on a region where the majority of the people
listen to very different drummers. In an article in 1964 entitled "The Security
of the Western Pacific," in a leading Western strategic journal, Peter Polomka

called attention to aspects and consequences of this myopic approach: "The dangers of seeing Asia through European eyes, of sinking into the quicksands of over-simplification which Western political systems seem to require to function, and of being over-influenced by the political dynamics of one's own environment rather than the forces at work in Asia itself, may well explain a great deal of what went wrong with U.S. policy in Asia in the post-1945 period." The American involvement in Asia, Polomka believes, "foundered essentially through a failure to understand the region's own dynamics and, in particular, in miscalculating the power and importance of the forces of nationalism which had been unleashed in the Asian Pacific region."[4]

This is the thrust of many of those who argue that the United States has shown a deplorable lack of understanding and empathy in its approach to Asia. Others would carry the argument further by insisting that Americans, with some outstanding exceptions, have not even attempted to understand the history and culture of the Asian peoples and have therefore been poorly prepared to deal with Asians in terms of mutual interests and concerns. Certainly there have been, and still are, few Asia specialists—specialists by virtue of extensive experience, study, and interest—among responsible policymakers in the United States, and the higher up one looks on the policymaker ladder the fewer qualified specialists there are. This is a particularly deplorable situation in the emerging Asian-Pacific era. As Secretary of State Shultz declared after a visit to the Western Pacific in the spring of 1983, ". . . if you want to understand the future, you must . . . understand the Pacific region."[5] Doubtless the secretary realizes that this regional imperative calls for some basic retooling and reorientation on the part of those immediately around him.

All kinds of qualifications of this kind of criticism immediately come to mind. Many thousands of Americans, ever since the first significant contacts between the United States and Asia began well over a century and a half ago, have had long experience in Asia and have taken a special interest in the affairs of that part of the world, especially in East Asia. Certainly top-level U.S. policymakers should have understanding of and empathy with cultures and values and goals quite different from their own; but these are only some of the many qualifications that top leaders should possess and that many area specialists do not. The greatest need at the top is not for more "area specialists." The old rule about "the amateur on top, and the expert on tap" still has considerable validity. U.S. leaders can hardly be faulted for failing to have an adequate understanding of Asian cultures and of the forces at work in this vast continent. Few Asians themselves really understand their own complex cultures, and even fewer the cultures of other Asian peoples. The failures of U.S. policies in Asia over the years have been due to many factors, of which the lack of adequate understanding and empathy have seldom been the most determining. Moreover, the American record in Asia has many successes and achievements, despite its many reverses, to its credit. At the present time, in particular, the United States has made many recognized contributions to the security and development of the region and of many of the countries in it, and its relations with most of the countries of the region have been generally satisfactory, at least on official levels. But many problems remain, and many more are on the horizon or will develop in the future. Hence there is as little justification for resting on one's laurels in U.S.– Western Pacific relations as there is in lamenting past disappointments or present problems.

Some of the prevailing criticisms of U.S. policies in the Western Pacific have been suggested in the preceding paragraphs, and many others could be mentioned. For example, three standard criticisms that have special relevance for political and security analysis are that the U.S. involvement and commitments in the Western Pacific lack reliability and credibility; that the United States still seems to conceive of its relations with the nations of the region in terms of its old patron-client or dominant-subordinate relationships rather than in terms of genuine mutuality of interests and genuine partnership; and that, in essence, the fluctuations of U.S. policy in the Western Pacific have been due more to a basic lack of policy and strategy than to any failure to comprehend or to make adjustments to changing conditions and circumstances.

This last criticism—that the United States has no policy for the Western Pacific—is one that is difficult to evaluate in any objective way. Basically, the United States, as a superpower that is deeply involved in the Western Pacific, has to have overall policies and strategies, if not a single overall policy, to guide its actions toward the countries of the region, which include some of the most important actors in the international system. On the other hand, it is not easy to define the foreign policy of any nation in very specific terms, or to relate the innumerable general statements on foreign policy to specific aspects of that policy or to particular regions and countries. Most of the responsible U.S. policymakers have consistently maintained that the United States does have well-understood and to a lesser degree well-defined foreign and strategic policies. Those who have been primarily responsible for shaping and carrying out policies in the Western Pacific insist that this increasingly important region is not outside the perimeter of these policies and strategies.

FUTURE SCENARIOS

This concluding chapter will suggest possible future scenarios regarding U.S. relations, with emphasis on security aspects, with some of the key nations of the region. One might logically start with relations with the other major actors in the Western Pacific, the Soviet Union, Japan, and the People's Republic of China.

The United States and the Soviet Union in the Western Pacific

Any discussion of security relationships with the Soviet Union in the Western Pacific must emphasize their central importance, their dangerous confrontational character, and their global dimensions. Primary security objectives of the United States in the region are to maintain a military posture adequate to meet any major threat from the expanding military presence and power of the Soviet Union, and to cooperate as closely as possible with its Western Pacific allies, and with other nations in the region that are also concerned about the Soviet threat even if less so than the United States, including the People's Republic of China.

Clearly, Soviet–American relations in the area are a part of a wider pattern of relations, and can be properly assessed only within this larger framework. The Western Pacific is probably the second most important theater of confrontation. Indeed, in some respects it is an area of even more direct military confrontation between the superpowers than is the European theater. More military power of both countries is present in this region than in any other part of the world except Europe. Each country is disturbed by the growing military presence of the other in the region, which is the central conflict zone between them in the entire Asia-Pacific area. Each regards the other as the major threat in the Western Pacific, and each justifies its substantial, expensive, and growing military presence in East Asia and the adjacent Pacific Ocean waters largely in terms of its global assessment of the other's intentions and power.

One could argue that in the Western Pacific the two superpowers maintain such formidable military strength primarily to enhance their security against each other, rather than to provide security against potentially hostile nations in the region or to assist regional states in improving their own security position. This is another reason why the military activities and security measures of each country in the Western Pacific might more properly be analyzed in global rather than in regional terms. It also helps to explain why so many of the nations of the region, whatever their relations with the superpowers, regard these giants as threats as well as possible supporters and are fearful that they may be dragged into the conflicts and rivalries of the giants and become pawns or victims in a power game with which they are quite unequipped to cope. In other words this helps to understand the uneasy feeling prevalent throughout the Western Pacific that the superpowers are more part of the problem than part of the solution. But the nations of the region realize that, for better or for worse, the superpowers are and will continue to be major actors in the region. The best they can hope for is that these giants will help to counteract each other, that they can be persuaded to refrain from making the region a cockpit of their rivalries, and that they will recognize their common interests in contributing to the region's peace, stability, and development.

Each superpower will continue to be very suspicious about the other's relations with the People's Republic of China. The likelihood is that U.S. relations and contacts with China will continue to develop, but that they will remain essentially limited and rather disappointing to both countries. The Soviet Union and China will probably continue to move away from their very hostile and inflexible positions *vis-à-vis* each other. The contacts that are slowly beginning to be reestablished will continue, well short of any renewal of the old pattern of ideological affinity and alliance relationships. Limited but developing relations of both superpowers with China should help to promote peace, stability, and development in the Asia-Pacific region. This is a view, however, that will not be widely held in either superpower. Certainly each will look with suspicion upon any signs that China is developing closer relations with the other.

In the Korean Peninsula both powers want to prevent the tense relations of the two Korean regimes from flaring up into another military conflict. If such a conflict broke out, both would probably seek to confine it within the Peninsula; but obviously the Soviet Union would support the North Korean regime, probably well short of direct military intervention, and the United States would support the Republic of Korea, perhaps even to the extent of committing U.S. troops to the defense of the South Koreans. This could create a dangerous possibility of an armed clash between the superpowers, which might rapidly spread far beyond the Korean Peninsula.

In Indochina, another danger zone, the Soviet Union is supporting Vietnam and the Vietnamese occupation and control of Kampuchea, whereas the United States has refused to establish official relations with the Communist regime in Vietnam and is a strong critic of the Vietnamese role in Kampuchea. It is supporting the efforts of the ASEAN countries to secure Vietnamese withdrawal from Kampuchea, and is providing assistance to the noncommunist Cambodian resistance forces based in Thailand and to Thailand to enable that country to deal more effectively with its problem of defense against possible Vietnamese thrusts and of handling the Cambodian refugees on its soil. The United States is also concerned about the availability of American-built bases in Vietnam—Cam Ranh Bay and Danang—for Soviet use. These bases provide facilities for the Soviets to extend their reach more effectively over vital sea-lane routes through Southeast Asian waters and still further into the Pacific and Indian Oceans.

In the Western Pacific, as elsewhere, U.S.–Soviet relations will almost certainly continue to be more conflictual than cooperative. The growing military buildup of both superpowers in the region, especially in North Pacific waters and the adjoining littorals, and the increasing militancy and provocativeness of the rhetoric as well as the actions of both countries are particularly disturbing and ominous factors. But it is in the interest of the United States to attempt to work out at least some cooperative relationships with the Soviet Union in the Western Pacific, such as parallel efforts to prevent the explosive situations in the Korean and Indochinese peninsulas from escalating into major threats in their regions and beyond. Major objectives should be to prevent Soviet–American competition and confrontation from developing into major conflict situations, and to reduce the level of armaments and military forces that the two superpowers maintain in the region (a goal that will probably be feasible only if and when the two superpowers agree on major military de-escalation on a global scale).

The United States and Japan: Security Aspects of the Relationship

The U.S. security presence in the Western Pacific and its entire policies in the region will continue to be anchored on Japan, its most important Asian ally and its second most important trading partner. But all is not well with this "core relationship." Its security aspects, which have been central, are being adversely affected by the uncertainties and disagreements over security needs and priorities, and over the relative role of the two allies in the defense of Japan and in the larger task of security in the Western Pacific. On the issue of burden sharing, basic differences still remain, although the United States remains committed to bearing the brunt of the security responsibilities in the region as a whole, and Japan is slowly and reluctantly moving toward assumption of a greater share of its own defense. The major and growing differences on a wide variety of economic, and especially trade, issues and policies have adversely affected U.S.–Japanese cooperation in the security and political fields. These differences are a major cause of U.S.–Japanese tensions. They constitute a security as well as an economic threat and may indeed be regarded as one of the major security threats in the Western Pacific region. This conclusion may be advanced without subscribing to the view of one commentator that "the emerging Cold War between the United States and Japan" is a "much greater threat to the entire Asia-Pacific region" than the Soviet threat.[6]

Certainly, the U.S.–Japanese relationship will continue to be important for both countries; but there are obvious storm clouds ahead. It needs to be carefully nurtured, with a greater degree of agreement on mutual interests and responsibilities on national, regional, and international levels and a greater degree of realism in dealing with the very real differences that are becoming increasingly apparent. The changing roles, outlooks, and policies of Japan and the United States in a changing regional and global environment provide a central theme for any analysis of the security picture in the Western Pacific and of the course of international relations generally.

Security Aspects of the U.S.–China Relationship

The People's Republic of China and the United States seem to have at least some parallel security interests, especially in coping with the Soviet threat and in assisting China to modernize its large but ill-equipped military establishment; but it is already apparent that progress in these directions will continue to be limited and tenuous, always with the possibility that it will be one of the first casualties of any major adverse trends in the fragile and still tentative relations that the two countries have been slowly forging since the early 1970s. In developing any security relationships with the People's Republic of China, moreover, the United States must be especially sensitive to the reservations and apprehensions of other states of the region regarding an increasingly assertive and powerful China. Possibly the fears of some of China's neighbors are based more on historical memory than on China's likely behavior in future years, but the United States should remember that such fears exist and that they will be accentuated and will constitute real roadblocks in the relations of the United States with other Asian nations if the United States does not tread warily in its security relationships with China.

In spite of the great divides between the two countries, U.S. relations with the People's Republic of China will continue to expand and will become an increasingly important dimension of U.S.–Western Pacific relationships. But they will be far more limited than many Americans anticipated in the brief period of euphoria and suddenly expanding contacts that accompanied and followed the gradual normalization of relations in the 1970s. This realization is causing some disappointment in the United States, but it is probably a sounder and more realistic basis for long-time relations between two such different countries, governments, social systems, and cultures than any Sino–American relationship in the recent past. As Parris H. Chang has observed, since the Communists came to power in China, nearly four decades ago, relations between the United States and China have evolved "from hostility to euphoria to realism."[7] It remains to be seen, of course, how "realistic" the present "realism" will prove to be, especially in terms of Western Pacific security. From an American point of view, however, as long as China maintains its present course it will be more of a positive than a negative factor in the security picture in the Western Pacific. This is a major change both in the security environment in the region and in U.S. perceptions and approaches to China.

The Taiwan issue will continue to cast a cloud over developing Sino–American relations, even though it has been on the back burner of these relations ever since the Shanghai Communiqué of February 1972. It is an issue on which the leaders of China have expressed the strongest views, quite at variance with those of the United States, and one which could be revived by China's leaders at any time if they choose to revert to an openly anti-American stance. Ever since the Shanghai Communiqué they have tacitly, if reluctantly, acquiesced in the extensive "unofficial" contacts that the United States has maintained with the regime on Taiwan. Once the United States agreed to withdraw official recognition of the Republic of China on Taiwan, to abrogate its security treaty with that regime, to withdraw its military contingents from Taiwan, and to reduce and eventually cease to provide military assistance to the Taiwan regime, the People's Republic of China no longer insisted that the Taiwan issue was an insuperable barrier to the normalization of relations with the United States. But quite obviously China's leaders are not reconciled to the U.S. position on Taiwan, even though that position has been considerably modified in the directions that they desire. In all probability they will not resort to military means to force the reunion of Taiwan with the Chinese mainland, although they have refused to forgo this option. If such a military move materializes, the United States will probably come to the aid of Taiwan and the whole security environment in the Western Pacific, and perhaps even beyond, will be adversely affected. This is the kind of gamble that the People's Republic of China will probably not take, and that it may not feel obliged to take, because it is willing to be patient on this issue and believes that the eventual reunion of Taiwan with the rest of China will come about without the necessity of a resort to direct military operations. But the Taiwan issue will continue to be a potential "flash point" in East Asia.

The United States and the Security of South Korea

The most continuously dangerous conflict zone in the Western Pacific is in the Korean Peninsula, and specifically along the Thirty-eighth Parallel and in the DMZ, where North and South Koreans face each other directly, each possessing formidable military power. Moreover, South Korea is backed by nearly 40,000 American air and land forces stationed in the DMZ and in nearby bases, and the Soviet Union and China provide backing, tangible and intangible, to the North Koreans, while competing with each other for influence with the North Korean regime. With all the major powers of the Western Pacific directly involved in the Korean Peninsula, and with the two regimes in the Peninsula in a state of continuing confrontation, it is difficult to see an end to this explosive situation, with its alarming spillover potentialities.

The United States will certainly remain directly and indirectly involved in the defense and security of South Korea. Since the reversal of President Carter's decision to withdrawn gradually all U.S. ground troops from South Korea, a decision that created alarm in Japan and elsewhere in noncommunist East and Southeast Asia and in the United States as well, there seems to be little likelihood that the American troops in South Korea will be withdrawn as long as the South Koreans wish them to be there and as long as the dangers to South Korea's security are so great and ever-present. Conceivably the American military presence could be reduced substantially if the South Koreans, with U.S. assistance, are able to gain greater relative military strength *vis-à-vis* their North Korean adversaries, or if relations between North and South Korea should substantially improve.

The United States is encouraging the South Koreans to make every possible effort to improve these relations, and presumably the Soviets and Chinese, in varying degrees and ways, have let Kim Il Sung know that they too hope for the peaceful reunification of the divided country. The United States is pressuring South Korea to continue its talks with North Korea, which resumed in 1984 after a long hiatus, and to seek other ways of establishing less hostile relations with the North. In the meantime, the United States recognizes that even major and sincere efforts in this direction may lead nowhere and is reconciled to a long military and other kinds of involvement in South Korea. The United States is beginning to work more closely with Japan, which also has a major stake in the security of South Korea, and there have been some discussions, and apparently some agreements, among these three states, which the Soviets have interpreted as further proof that a tripartite U.S.–Japan–South Korea triangle or alliance, anti-Soviet in nature, is already in the process of formation.

The United States will continue to work with existing regimes in South Korea, even though it is under constant criticism for its support of authoritarian regimes that seem to lack real legitimacy and are opposed by many South Koreans. It will try to avoid too close association with these regimes and will put pressure on them to institute more fully and more sincerely their promised reforms and to broaden political participation. Much will depend on the evolution of the present Chun Doo Hwan regime. If Chun steps down in 1988 and keeps his promise to permit free elections to determine the choice of his successor and perhaps even the character of the future political system, the political situation in South Korea may improve perceptibly, especially because that country will be on good behavior before and during the scheduled Olympic Games in Seoul in 1988. But there is always the possibility that the internal political situation may become more confused, unstable, and even anarchic before as well as after South Korea's latest strongman bows out voluntarily, leaves under pressure that he can no longer resist, or is removed by an assassin's bullet.

In any event, the United States will continue to be concerned about the security of South Korea and to be committed to help to preserve that security, even if the internal situation in that troubled country deteriorates instead of improves. There is also the possibility that whatever its political future South Korea will continue to experience an impressive rate of economic growth, after its slowdown in the mid-1980s, and will follow a more independent foreign policy, as a result of which its relations with the United States will take on many new directions, some favorable and some unfavorable from the American point of view.

The United States and the Security of Southeast Asia

In Southeast Asia the United States has not yet developed a clearly articulated or understood policy since its withdrawal from Vietnam in 1975, unless its growing interest in and support of the ASEAN states, its continued refusal to establish diplomatic or other relations with Vietnam, and its opposition to Vietnamese policies generally, especially the occupation of Kampuchea and continued pressures on Thailand, may be said to add up to a policy. These trends will probably continue and strengthen. If the ASEAN states and Vietnam and Kampuchea develop more satisfactory relations, the United States will certainly welcome this trend, and will probably then move toward a "normalization" of relations with the Indochinese states.

Contacts with ASEAN will be an increasingly important dimension of U.S. relationships in Southeast Asia. These contacts, which are already quite extensive, will facilitate exchanges between the United States and ASEAN member states on security as well as on many other matters, even though ASEAN from its inception has sought to exclude security issues from its formal agenda. The post-ministerial consultations between the foreign ministers of ASEAN countries and their dialogue partners, including the United States, provide an appropriate forum for such exchanges, which will put mutual security concerns and cooperation within the broader framework of overall foreign policy and mutual national interests.

ASEAN states, especially Indonesia and Malaysia, often complain that the United States does not give them adequate recognition and priority, but they also often allege that the United States is interfering in their internal affairs and in their efforts to develop more independent external policies and more adequate security for the region. They also seem to feel that the strongly anti-Soviet and pro-Japanese positions of the United States may complicate the relations of the Southeast Asian nations with the major powers that are active in their region.

Other complicating factors in U.S. relations with all of the ASEAN states, and especially with Indonesia and Malaysia, are differences in policies and approaches to the People's Republic of China, and different assessments of the vast changes that are under way in China and the implications of these changes for the security of Southeast Asia and the entire Western Pacific area. The United States must take the special sensitivities and apprehensions regarding China that prevail in ASEAN countries into account in its relations with these countries and in its overall Western Pacific policies.

With all of the noncommunist states of Southeast Asia except Burma, the United States has developed extensive contacts and generally satisfactory relations. In general, it is more sympathetic toward the foreign policy orientations and security views of Singapore and Thailand than with those of other states of the region.

The United States is giving considerable support to the efforts of Thailand to improve its defense posture *vis-à-vis* a hostile Vietnam and to deal with the problems created by the presence on its soil of hundreds of thousands of refugees from Indochina, especially from Kampuchea. These steps have helped to reverse the previous trends toward growing coolness and alienation between the United States and the mainland nation of Southeast Asia that was once its closest ally. The United States should give greater attention to the present concerns of Thailand, and should seek to cultivate closer relations, while recognizing that relations will not be as close as they were when the two nations were allied in SEATO and when Thailand was allowing the United States to operate from Thai bases during the Vietnam War.

U.S. relations with Malaysia are less extensive, but seem to be growing and improving. This may be attributed in part to the growing realism in Malaysia's external as well as internal policies since Mahathir bin Mohamad became Prime Minister in July 1981, and to a greater recognition in the United States of Malaysia's growing regional and international role, as well as to increasing economic and other contacts and relations, on bilateral, regional, and international levels.

With the Philippines the United States has a special relationship that in various forms goes back to the turn of the century, and that has taken on new dimensions since World War II and the granting of independence to the Philippines by the United States in 1946. The aspects of the special relationship that have received the most attention in recent years, in addition to very extensive economic, financial, and business contacts, are the issues of the American bases on Luzon and the relations of the U.S. government with the authoritarian and increasingly unpopular regime of Ferdinand Marcos, during his long rule from 1965 to 1985. For the United States both issues have been particularly important and particularly sensitive. The same observation may now be made about U.S. relations with the post-Marcos regime headed by Corazon Aquino.

For some years, following the original agreement between the Philippines and the United States for the development of two major U.S. bases on Philippine soil—the huge naval base at Subic Bay and the air base at Clark Field—there seemed to be little question that the United States would be able to use these bases for as long as it desired, if it was willing to pay the financial and political costs. But even during the Marcos era difficulties and uncertainties developed. When the lease on the bases was renewed and revised in 1983, Marcos demanded and received a sizable payment and other concessions, and he let it be known that continued Philippine approval was subject to possible reconsideration. Many opponents of Marcos, in the United States as well as the Philippines, charged that the United States had paid too high a price in monetary terms and other concessions and especially in its continued support of an unpopular authoritarian regime. In the post-Marcos era the future of the bases is even more uncertain, and this is a matter of great concern to the United States. Some consideration is being given to possible alternative sites, such as the development of stronger bases and facilities on Guam, or in the Northern Marianas, but all of these would be rather unsatisfactory and very expensive replacements for the Philippine bases and would greatly complicate the already difficult task of supporting U.S. military missions and overall objectives in the Asia-Pacific Ocean–Indian Ocean regions.

The issue of official and unofficial attitudes toward the Marcos regime was a thorny one that called for a more searching review and probably more marked reorientations than were in fact undertaken. After the assassination of Marcos's leading political opponent, Benigno Aquino, in August 1983, the United States tried to distance itself from the Marcos regime, without jeopardizing its extensive interests in the Philippines. It intensified these efforts during and after the national elections in the Philippines of February 7, 1986, which it regarded as so marred by fraud and strong-arm tactics by Marcos supporters as to provide a dubious basis for Marcos's continued legitimacy.

Marcos claimed that the elections had given him a six-year extension of his long rule; but soon after the results were announced, the Marcos era came to a speedy and ignominious end. The United States urged him to abdicate gracefully, and when he eventually agreed to bow to the inevitable, he was flown out of the country (allegedly against his wishes) in an American plane, and given refuge—at least temporarily and rather reluctantly—in Hawaii. The United States immediately recognized the successor government, headed by Corazon Aquino. It has established close and extensive—if still tentative and mutually reserved—relations with the new order in the Philippines. But the future of the new regime, and of U.S. relations with it, is still in doubt; and the question of U.S. relations with subsequent regimes is of course an even greater uncertainty.

All of the recent changes in the Philippines have demonstrated the need for more attention, more sensitivity, and more understanding on the part of the United States, on both official and unofficial levels. Clearly the United States needs to give a great deal of extra attention, now and in the immediate future, to the situation in the Southeast Asian nation with which it has had the longest and closest relations, with which it has such extensive ties, and in which it has such a tremendous stake. It needs to reconsider, and probably reorient in major ways, its basic policies and approaches toward that country.

The United States and the Security of the Southwest Pacific and Oceania

Australia and New Zealand face less pressing and less serious security problems than do the nations of East and Southeast Asia; but even in the region in which they are located and in which they are clearly dominant, the Southwest Pacific, the security environment is changing in many favorable and unfavorable ways. There are growing security and other kinds of linkages between this region and the two other major subregions of the Western Pacific, especially with Southeast Asia but increasingly with East Asia, most notably with Japan.

The security environment has been altered by developments elsewhere in the Western Pacific and in the global arena, and also by some significant changes in the region itself. Among these changes are the increasing independence and confidence in Australia and New Zealand, the advent of Labor governments in both countries, the growth of pacifist and especially of anti-nuclear sentiments in both, and the at least temporary breakup of the ANZUS alliance.

In New Zealand pacifist and antinuclear sentiments have been so strongly endorsed by the Labor government that they have become national policy. As a result serious strains have developed between New Zealand and the United States, especially over the issue of port calls by U.S. warships. This impasse could not be resolved, and in 1986 the United States in effect abrogated the ANZUS alliance and its defense commitments to New Zealand, while professing a desire to maintain and strengthen its ties with Australia on a bilateral basis. Australia has been showing some reluctance to permit the use of its territory for some kinds of U.S. military activities, notably the testing of MX missiles. But in spite of some internal demands and pressures the Labor government of Australia has announced that Australia will continue to be a firm ally of the United States and will continue to allow the United States to use the numerous Australian naval, air, and communications bases and facilities that have long been available to it.

The United States is understandably concerned about the deterioration of its relations with New Zealand, a long-time friend and ally, and about the possible effects of this deterioration on its relations with Australia, which have an even higher priority and importance. It is disturbed by the suspension of the ANZUS alliance, one of its hitherto most stable alliance relationships. Australia has tried to help to resolve the impasse between its ANZUS allies. It recognizes the importance of its associations with the United States, but it also has special ties with its antipodean neighbor.

Because of the U.S. need to reassess its relations with its ANZUS allies, including its security relationships, an immediate task would be to seek a mutually satisfactory compromise in the present dispute with New Zealand to prevent this dispute from impairing U.S. relations with a long-time friendly nation and from blocking efforts to revive the ANZUS alliances. The United States must also seek to continue its cooperative relationships with Australia.

A major challenge is to deal realistically with the unexpected crisis in ANZUS. This crisis has forced all ANZUS members to reassess the value of this long-time alliance to them, and to consider the relative significance of the tripartite security arrangement in the context of the totality of their relationships. It has also forced them to reassess the entire range of their mutual relations and to seek to evolve satisfactory substitutes for the relationships and protection that they enjoyed under ANZUS.

In the thinly populated islands of Oceania many changes have been and are affecting the security environment in the Southwest, South, and Central Pacific. These include the emergence since World War II of nine independent island nations that gradually have assumed at least minor roles in the Pacific region and have increasingly practiced cooperation through several important regional associations, most notably the South Pacific Forum, of which Australia and New Zealand are also members. Events calling for change are the nations' rising protests against great power activities and rivalries in the region, including naval and other military presence and operations and the testing of nuclear weapons; the strong pacifist and antinuclear sentiments throughout the region; and the change of status of most of the islands of Micronesia—the Mariana, Marshall, and Caroline islands—from incorporation in the Trust Territory of the Pacific Islands, under U.S. trusteeship in the United Nations Trusteeship System, to various patterns of semi-autonomous or nearly autonomous association with the United States.

With the continuance of a strong military presence in the Western Pacific, and with expanding Soviet naval and air activities and capabilities in Pacific waters, the entire region of Oceania, although geographically remote from most of the centers of world power, will be more affected than previously by external contacts and developments as well as by the many changes that are taking place in it. The United States will continue to be a major actor in Oceania, as elsewhere in the Pacific Basin, and it must reorient its policies and activities there accordingly. Above all, the United States must show greater understanding of the interests and sensitivities of the peoples in the multitude of scattered islands in this vast oceanic region.

THE UNITED STATES AND THE WESTERN PACIFIC IN "A RADICALLY DIFFERENT ERA"

The imperative of reorientation and reassessment is a theme dictated by any review and analysis of the U.S. role in the Western Pacific and U.S. security relationships in the region. It is dictated because of the changing political and security environments in the region and in the international system as a whole, the problems and opportunities that these changes present, the growing feeling that the United States still lacks well-defined policies and strategies for dealing with the region, and a realization that while its political and security relations with most of the nations of the region are on the whole relatively satisfactory and relatively stable, problems of a potentially serious nature have arisen in almost all of these relations—problems that will not go away with inattention or status quo defensive postures and that indeed call for immediate attention and reassessment. The fact that the present time is a period of relative stability and relative lack of immediate crisis situations in the Western Pacific and in U.S. relations with the countries of the region is no reason for relaxation and inattention. Rather, it is a reason for serious review and reappraisal at a time when these can be undertaken in the relative absence of a crisis atmosphere.

For the United States, strategically and perhaps politically, the Western Pacific is probably the second most important region in the world—second only to the Atlantic–West European region, the traditional center of American contacts and concerns. It is the region of greatest interaction of four major world powers, the United States, the Soviet Union, Japan, and China. Yet in the United States this part of the world has been relatively neglected.

In spite of much talk about the coming Pacific era, about the importance of U.S. relationships with the countries of the region, about U.S. concern with the activities of the Soviet Union in the Asia-Pacific area, and about the growing interdependencies among the nations of the Pacific Basin, the Western Pacific, extending from Eastern Siberia and Japan to Australia and New Zealand, with three major sub-regions, East and Southeast Asia and the Southwest Pacific, sometimes extended to encompass vast areas of the Pacific Ocean and the island states of Oceania, is not even yet receiving the attention in the United States, in either official or unofficial quarters, that its growing importance as a major international region would seem to require. In its official and unofficial contacts with this vast region the United States is still handicapped by a lack of adequate knowledge and understanding of the peoples and nations of the region—of their history, cultures, values, and aspirations, as well as their present political, economic, and social policies and goals, and their new positions in the changing world environment. At the highest official levels the lack of real knowledge and understanding, as well as of clear-cut policies and genuinely cooperative approaches, is painfully obvious, and many concerned observers have argued that far too little is being done to improve this disturbing situation.

It is long past time for responsible American policymakers to include the Western Pacific in their orbits of primary concern and to undertake a long process of education regarding the realities of the underlying conditions and the changing scene in this region and the implications for U.S. policy. It is also long past time for these responsible decisionmakers to give serious consideration to the frequent suggestions that the United States should develop more coherent and understandable policies regarding the Western Pacific, featuring greater and more effective coordination of its policies within the labyrinthine governmental apparatus at home, greater cooperation and more genuine consultation with its allies and other friends in the region, and "a wider framework of cooperation in many spheres."[8] As Michael Armacost, U.S. under secretary of state for political affairs, pointed out when he used this phrase, this "wider framework of cooperation" should embrace cooperation among nations of North America, Western Europe, and Asia, as well as between the United States and the countries of the Western Pacific, bilaterally and multilaterally, nationally, regionally, and even internationally.

It is of course all too easy to advance such sweeping suggestions and all too difficult to implement them, even if there is a general acceptance of them in the United States and in the nations of the Western Pacific. Most American policymakers would argue that they are moving as rapidly as possible in these directions, but a prevailing feeling in unofficial American circles and in many quarters in Western Pacific countries is that the United States is not pursuing these professed goals with the dedication, skill, and intensity called for and that, on the whole, the United States has not yet given a sufficiently high priority to the Western Pacific—has not yet really begun to prepare for its new role in a changing and increasingly important world region.

U.S. security policies and relationships in the Western Pacific should obviously be considered within the framework of national interests and priorities and of changing regional and international realities. Security is, after all, only a part of overall national concerns, although it is necessarily a basic goal of any nation. In dealing with the Western Pacific, U.S. security policies and approaches must be both technical and comprehensive. They must be concerned with capabilities as well as with objectives, with implementation of policies as well as with their articulation. They must seek, as a major objective, to support and strengthen alliances and other special security relationships with some of the nations of the region. They must give a high priority to measures to counteract the growing Soviet military buildup in the Asia-Pacific region, but they must also include plans and preparations for dealing with other kinds of security threats in the region. Above all, in the Western Pacific the United States must take a much broader approach to security, embracing nonmilitary as well as military aspects and policies. In the pursuit of this broader approach, the Japanese concept of "comprehensive national security" and Michael Armacost's reminder of the need for "a wider framework of cooperation", within and beyond the region, must be borne in mind and perhaps used as yardsticks for measuring and evaluating both specific security policies and basic security approaches.

The security environment in the Western Pacific is a most complex one, and it is changing in many directions. Some of these are already discernible but others are still buried in the mists of the future. One must take into account the certainty of unexpected events as well as the implications for major changes that are already discernible. In this complex and changing environment U.S. security policies and relationships have already developed a most complex pattern, encompassing global and regional, bilateral and multilateral, military and nonmilitary aspects. Security relationships, it should be remembered, encompass not only the extensive and important U.S. alliance system in the Western Pacific, but also other patterns of alignment and cooperation with countries that are not formal allies. These include, as a major idiosyncratic case in the region, security dimensions, however limited, of the developing relations with the People's Republic of China and also relations, in the region and beyond, with the Soviet Union. The very limited, and essentially hostile, relations of the United States with North Korea and with Vietnam and the other Indochinese states revolve largely around security considerations. The growing U.S. relations with ASEAN countries are primarily nonmilitary in nature, but they have some military and security aspects, mainly because of the joint concern of the ASEAN states and the United States over the developments in Indonesia.

Looking at the situation in the Western Pacific, the United States may find more favorable than unfavorable trends, from the point of view of its security interests. But it must give special attention to the dangers that it does perceive. Obvious needs are to shore up its alliance system, and to seek greater agreement on threats to the region and ways for meeting these threats. Even though most of the existing U.S. bilateral alliances with Western Pacific nations—but not its major multilateral alliance in the region, ANZUS—are still in place and perhaps are basically stable, strains have developed in all of them that call for very prompt and very special attention. This applies particularly to the alliance with Japan—the core of U.S. security relationships in the Western Pacific, and perhaps its most important security relationship, as Ambassador Mansfield and others have argued. The need for special attention also applies to its alliances with South Korea and the Philippines, both of long standing and both of unusual strategic significance. Unexpectedly, with the new strains with New Zealand, that led to U.S. abrogation of ANZUS, it now applies to U.S. security relationships with Australia and New Zealand, especially the latter. Even with the new nations of Oceania, and with the emerging semi-autonomous states of the former Trust Territory of the Pacific Islands, special security problems for the United States are developing on an unexpected scale. The vast region of Oceania is a vital strategic zone for the United States and any major difficulties with the island nations and peoples of this zone would present serious complications for the United States in the promotion of its security and other objectives in the entire Pacific Basin region, and especially in the Western Pacific.

The present is no time for the United States to rest on its laurels as far as the Western Pacific is concerned. It should take advantage of the relative lull in the immediate situation in the region to reassess its past policies and approaches and its present orientation and objectives in the light of the underlying changes that are under way in the region, and in the world.

A summary of discussions at a major international conference on Asian security in the 1980s, held at the Rand Corporation in 1979, concluded by observing: "Conceptions of both national and regional security have been, and will continue to be, extensively recast throughout the area as a result of these changes. . . . While the past cannot be wished away, Asia and America on the verge of the 1980s confront a radically different era in terms of the nature of security issues and the forces propelling interstate and intrasocietal change and conflict."[9] These conclusions are even more relevant and compelling in the waning years of the twentieth century than they were when they were formulated. Will the United States be able to develop security and other relationships and policies that will be more adequate, and more responsive to the trends in the Western Pacific in this "radically different era"?

Notes

[1] George Shultz, U.S. Secretary of State, "The United States and East Asia: A Partnership for the Future," address before the World Affairs Council of San Francisco, March 5, 1983; Bureau of Public Affairs, U.S. Department of State, *Current Policy*, no. 459, March 5, 1983, p. 3.

[2] Michael H. Armacost, "NATO and the Challenges Ahead," address before the Atlantic Treaty Association, Toronto, October 10, 1984; Bureau of Public Affairs, U.S. Department of State, *Current Policy*, no. 620, October 10, 1984, p. 4.

[3] Michael H. Armacost, "The Asia-Pacific Region: A Forward Look," address before the Far East-America Council/Asia Society, New York, January 29, 1985; Bureau of Public Affairs, U.S. Department of State, *Current Policy*, no. 653, January 29, 1985, p. 4.

[4] Peter Polomka, "The Security of the Western Pacific: The Price of Burden Sharing," *Survival* 26 (January/February 1984): 8.

[5] Shultz, "The United States and East Asia," p. 1.

[6] Derek Davies, "Signs and Portents of a Future Full of Change," *Asia 1986 Yearbook* (Hong Kong: Far Eastern Economic Review, 1986), p. 14.

[7] Parris H. Chang, "U.S.-China Relations: From Hostility to Euphoria to Realism," *The Annals of the American Academy of Political and Social Science* 476 (November 1984).

[8] Armacost, "NATO and the Challenges Ahead," p. 4.

[9] Richard H. Solomon, ed., *Asian Security in the 1980s: Problems and Policies in a Time of Transition* (Cambridge, Mass.: Oelgeschlager, Gunn & Hain, 1980), p. 305.

Index

About the Author

Norman D. Palmer is professor emeritus of political science, University of Pennsylvania, where he taught for thirty-five years. He was chairman of the both the Political Science Department and the International Relations Graduate Program and the senior political scientist in the South Asia Regional Studies Program. He has been a visiting professor at many other universities in the United States and abroad. He is a member of the Council on Foreign Relations and the Association for Asian Studies, a former president of the National Council on Asian Affairs, and a former national president of the International Studies Association. During World War II, he served in the Pacific combat theater as a naval air combat intelligence officer. He has visited Asia frequently since then. He is the author or co-author of twenty-five books, including *Major Governments of Asia, Changing Patterns of Security and Stability in Asia, The United States and India: The Dimensions of Influence*, and *International Relations: The World Community in Transition*. A native of Maine, he is a graduate and a former member of the faculty of Colby College, with B.A. and L.H.D. (Hon.) degrees from that institution. He received M.A. and Ph.D. degrees from Yale University. Currently he and his wife reside in the San Juan Islands, in the State of Washington.